Learning from Economic Downturns

DIRECTIONS IN DEVELOPMENT
Human Development

Learning from Economic Downturns

*How to Better Assess, Track, and Mitigate
the Impact on the Health Sector*

Xiaohui Hou, Edit V. Velényi, Abdo S. Yazbeck,
Roberto F. Iunes, and Owen Smith

THE WORLD BANK
Washington, D.C.

RAPID SOCIAL RESPONSE

ISBN (paper): 978-1-4648-0060-3
ISBN (electronic): 978-1-4648-0061-0
DOI: 10.1596/978-1-4648-0060-3

Cover image: © Pete Ellis / Drawgood Illustration. Used with the permission of Pete Ellis / Drawgood Illustration. Further permission required for reuse.
Cover design: Naylor Design, Inc.

Library of Congress Cataloging-in-Publication Data

Hou, Xiaohui, author.
Learning from economic downturns : how to better assess, track, and mitigate the impact on the health sector / Xiaohui Hou, Edit V. Velényi, Abdo S. Yazbeck, Roberto F. Iunes, and Owen Smith.
    p. ; cm. — (Directions in development)
    Includes bibliographical references.
ISBN 978-1-4648-0060-3 (alk. paper) — ISBN 978-1-4648-0061-0
    I. Velényi, Edit V., 1972– author. II. Yazbeck, Abdo S., author. III. Iunes, Roberto F., author. IV. Smith, Owen, 1973– author. V. World Bank, issuing body, publisher. VI. Title. VII. Series: Directions in development (Washington, D.C.)
    [DNLM: 1. Health Care Sector—economics. 2. Economic Development. 3. Economic Recession. 4. Health Policy. W 74.1]
    RA395.A3
    362.1—dc23   2013022145

Contents

Boxes

Figures

Tables

Foreword

Many countries around the world are moving toward universal health coverage, while navigating through periods of economic crisis.

The impact of the economic downturn of 2008–09 on the health care sector has renewed efforts to make health systems more resilient during and after economic downturns. Health policy makers and development practitioners are grappling with how to better identify areas that make the health sector vulnerable to economic downturns, and how to track and mitigate the impact of economic downturns. To effectively manage the challenges resulting from economic uncertainty, the health sector must look at recent failures and successes as a learning opportunity for improvement, with the end result being greater health system resilience.

This book, financed by the Rapid Social Response Program at the World Bank, responds to these challenges facing the health sector. It introduces a framework for assessing, tracking, and mitigating (A.T.M. framework) the impact of economic downturns on the health sector. This framework provides policy makers and practitioners in the health sector with a more systematic way to design and implement policies that can protect people, particularly the poor, from the negative effects of economic downturns.

The A.T.M. framework includes a quantitative tool to help countries assess and identify areas within and beyond the health sector that render it vulnerable to economic downturns. This book illustrates the benefit of implementing rapid surveys to track the impacts of crises in real time as economies shrink, and emphasizes the importance of building effective health information systems that can regularly monitor system changes. Analysis of several country case studies in developing countries sheds light on the importance of linking the health sector with the social protection sector, particularly social safety nets, using the common identification and targeting methods to reach the poor and the vulnerable. The more recent lessons from several EU countries emphasize the importance of political economy in implementing policy reforms during economic downturns and again illustrate how the data can help facilitate more evidence-based policy making.

Policy makers from the health and social protection sectors in both developing and high-income countries have provided significant feedback for this work. The feedback focuses on policy makers' experience with the impact of the recent crisis and their views on the effectiveness of policies aimed at mitigating crisis impacts on health services for the poor and the vulnerable.

Sanjay Pradhan
Vice President
Change, Knowledge and Learning
The World Bank

Keith Hansen
Acting Vice President
Human Development Network
The World Bank

Acknowledgments

The authors first thank Maria-Luisa Escobar, Hideki Mori, Daniel Dulitzky, and Nicole Klingen for their guidance and support of this work. The book has benefited from a number of contributors. Logan Brenzel wrote a background paper on the impact of economic crisis on health and the four country case studies, which are summarized in chapter 1. Marc Smitz contributed to the analysis of chapter 2 on assessing vulnerability. The findings in chapter 3 draw from earlier work done by M. Ihsan Ajwad, Mehtabul Azam, Basab Dasgupta, Johannes Koettl, Yiyang Li, and Zlatko Nikoloski. Alexander Hamilton did much of the research for and the initial drafting of chapter 4.

The authors would like to thank the representatives from Colombia, Estonia, Georgia, Greece, Indonesia, Ireland, Mexico, Portugal, the United Kingdom, and the United States who presented in the Knowledge Exchange event on "The Health Sector and Economic Downturn" in September 2012 in Washington, DC, organized by the World Bank Institute and financed by the Rapid Social Response Program (RSR). The event has motivated the authors to document their knowledge and experiences. Particularly, we would like to thank John Yfantopoulos (professor of health economics, University of Athens, Greece); Steve Thomas (professor of health policy and management, University of Dublin, Ireland) and his colleagues Sara Burke (postdoctoral researcher at the Centre for Health Policy and Management, Trinity College Dublin, Ireland) and Sarah Barry (research fellow at the Centre for Health Policy and Management, Trinity College Dublin, Ireland); and Pedro Pita Barros (professor of economics, Universidade Nova de Lisboa, Portugal) for presenting their respective country case studies at the event and later providing the written case studies. We appreciate the valuable comments from participants of the Knowledge Exchange event and the session on the similar topic in the Second Global Symposium on Health Services Research held in Beijing in November 2012. The authors are indebted to the peer reviewers—Antonino Giuffrida, Amanda Glassman, and Robert Palacios—for their insightful written comments, and to Melody Molinoff for exceptional editorial service. The book was further edited for publication by Carolyn Goldinger, and its production and printing were handled by the World Bank's Publishing and Knowledge Division. Finally, we are especially grateful for the financial support provided by RSR and its donor countries: Australia, Norway, the Russian Federation, Sweden, and the United Kingdom.

About the Authors

Xiaohui Hou is a senior economist at the World Bank Institute. She has worked in both health and social protection sectors in the South Asia, East Asia, Eastern Europe, and Central Asia regions in the World Bank. She has led a number of World Bank reports and published in both economics and medical peer-reviewed journals. She teaches in several universities in China as a visiting scholar. She received a PhD in health services and policy analysis and an MA in economics from the University of California, Berkeley, and an MA in health policy and administration from Washington State University.

Edit V. Velényi is an economist with the HNP Anchor of the World Bank, where she has focused on the relationship between the macro economy and health financing. Previously, she worked with the Development Impact Evaluation Initiative to coordinate the health portfolio. In 2007, she was a field-based manager for the evaluation of the Lagos Community Health Plan with the Amsterdam Institute for International Development. While with the Africa Region, she coedited *Public Ends, Private Means* and coauthored chapters on health insurance. Velényi received a PhD in economics from the University of York, an MA from the Johns Hopkins University School of Advanced International Studies, and an MA from the Budapest Business School.

Abdo S. Yazbeck is lead health economist for the Africa Region and has a PhD in economics (health and labor). He was a health sector manager in Europe and Central Asia and previously a program leader at the World Bank Institute. He worked for seven years in South Asia operations. Yazbeck also worked as a senior health economist in the private sector, focusing on Africa, the Middle East, and the former Soviet Union after being part of the *World Development Report (WDR) 1993: Investing in Health* team and teaching economics at Rice University and Texas A&M University. He has authored or edited five books, including *Attacking Inequality in the Health Sector*.

Roberto F. Iunes is a senior health economist at the World Bank Institute. Before joining the World Bank, he worked at the Inter-American Development Bank in health sector operations and at the Office of Evaluation and Oversight. His academic experience includes working as faculty and researcher in the economics of health and nutrition at the School of Public Health at the University of São Paulo, as well as Takemi Fellow and research fellow in the health care financing program at Harvard University. His public sector experience includes work with the three levels of government in his native Brazil.

Owen Smith is a senior health economist in the Europe and Central Asia Department of the World Bank, where he has worked on health financing and policy issues across the region. Prior to joining the World Bank, he worked as a health economist at Abt Associates, with a focus on Sub-Saharan Africa, and as a country economist at the Canadian Ministry of Finance, working on East Asia. He studied economics and international development at Queen's University in Kingston, Ontario, and at Harvard's Kennedy School.

Abbreviations

ADSE	Assistência na Doença aos Servidores do Estado (civil servants' health insurance plan, Portugal)
APIFARMA	association of the pharmaceutical industry (Portugal)
A.T.M.	assessing, tracking, and mitigating
CBT	community-based targeting
CPIA	country policy and institutional assessment
CRW	Crisis Response Window
DAH	development assistance for health
ECA	Europe and Central Asia
ECB	European Central Bank
ECHE	European Conference on Health Economics
EF	external factors
ESRI	Economic and Social Research Institute
EU	European Union
FDI	foreign direct investment
GDP	gross domestic product
GEC	global economic crisis
GGE	general government expenditures
GHE	government health expenditures
GNI	gross national income
GP	general practitioner
H4A	height for age
HEFPro	Health Equity and Financial Protection
HF	health financing
HHF	household-level factors
HIC	high-income country
HIFs	health insurance funds
HNP	Health, Nutrition, and Population (sector of the World Bank)
HSE	Health Service Executive (Ireland)
ICRG	International Country Risk Guide
ICT	information and communication technology
IDA	International Development Association
IG-C30	income group closest 30
ILO	International Labour Organization

IMF	International Monetary Fund
IMR	infant mortality rate
JPS-BK	Jaring Pengaman Sosial Bidang Kesehatan (Social Safety Net Program, Indonesia)
LIC	low-income country
MDGs	Millennium Development Goals
MHIF	Mandatory Health Insurance Fund (Kyrgyz Republic)
MIC	middle-income country
MIS	management information system
MMR	maternal mortality rate
MOF	Ministry of Finance
MOH	Ministry of Health
MoU	memorandum of understanding
NHA	National Health Accounts
NHS	National Health Service
ODA	official development assistance
OECD	Organisation for Economic Co-operation and Development
OOP	out-of-pocket
PC	per capita
PEIR	Public Expenditure and Institutional Review
PHE	public health expenditure
RSBY	Rashtriya Swasthya Bima Yojna (health insurance program, India)
RSR	Rapid Social Response Program
SAR	special administrative region
SAS	South Asia
SISBEN	Selection System of Beneficiaries for Social Programs (Colombia)
SOPAC	South Pacific Applied Geoscience Commission
SPF	Social Protection Floor Initiative
SR	senior
SSF	Sub-Saharan Africa (now SSA)
SWAp	sectorwide approach
THE	total health expenditure
UNICO	Universal Coverage for Health
VZ	vulnerability zone
W4A	weight for age
WDI	World Development Indicators
WHO	World Health Organization

Overview

There is increased recognition that health and economic development are inter-connected. Both macro and micro studies show that better health status leads to more productivity, which in turn leads to increased economic growth. Conversely, the faster the economy grows, the greater the demand for health care and health sector spending. Over the past several decades, the health sector has become an increasingly important component of the global economy, evinced by the growing trend of health expenditures as a share of gross domestic product (GDP), especially in high-income and emerging middle-income countries.

Due to the cyclical nature of economic performance, building health sector resilience is critical to preparing for inevitable economic downturns. The global economic crisis (GEC), which began as early as 2007, brought renewed attention to the impacts of economic downturns on health sectors worldwide and revealed that no country is immune to external challenges, even those with advanced economies and AAA credit ratings.

In recent years the GEC has driven further research to better understand the pathways from crises to population health. At a high-level consultation on the financial crisis and global health organized by the World Health Organization (WHO), the director-general provided three objectives that the development community should aspire to attain in this area (WHO 2009):

1. Build awareness of the ways in which an economic downturn may affect health spending, health services, health-seeking behavior, and health outcomes.
2. Make the case for sustaining investments in health.
3. Identify actions—including monitoring of early warning signs—that can help mitigate the negative impact of economic downturns.

Despite sustained fiscal pressures and the expected continuation of stagnation in Europe, there have been limited efforts to gather systematic evidence and develop frameworks that would guide policy makers on how to design and implement more effective mitigation responses and build health system resilience.

The A.T.M. Approach

This book aims to respond particularly to two objectives on the global health policy agenda by building more awareness as to how economic downturns may affect the health sector and by identifying tools and actions that can help mitigate the negative impact of economic downturns.

Compared to other areas, such as social protection or response to natural disasters, the health sector has lagged behind in developing and offering systematic tools for vulnerability assessment, tracking, and crisis mitigation.

The *A.T.M. framework* outlines the importance of Assessment, Tracking, and Mitigation and the interdependence of these methods for effective crisis response and strengthening health system resilience to economic shocks. The framework proposes that in order to be effective in mitigation, governments and policy makers must possess or develop:

1. Tools to assess the health sector vulnerability to economic crisis
2. Tools, information systems, and data sources to track system and population-level effects quickly during a crisis
3. Ability to implement effective policies that can be used to mitigate effects when a crisis hits

The objective of this book is to raise awareness of the challenges that health systems, in both developing and developed countries, face in times of economic crisis and provide a framework by which governments and policy makers can meet the critical challenge of health sector stabilization and resilience building. The successful implementation of these tools can positively affect not only population health, but long-term development trajectories as well.

Assessment

Chapter 1 discusses the lingering effects of the GEC, especially in terms of health care, and elaborates on the A.T.M. framework. Chapter 2 maps out and tests a new way of assessing the vulnerability of health sectors to economic downturns. It explores a thus far uncharted territory by: (a) offering a definition of crisis-related health system vulnerability; (b) presenting a vulnerability assessment framework to conceptualize the drivers of system vulnerability in a way that can be applied for quantitative analysis; and (c) proposing a global vulnerability assessment tool to enable benchmarking country performance against peers and over time, help identify weak spots that reduce a country's ability to manage and mitigate crisis effects on the sector and health outcomes, focus attention and resources, and, consequently, strengthen system resilience.

Extensive research found that a standardized definition of crisis-related health system vulnerability did not exist prior to this book. Drawing on vulnerability definitions from other areas and adapting them to this context, crisis-related vulnerability in the health system is framed as *the full range of factors that place people at risk of becoming "health insecure" and threaten universal and permanent access to quality health care services.*

Health system vulnerability to crisis is multidimensional and, as such, requires examination of factors outside the health sector to better understand the likelihood and expected depth of vulnerability. The assessment framework captures the complex relationship between three levels: external factors, which include macro, fiscal, and demographic variables; health system–level factors, which include variables on health financing and coverage; and household-level factors. These vectors jointly determine health sector resilience and health outcomes during crisis.

The assessment framework was conceptualized to guide the development of a global vulnerability assessment tool, which relies on data from the Fiscal Health Database (World Bank 2012). This macro database covering 183 countries over 16 years (1995–2010) compiles a number of international data sources with the ambition to offer a synthetic data source, which, with updates, can provide continuous and standardized data for future vulnerability assessment efforts.

The proposed global health system vulnerability assessment tool will help build more awareness of the impact of economic downturns on the health sector. Further, it will provide quantitative evidence to guide decision making and policy response that will help mitigate the negative impact of economic downturns. It is expected that the presented framework and global assessment tool can catalyze a process that may produce more refined instruments and increasingly more relevant data.

Despite recognized limitations and constraints, this first attempt at a vulnerability assessment tool can be used to identify: (a) countries that have fragile macrofiscal conditions, which make health systems more prone to contraction; (b) how the health system performs on financing and coverage; (c) how countries perform on final outcomes measures; and (d) where a country is placed in overall system vulnerability.

Undoubtedly, global tools and league tables that are based on reduced dimensions of determinants to compare country performance suffer from limitations. For example, both the Human Development Index and the Doing Business Index have been heavily debated in regard to their methodological robustness and interpretation of the rankings. Such tools are not perfect, but they have been important in focusing the attention of policy makers and the development community on shortcomings in critical areas and caused the leveraging of significant resources to remedy weaknesses at the country level. Similarly, the policy-multiplier effects of a system vulnerability assessment tool are expected to be high. Overall, the application of vulnerability assessment tools at the global and country levels are expectedly good and are relatively small investments with potentially high human capital returns.

Tracking

Chapter 3 explores the importance of checking the "vital signs" of the health system to see how an economic downturn affects system performance and health outcomes. Tracking is critical for detecting warning signals and drawing policy attention to areas that could further aggravate the effect of the crisis on the health sector and population health outcomes.

Continuous tracking and monitoring can occur at different levels, and require a variety of methods, tools, and data sources. Among the methods, tracking primarily refers to the use of contemporaneous data flows, such as administrative data from management information systems (MIS), or ex-post analysis of data that can be accessed with a short lag, for example, a dedicated survey with a fast turnaround.

In contrast with the proposed global assessment tool that relies on standardized macro data from a variety of international sources, tracking predominantly draws on micro data collected from the system through MIS (for example, health insurance fund), facility-level data, or household surveys to assess population-level effects. The global assessment tool is designed to provide information for global policy discussions, draw attention to areas of system vulnerability, and identify limitations in global data sources that can help system vulnerability assessment. Tracking, on the other hand, takes vulnerability assessment to the country level and harnesses more granular and higher frequency data. Thus, tracking is more dynamic and can more precisely inform policy making through the identification of specific system bottlenecks. Combining the assessment and tracking tools will provide more comprehensive data to help policy makers and governments deal with negative impacts and build health system resilience.

Chapter 3 explores different tools used to track the impact of the economic downturn on the health sector in Europe and Central Asia (ECA). The discussion focuses on both "what" and "how" to track the impact of a crisis on health systems and illustrates with selected findings from a range of data collections efforts that were specifically initiated to track the short-term impact.

ECA's challenge to deal with the GEC further illustrates the important lesson that no country is impervious to the impact of economic downturn. Extending this lesson to other regions, most of which are poorer than ECA, should raise concerns about the ability of health sectors in low- and middle-income countries to prepare for future economic downturns. The experience of ECA's health systems, and in particular the limited ability to quickly track developments and respond by mitigating the impact of the downturn, should provide a clear signal to other countries and to development agencies that there is significant scope for health sectors to take on a much more effective role and to become a better steward of the health status and health needs of the population.

Mitigation

Chapters 4 and 5 examine the development and implementation of health sector policies and instruments that can mitigate the impact of economic downturns on populations. A series of country case studies represent experiences in Europe, South America, and Asia. The studies provide important lessons from both developed and developing countries that can be instructive in policy reform. While reforms to improve efficiency and resilience within a system are critical, there are additional ways to mitigate the impact of economic crisis on poor and vulnerable populations.

A key lesson, explored in chapter 4, is the important nexus between the health sector and the social protection sector, specifically through social safety net programs. Actually, the most successful mitigation programs in the health sector are those that are able to link with social safety net programs and use existing targeting instruments to scale up the coverage during economic downturns.

Significant similarities exist among different types of social programs in the delivery of services or transfers to the poor. An effective management system can further enable the collaboration of these programs and improve the overall governance and transparency of the delivery system. Such integrated information system can assist all the relevant programs across different aspects of operations, including eligibility assessment, beneficiary identification and registration, tracking services utilizations and delivery of benefits, and facilitating coordination of different programs at different levels.

In chapter 5, lessons from two European Union (EU) country case studies lead to two main conclusions. First, the political economic dynamics of reform processes between the health sector and the Ministry of Finance, as well as within the sector, are critical. Political economy is especially important if there is not enough time for evidence-based priority setting. Second, further developing and applying country-level monitoring tools and early warning systems could help evidence-based responses. These tools must consider changes in inputs (for example, health financing), outputs (for example, utilization), and outcomes (for example, mental health, suicide rates, chronic conditions, and so forth) to understand the effects throughout the result chain. Thus, crisis effect monitoring is not a short-term engagement. It requires a systematic and long-term impact assessment approach.

These findings lead back to the A.T.M. framework, which may serve as a valuable tool irrespective of which income group a country is in. While advanced economies have relied more on automatic stabilizers and have more developed social safety nets, the global crisis has shown that there is no place for complacency.

Conclusion

The cyclical nature of economic performance makes economic downturns a recurring phenomenon. Crises vary in terms of their trigger, geographic origin and scope, length, and depth. These parameters, the extent of structural preparedness, and policy reactions by governments jointly determine the severity of outcomes and the length of the impact horizon. A global lesson from these crises is that the health sector must build systems that can effectively assess vulnerability, track system changes, and synthesize the information to improve mitigation efforts. These structural changes can, and must, happen and cannot come soon enough.

Bibliography

WHO (World Health Organization). 2009. *The Financial Crisis and Global Health*. Report of a High-Level Consultation. Geneva, Switzerland: World Health Organization. January 19.

World Bank. 2010. "Lessons from Past Crises—and How the Current Crisis Differs." In *Global Monitoring Report 2010: The MDGs after the Crisis*. Washington, DC: World Bank. http://siteresources.worldbank.org/INTPROSPECTS/Resources/334934 -1327948020811/8401693-1327957257247/8402460-1328631318777 /GMR2010WEB.pdf.

———. 2012. Fiscal Health Database. Health and Economy Program, Health, Nutrition, and Population Anchor, World Bank, Washington, DC.

CHAPTER 1

A Framework for Health Sector Resilience

The cyclical process that characterizes economic performance suggests that economic downturns have been and are likely to continue to be recurring phenomena.[1] It is of concern, however, that in the last two to three decades, the world economy has been hit by very large and growing recessions. These are a result of globalization's economic integration. Thus, the devastating Latin American economic crisis of the 1980s was later followed by the Asian financial crisis that began in mid-1997. The resulting recession, considered by many to be the most serious global economic crisis (GEC) of the post–World War II period (Stiglitz 2000), was surpassed only 10 years later by the even more severe global financial crisis that began in 2007–08. This crisis has led to the 2008–12 global recession and contributed to the European sovereign-debt crisis (Held, Kaldor, and Quah 2010).

Global economic integration coupled with the volatility of economic growth has fundamentally altered the nature of risks facing the poor, particularly in developing countries, given their relative weak institutional and governance structures (Heltberg, Hossain, and Reva 2012). Output fluctuation has been found to be much higher and more persistent in developing countries than in developed countries, and historically, the most volatile economies in the world are those in developing countries[2] (Agénor, McDermott, and Prasad 2000; Hnatkovska and Loayza 2003; Pallage and Robe 2003). In addition, the negative correlation observed between macroeconomic economic volatility and long-run economic growth is greater in developing countries than in industrialized economies (Hnatkovska and Loayza 2003), and the welfare costs of such volatility are quite significant, at least ten times that of the United States. In fact, "removing consumption volatility is equivalent to increasing consumption by at least 0.34% in perpetuity" (Pallage and Robe 2003, 678). That being said, one of the significant developments of the recent GEC is the wide and deep negative impacts that high-income countries (HICs) have experienced. Therefore, the lessons that can be learned are equally important for both developing and developed countries

(Brahmbhatt and Canuto 2012; Foxley 2009; Frankel, Végh, and Vuletin 2011; WHO 2009; World Bank 2010).

Just as no country has been immune to the far-reaching effects of the global economic downturn, no sector has been unaffected. As the health sector continues to play an increasingly important role in the global economy, vulnerabilities, both within the system and through direct economic impacts on households, present greater challenges for those tasked with building health system resilience. The remainder of this chapter explores the growing importance of health in a global economy, the transmission pathways of the impact of economic downturns on the health sector and population health, and then introduces the Assessing, Tracking, and Mitigating (A.T.M.) framework and the overall objective and structure of the book.

The Growing Importance of Health in a Global Economy

The increasing importance of the health sector in the global economy is the result of the two-way relationship between health and income and the alarming increase in both public and private expenditures on health.

It has been long established that higher income can promote better health. The evident mechanisms are through the purchase of better health-related goods and services, such as better nutrition and better access to safe water and sanitation. In recent years, more evidence has emerged to test the causality from the other direction, that is, how health can affect income. The growing evidence, both micro and macro, has shown that health is also a determinant of income. For example, Bloom and Canning (2005) found that health makes a positive and statistically significant contribution to aggregate output. Their estimates showed that a one percentage point increase in adult survival rates increases labor productivity by about 2.8 percent. Several mechanisms were suggested, including increased labor productivity from a healthier and more vigorous workforce, higher returns on investment in schooling due to better cognitive development in early childhood and improvement in adult health, and increased incentive for saving and investment due to longer life expectancy. This is important because "to the extent that health follows income, income growth should be the priority for developing countries. To the extent that income is a consequence of health, investments in health, even in the poorest developing countries, may be a priority" (Bloom and Canning 2008, 1).

In addition to the two-way relationship between health and income, the rapidly increasing public and private expenditures on health are also putting health in the center of political debate in a number of countries. Recent analysis by the International Monetary Fund (IMF) and the Organisation for Economic Co-operation and Development (OECD) showed alarming growth in health spending in HICs and rapid growth in emerging middle-income countries (MICs) (figure 1.1). This empirical fact reflects a high demand by populations in these countries for increased spending on health.

Figure 1.1 Health Spending as a Percentage of GDP in Advanced (HIC) and Emerging (MIC) Countries

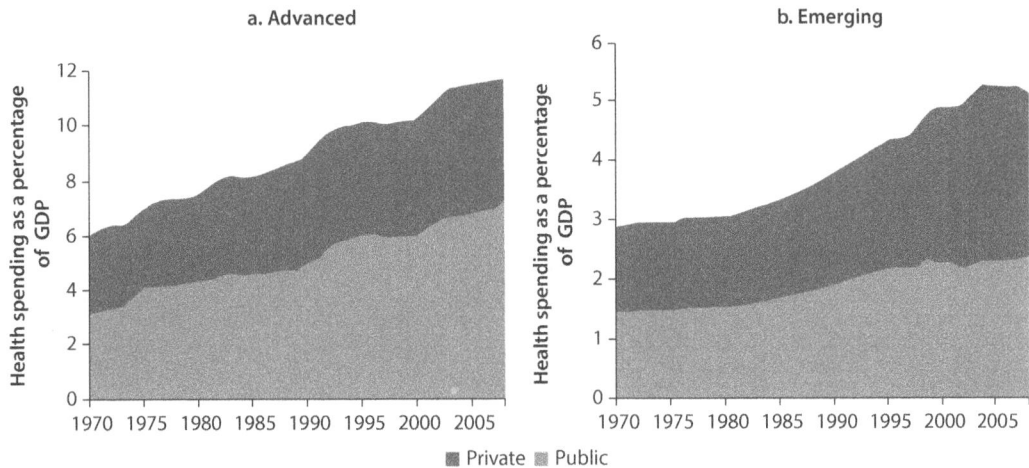

Source: Clements, Coady, and Gupta 2012.
Note: GDP = gross domestic product; HIC = high-income country; MIC = middle-income country.

A prefinancial crisis regional population household survey in Europe and Central Asia also confirmed this high demand by the population. Despite health spending being relatively high in this emerging region, 22 of the 28 countries surveyed ranked increased public investment in health as their first priority when the options given were *"Education, Health, Housing, Pensions, Environment, Public Infrastructure, Other."* The remaining six countries ranked education first and health second, which means that the population of every country in the region ranked additional public investments in the health sector as first or second priority (EBRD 2010).

It is apparent from the consistent and sizable increases in public and private spending in the health sector that the fiscal footprint of the health sector is already large in many countries and will only continue to grow as countries develop and become wealthier. Clearly, the faster the economy grows, the larger the demand for health care and health sector spending, which raises the question: What happens to the health sector when the economy experiences a downturn?

The Impact of Economic Downturns on the Health Sector and Population Health

Economic crisis can manifest itself in many different ways.[3] The global crisis that began in 2007–08 exemplifies the varied and far-reaching effects of economic crisis. The countries of Eastern Europe experienced the sharpest decline in gross domestic product (GDP), while Central Asian countries were for the most part indirectly affected through the decline in oil prices and the banking crisis that hit the Russian Federation. In East Asia, the crisis had a major negative impact on the labor market due to the decline in global demand for garments

Figure 1.2 Multiple Transmission Paths from Economic Crisis to Health Outcomes

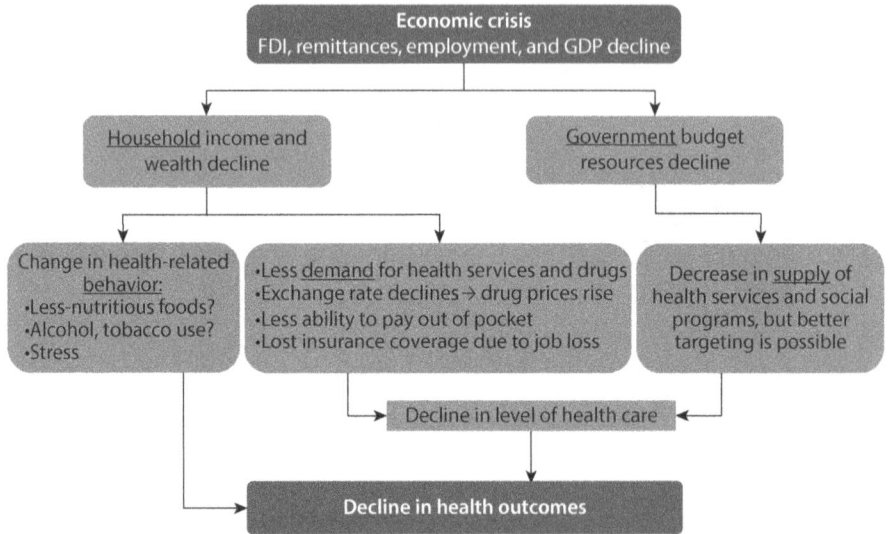

Sources: Adapted from Musgrove 1987; Waters, Saadah, and Pradhan 2003.
Note: FDI = foreign direct investment; GDP = gross domestic product.

and electronics. In Sub-Saharan Africa, Latin America, and the Pacific Islands, the decline in revenues from the exports of commodities and from general trade led to important fiscal pressures (Green, King, and Dawkins 2010). Understanding the type of crisis is critical because it is the nature of a given crisis that defines how its economic manifestations are transmitted to the health sector or to the health of the general population.

The underlying framework for understanding the transmission paths of economic downturn to the health sector and population health is shown in figure 1.2. An economic downturn will have an impact on employment and access to capital, among other drivers of growth. This impact will then have a dual effect on both households and the health sector due to changes in budgets and resource availability both at the household and government levels. In other words, the pathways impacting health and health systems address the supply of health care services, the demand for health services, and household behaviors that could directly impact health.

In a period of economic downturn, household income is likely to decline, exposing a number of vulnerabilities, which fall into two channels. The first channel is through household behaviors, particularly household food consumption and nutritional intake. For poor families, over half of household expenditure is on food. Reduced income usually leads to an initial reduction in the consumption of more expensive food items, followed by a reduction in the size and frequency of meals (Brinkman et al. 2010). Evidence shows that the Asian crisis of the late 1990s led to an increase in childhood anemia and wasting among the Indonesian urban poor, and to vitamin A deficiency in pregnant women and children (Block 2004; Brinkman et al. 2010; Kwon et al. 2010). In the region as a whole, maternal anemia rates increased by 10–20 percent; prevalence of low birth weight rose by 5–10 percent; childhood stunting by 3–7 percent; and wasting by 8–16 percent (Bhutta et al. 2009).

The other channel is through household interaction with the health sector. During periods of crisis, unemployment and declining real wages lead to reductions in health insurance coverage, particularly in health financing systems where social health insurance is dominant. For example, in Central Asia, there were statistically more significant cancelations in health insurance among households affected by the recent economic crisis than in matched control groups (Dasgupta and Ajwad 2011). In Mongolia, health insurance coverage declined from 84 percent to 81 percent between 2008 and 2009 (Bredenkamp, Sølve Sande Lie, and Brenzel 2011). Diminished household income and lack of health insurance may also result in significant declines in health services utilization, particularly preventive care visits. Estimates from Peru, related to the crisis of the late 1990s, indicate that a 1 percent decline in GDP is related to a 0.28 percent decline in the number of antenatal visits and a 0.31 percent decline in the probability of women attending four or more antenatal visits (Agüero and Valdivia 2010). In Armenia, 52 percent of households affected by the 2008–09 crisis postponed visits to a doctor or health care center. In Turkey, this figure was 27 percent and in Romania, 24 percent (Dasgupta and Ajwad 2011). In Bulgaria, preventive care was postponed by 12 percent of households affected by the crisis (Dasgupta and Ajwad 2011).

On the supply side, an economic downturn is likely to impact resources available to all public services, including health. As expected, governments tend to reduce the level and composition of spending due to tightened fiscal constraints. In Peru, the financial crisis led to a 58 percent reduction in public health expenditure between 1985 and 1990 (Paxson and Schady 2004). In Thailand, public and private health expenditure fell by 36 percent during the Asian financial crisis of 1997–98 (Hopkins 2006). In Central Asia, public health expenditure fell as a proportion of total health expenditure between 2008 and 2009, while the real growth rate of per capita public health expenditure declined by 28 percent in Georgia, the Kyrgyz Republic, Moldova, and Ukraine (Chubrik et al. 2011). In Jamaica, government health expenditure experienced a 6.5 percent negative growth during the crisis period of 2009–10. If health services are not strategically targeted to the most vulnerable, the downturn may have a strong impact on those who cannot afford alternative sources of care (Brenzel 2012b).

The potential overall impact of the three linkages could be a decline in health outcomes. It has been estimated that in developing countries, a 1 percent GDP decline is associated with a rise in mortality of between 0.24 and 0.40 infants per 1,000 children born (Baird, Friedman, and Schady 2011). A similar phenomenon was observed in the countries affected by the Asian crisis, as they experienced a 3–11 percent increase in under-five mortality rates. Several studies have been conducted on the impact of economic shocks and the current GEC on child nutritional status in Africa. An additional 27,000 deaths in children less than five years of age are expected in Sub-Saharan Africa because of the recent global crisis (Cornia, Rosignoli, and Tiberti 2011).

It is clear from the existing evidence that negative external shocks, such as those emerging from economic crises, have had significant impacts on population health and the health sectors in developing countries.

The A.T.M. Framework: A Positive Transmission Mechanism

Health is not just an outcome of income; it is also a determinant of income. Both theoretical and empirical evidence have shown that a population's individual and collective health affect a nation's economic development and performance. The challenge to make health sectors more resilient and prepared to face economic crises is, therefore, critical for developing countries. To meet this challenge the A.T.M. framework was developed to break the negative transmission through the three-step process of *assessing* the health sector vulnerability to economic crisis, *tracking* the impact quickly during the crisis, and *mitigating* the impacts of the crisis through countercyclical policy instruments (see figure 1.3).

In the following chapters the A.T.M. framework is examined in depth to provide a blueprint for increasing health sector resilience during economic downturns.

Chapter 2 focuses on assessing the vulnerability of the health sector to downturns. An empirical instrument was developed and applied to a global database to capture the extent to which health sectors are prepared for economic downturn. A vulnerability framework and instrument was developed and applied with specific examples from European countries that were strongly impacted by the 2008–09 financial crisis. A vulnerability zoning approach was used to situate countries relative not only to neighboring and similar income countries, but also

Figure 1.3 The A.T.M. Framework

Assess the vulnerability of the sector to downturns

Global assessment | Country-specific assessment

Track the impact of the crisis in real time

Global and regional tracking | Country-specific tracking

Mitigate the impact of the crisis on the vulnerable

across a range of factors that are external to the health sector, characteristics of the sector, and related to household risks.

Chapter 3 focuses on tracking the impact of the crisis in real time as economies shrink. The Europe and Central Asia (ECA) experience that began in 2008 and 2009 exposed the health sector in most countries as unable to quickly and effectively track the short- and medium-term impact of the economic downturn. With the exception of a few countries, there were no national instruments that could capture how households were being impacted or how insurance funds were being affected. The ECA Human Development team at the World Bank fielded snap household surveys in six countries and an insurance survey in 10 ECA countries to track the impact. The ECA experience allows for discussions of how such tracking mechanisms can be mainstreamed to ensure that health sectors are not caught unprepared in future downturns.

Chapter 4 examines the development and implementation of health sector policies and instruments that can mitigate the impact of a downturn on the most vulncrable. The ability of any sector to mitigate the impact of an economic downturn is contingent on the existence of instruments prior to the downturn that allow identification of the most vulnerable and the ability to target interventions to them. The recent ECA experience in 2008 and 2009 points to the dearth of such instruments in the health sector (with the possible exceptions of Turkey and Georgia). Previous economic downturns in East Asia and Latin America have led to considerable improvements in identification and targeting of the poor. Chapter 4 discusses four country case studies and summarizes the lessons that can be used in other countries. The chapter puts a particular emphasis on the important nexus between the health sector and the social protection sector, especially the targeted transfers.

The last chapter, chapter 5, presents the experiences of two European countries (Ireland and Portugal) to illustrate how the health systems of these developed countries responded to the crisis with policy changes that affected their systems and health outcomes during the prolonged negative economic cycle that began in 2008. The studies explored the data, monitoring, and warning signs that were used to inform health policy discussions and the ways in which system resilience has been affected. The cases also illustrate the differences in the political economic dynamics of country responses, their priority-setting processes, and reform management.

The overall aim of this book is to provide policy makers and practitioners in the health field a more systematic framework (A.T.M.) to design and implement policies that can protect people, particularly the poor, from the negative effects of economic downturns on health and health services utilization. The critical challenge to track and mitigate negative shocks on health brings to light the importance of strategic cross-sector partnerships such as between the health sector and the social protection sector. These strategic partnerships will allow more effective identification and delivery of transfers and essential services to the poor and vulnerable and bring greater stability and resilience to health systems globally.

Learning from Economic Downturns • http://dx.doi.org/10.1596/978-1-4648-0060-3

Notes

1. The terms "economic downturns" and "crisis" are being used interchangeably. Noneconomic shocks, such as natural disasters, are excluded from the analysis.
2. Inversely, nine of the ten less volatile economies are OECD countries (Hnatkovska and Loayza 2003).
3. See Ishihara (2005) for a crisis typology.

Bibliography

Agénor, P. R., C. J. McDermott, and E. S. Prasad. 2000. "Macroeconomic Fluctuations in Developing Countries: Some Stylized Facts." *World Bank Economic Review* 14 (2): 251–85.

Agüero, J. M., and M. Valdivia. 2010. "The Permanent Effects of Recessions on Child Health: Evidence from Peru." *Estudios Económicos* 1: 247–74.

Baird, S., J. Friedman, and N. Schady. 2011. "Aggregate Income Shocks and Infant Mortality in the Developing World." *Review of Economics and Statistics* 93 (3): 847–56.

Bhutta, Z. A., F. A. Bawany, A. Feroze, A. Rizvi, S. J. Thapa, and M. Patel. 2009. "Effects of the Crises on Child Nutrition and Health in East Asia and the Pacific." *Global Social Policy* 9: 119–43.

Block, S. A. 2004. "Nutrition Knowledge and the Demand for Micronutrient-Rich Foods: Evidence from Indonesia." *Journal of Development Studies* 40: 82–105.

Bloom, D. E., and D. Canning. 2005. "Health and Economic Growth: Reconciling the Micro and Macro Evidence." Working Paper 42, Center on Democracy, Development, and the Rule of Law, Stanford Institute on International Studies, Stanford, CA.

———. 2008. "Population Health and Economic Growth." Commission on Growth and Development Working Paper 24, Commission on Growth and Development, Washington, DC.

Brahmbhatt, M., and O. Canuto. 2012. "Fiscal Policy for Growth and Development." *Economic Premise* 91, Poverty Reduction and Economic Management, World Bank, Washington, DC.

Bredenkamp, C., G. Sølve Sande Lie, and L. Brenzel. 2011. "Rapid Assessment of the Effect of the Economic Crisis on Health Spending in Mongolia." Health, Nutrition, and Population (HNP) Discussion Paper, Human Development Network, World Bank, Washington, DC.

Brenzel, L. 2012a. "Literature Review on the Impact of the Global Financial Crisis on Health." Unpublished background paper provided for *Learning from Economic Downturns: How to Better Assess, Track, and Mitigate the Impact on the Health Sector*, World Bank, Washington, DC.

———. 2012b. "Jamaica Case Study." Unpublished background paper provided for *Learning from Economic Downturns: How to Better Assess, Track, and Mitigate the Impact on the Health Sector*, World Bank, Washington, DC.

Brinkman, H. J., S. de Pee, I. Sanogo, L. Subran, and M. W. Bloem. 2010. "High Food Prices and the Global Financial Crisis Have Reduced Access to Nutritious Food and Worsened Nutritional Status and Health." *Journal of Nutrition. Supplement: The Impact of Climate Change, the Economic Crisis, and the Increase in Food Prices on Malnutrition* 10: 153–61S.

Chubrik, A., M. Dabrowski, R. Mogilevsky, and I. Sinitsina. 2011. "The Impact of the Global Financial Crisis on Public Expenditures on Education and Health in the Economies of the Former Soviet Union." CASE Network Report No. 100, Center for Social and Economic Research, Warsaw, Poland.

Clements, B., D. Coady, and S. Gupta. 2012. *The Economics of Public Health Care Reform in Advanced and Emerging Economies.* Washington, DC: International Monetary Fund.

Cornia, G. A., S. Rosignoli, and L. Tiberti. 2011. "The Impact of the Food and Financial Crises on Child Mortality: The Case of Sub-Saharan Africa." Innocenti Working Paper, UNICEF Innocenti Research Centre, Florence, Italy. http://www.childimpact .unicef-irc.org/documents/view/id/86/lang/en.

Dasgupta, B., and M. I. Ajwad. 2011. "Income Shocks Reduce Human Capital Investments: Evidence from Five East European Countries." Policy Research Working Paper 5926, World Bank, Washington, DC.

EBRD (European Bank for Reconstruction and Development). 2010. *Life in Transition Survey.* http://www.ebrd.com/pages/research/publications/special/transitionII.shtml.

Foxley, A. 2009. *Recovery: The Global Financial Crisis and Middle Income Countries.* Washington, DC: Carnegie Endowment for International Peace.

Frankel, J., C. Végh, and G. Vuletin. 2011. "On Graduation from Procyclicality." Preliminary Draft, National Bureau of Economic Research Working Paper 17619. http://www.nber.org/papers/w17619.

Green, D., R. King, and M. M. Dawkins. 2010. *The Global Economic Crisis and Developing Countries.* Oxfam International Research Report, Oxfam International.

Held, D., M. Kaldor, and D. Quah. 2010. *The Hydra-Headed Crisis.* LSE Global Governance. London School of Economics.

Heltberg, R., N. Hossain, and A. Reva, eds. 2012. *Living through Crises: How the Food, Fuel, and Financial Shocks Affect the Poor.* New Frontiers of Social Policy. Washington, DC: World Bank.

Hnatkovska, V., and N. Loayza. 2003. "Growth and Volatility." Policy Research Working Paper 3184, World Bank, Washington, DC.

Hopkins, S. 2006. "Economic Stability and Health Status: Evidence from East Asia before and after the 1990s Economic Crisis." *Health Policy* 75: 347–57.

Ishihara, Y. 2005. "Quantitative Analysis of Crisis: Crisis Identification and Causality." Policy Research Working Paper 3598, World Bank, Washington, DC.

Kwon, S., Y. Jung, A. Islam, B. Pande, and L. Yao. 2010. "The Impact of the Global Recession on the Health of the People in Asia." In *Poverty and Sustainable Development in Asia: Impacts and Responses to the Global Economic Crisis,* edited by A. Bauer and M. Thant. Metro Manila: Asian Development Bank.

Musgrove, P. 1987. "The Economic Crisis and Its Impact on Health and Health Care in Latin America and the Caribbean." *International Journal of Health Services* 17 (3): 411–41.

Pallage, S., and M. Robe. 2003. "On the Welfare Cost of Economic Fluctuations in Developing Countries." *International Economic Review* 44 (2): 677–98.

Paxson, C., and N. Schady. 2004. "Child Health and the 1988–92 Economic Crisis in Peru." Policy Research Working Paper 3260, World Bank, Washington, DC.

Stiglitz, J. E. 2000. "What I Learned at the World Economic Crisis." *New Republic,* April 17.

Waters, H., F. Saadah, and M. Pradhan. 2003. "The Impact of the 1997–98 East Asian Economic Crisis on Health and Health Care in Indonesia." *Health Policy and Planning* 18 (2): 172–81.

WHO (World Health Organization). 2009. *The Financial Crisis and Global Health.* Report of a High-Level Consultation. Geneva, Switzerland. January 19.

World Bank. 2010. "Lessons from Past Crises—and How the Current Crisis Differs." In *Global Monitoring Report 2010: The MDGs after the Crisis.* Washington, DC: World Bank. http://siteresources.worldbank.org/INTPROSPECTS/Resources/334934 -1327948020811/8401693-1327957257247/8402460-1328631318777 /GMR2010WEB.pdf.

CHAPTER 2

Assessing the Vulnerability of the Health Sector to Economic Downturns

During the 2008–09 financial crisis and economic downturn, no region suffered more than Europe and Central Asia (ECA). Surprisingly, in most countries in the region, health sectors were completely unprepared and almost entirely absent from actions to mitigate the impact of the downturn. The World Bank team covering human development sectors (Education, Health, and Social Protection) responded by fielding snap household and insurer surveys, providing timely technical assistance and funding. Two important lessons stand out when examining the recent ECA and previous health sector experiences during economic downturns. The first lesson revealed that responses are far less effective if they take place "at the height of a crisis" and, therefore, preparedness is critical. Second, the considerable heterogeneity of response makes learning and sharing knowledge critical.

There is little doubt that future systemic and unpredictable global economic downturns will occur. There is also no doubt, and the ECA evidence confirms, that such shocks will have a direct and more significant impact on the poor and vulnerable. Part of this impact will take the shape of health-related behaviors and risks (for example, use of health services, purchasing of drugs, access to insurance, nutritional status) triggered by the impact of the downturn on health systems, employment-related insurance mechanisms, and access to affordable food.

"A" in A.T.M.: Assessment of Vulnerability

The A.T.M. (assessing, tracking, mitigating) approach was designed to guide countries in their efforts to build health system resilience to economic crises. The approach starts with vulnerability assessment, which involves measurement of system performance relative to quantitative benchmarks. The second component encourages continuous tracking of crisis impact, especially variables that can serve as early warning signals to raise system alerts and help timely action. These first areas of focus enable informed mitigation strategies, which include both immediate actions to increase efficiency and attenuate the effect of the shock, as well as medium- to long-term structural changes.

As the entry point for successful mitigation strategies, this chapter examines the first area of focus of the A.T.M. approach. It proposes a Conceptual Framework for a health system vulnerability assessment that examines the drivers of system vulnerability in a way that can be applied for quantitative analysis. A Global Quantitative Tool is introduced to benchmark country-specific health system vulnerability to economic crises in comparison to peers and over time.

When considering the need for, and usefulness of, such an instrument the following questions may arise: Why should countries engage and invest in developing an assessment tool? Could such a tool help to strengthen systems and move countries toward universal health coverage? Who would use this tool, and how? If coupled with policy backing as well as global and country-level application, assessment and benchmarking will help identify weak spots, focus attention and resources, and strengthen system resilience.

Assessment is important because the proposed Global Assessment Tool could contribute to health system stability in the following ways:

1. Charting a New Territory: Compared to other fields, such as food security (Food Price Watch 2012; Messier et al. 2012) and environmental vulnerability (SOPAC 2010), the health system lags behind in providing standardized definitions, metrics, and applied tools that would help assess crisis-related vulnerabilities. There are no descriptive tools that would allow for retrospective comparison, let alone predictive tools that would enable early warning signals.

2. Investments to Improve Readiness and Resilience: Evidence has shown that when it comes to crisis mitigation, readiness matters. A system that has more reserves is more likely to withstand shocks. Investing in an assessment tool can yield returns by providing actionable data to reduce the population's vulnerability to economic crises and, thereby, mitigate the negative effect of shocks on human capital.

3. Methodological Rigor vs. Policy Multiplier: Undoubtedly, global tools and league tables that are based on reduced dimensions of determinants to compare country performance suffer from limitations. For example, the methodological robustness and interpretation of the rankings of both the Human Development Index[1] and the Doing Business Index[2] have been heavily debated. Although such tools are not perfect, they have played an important role in focusing the attention of policy makers and the development community on shortcomings in these areas and leveraging significant resources to remedy weaknesses at the country level. Similarly, the policy-multiplier effects of a system vulnerability assessment tool are expected to be high. Even when measurement and tracking focus on simple targets, such as the health targets of the Millennium Development Goals (MDGs), the policy and resource mobilization implications are invaluable.

4. Reducing Threats of Social Crisis and Rollback of Universal Health Coverage by Improving Harmonization between Macro and Human Development Objectives: The full effects of the global economic crisis, which started in 2007 in the developed world, have likely not yet fully materialized.[3] In affected Organisation for Economic Co-operation and Development (OECD) countries, with some lag, the shock has already started to hit the social sectors. On the positive side, crisis is an opportunity for efficiency gains. However, one challenge is that where system reforms have already squeezed efficiency, essential services can suffer. Given the tension between short- and long-term objectives, when system vulnerability is increasing, coordination and harmonization between macro stabilization and sectoral needs become more important because what "penny-wise can be smart, may well end up being pound-wise foolish" by undermining long-term investments in human capital (Gené-Badia et al. 2012). The case studies in chapter 5 illustrate how difficult it is to balance short- and long-term objectives and the dynamics between macro stability and sectoral objectives. Despite the difficulties, there are a number of countries that have effectively managed to cope with crises, used downturns to strengthen resilience, and catalyzed structural changes in the sector.

5. Breaking the Cycle: At the time this chapter was written, the Global Business Leader Survey's[4] confidence measure had declined to 46 percent. Anything below 50 percent is considered contraction. Through various pathways, such as foreign direct investment (FDI), remittances, trade, and foreign aid, the continued downturn can trickle further to developing economies. Macroeconomists and fiscal and monetary policy makers are working to break the downward cycle, but the efforts are not as articulated or visible on the social side. The proposed vulnerability assessment approach could serve as an empirical tool to inform health sector policies and reform efforts that aim to strategically strengthen system resilience.

6. Alignment with Global Development Priorities: Beyond being aligned with global development priorities, this chapter adds a sector-specific perspective on what risks economic crises pose for the health sector and how the sector could help mitigate these. As an example, the *World Development Report 2014*,[5] which focuses on managing risk for development, proposes that risk management should be a central concern at all levels of society. Viewing it from the health system's perspective, there are a number of instruments that can contribute to effective risk management at the sectoral level, including development and/or strengthening of general taxation and insurance for pooled financing; development and/or strengthening of targeting mechanisms, which ideally take advantage of existing structures of safety nets or, in case of gaps, strategic build-up and extension of safety nets in coordination and collaboration with other social sectors; and continuous risk assessment and tracking of progress to help policy makers and system designers keep their fingers on the pulse of ever-changing system vulnerabilities.

Undoubtedly, some regions and countries are more in need of vulnerability assessment than others. These countries are already doing their share to understand and map crisis pathways and effects, and devise policies and strategies that can attenuate the economic and social effects of negative shocks. Yet, often not enough is done. The development and introduction of assessment methods and tracking systems are important and worthwhile even in countries where the impacts of economic crisis have been less significant. As crises are unpredictable recurring events, early diagnosis and mitigation are critical to decreasing their effects. Building a tool and applying it is a relatively small investment with potentially high human capital returns.

Literature Review

The question to explore in the literature review is how far we have come in defining, understanding, and measuring health system vulnerability to economic crises. Even before the recent global economic crises (GEC), which started as early as 2007, a significant body of work was dedicated to exploring the human cost of various economic crises globally, including the consequences of macro shocks on health.[6] In recent years the GEC has driven further research to better understand the pathways from crises to population health. Two approaches have been widely applied to understand the relationship and transmission between economic crises and health. The "finalist" approach focuses on the effect of economic shocks on final health outcomes and the population-level financial effects, such as catastrophic expenditures and the poverty effects of health shocks, of ill health during crises. The "intermediary" approach focuses more on system-level factors and intermediary outcomes that constitute part of the result chain from crisis to health outcomes.

The Micro School: Final Health Outcomes Approach

One school of the crises-and-health literature has focused on estimating changes in final health outcomes as a result of economic crises, using micro data. Findings from applied micro studies diverge depending on whether the crisis occurs in a low-, middle-, or high-income country (Ruhm 2000, 2012; Smith and Yazbeck 2011). Further, controlling for income level, there is evidence of systematic difference in the impact of crises on health as a function of the social sensitivity and preferences of the government.

In low-income countries (LICs) crises have been associated with higher infant mortality and malnutrition. The evidence indicates that malnutrition has increased in countries of South Asia (Skoufias, Tiwari, and Zaman 2011) and Sub-Saharan Africa (Bhalotra 2010; Carter and Maluccio 2003) during macroeconomic downturns.[7] Infant mortality has been found to be countercyclical in developing countries; increasing when there are negative economic shocks (Conceição, Namsuk, and Yanchun 2009; Mendoza and Rees 2009; Paxson and Schady 2004; Rukumnuaykit 2003; Simms and Rowson 2003). In many cases, girls are disproportionately affected by negative outcomes (Baird, Friedman, and Schady 2007; Friedman and Schady 2009).

Evidence from high-income countries (HICs) suggests that economic downturns are "good for your health" (Ruhm 2000). For example, in the United States, infant mortality is pro-cyclical, decreasing when there are negative economic shocks. During recessions individuals are more likely to exercise[8] and less likely to smoke, drink, or engage in other health-damaging behaviors. On the other hand, Zaridze et al. (2009) found an increase in alcohol-related deaths in the Russian Federation during the crisis in the 1990s, as did Kwon and Jung (2009) in the developing context of Nepal and Bangladesh (Brenzel 2012). There are fewer traffic accidents and related deaths when the economy is weak. In contrast, the sign of coefficient estimates for mental health and suicide are mostly positive during crises. The Asian economic crisis was associated with a rise in suicide mortality in Japan, Hong Kong, and the Republic of Korea in 1998. Similarly, Kentikelenis et al. (2012) reported a 40 percent increase in suicides and increases in psychiatric morbidity in Greece as a result of the GEC. However, Stuckler et al. (2009) showed that despite rising unemployment, suicide rates were dropping in Finland and Sweden due to government commitment to social protection and use of active labor market programs.

Findings from middle-income countries (MICs) are indicative of an overall negative impact of economic crises on health. However, the evidence is stronger for intermediate indicators (government health spending and utilization of services) than for health outcomes such as prevalence of malnutrition and infant mortality, although in cases there is evidence of the latter. Positive policy responses in Argentina and Thailand are noteworthy examples of how countries can mitigate the adverse effect of macro shocks on population health and financial protection (Gottret et al. 2009; Smith and Yazbeck 2011). As to health effects, Schady and Smitz (2010) provide country-specific estimates of the effect of macroeconomic shocks on infant mortality for a sample of mainly MICs. In most countries, infant mortality appears to be pro-cyclical or a-cyclical. Only when shocks to gross domestic product (GDP) are very deep, 15 percent or larger, are they consistently associated with higher mortality.

The Health System School: Intermediary Outcome Approach

The other school of the crises-and-health literature has focused on understanding how the government and system pathways affect and contribute to decline in key health outcomes during crises.

By nature, work that falls under this category tends to apply a broader analytical framework, draw more on macro data and more detailed system-level data, and incorporate reviews of regional or global evidence. These types of analytical papers are often explicitly structured to inform and aid policy making regarding crisis monitoring, tracking, and mitigation in the context of the health sector. Because the social protection function is multidimensional and operational mechanisms across sectors are similar or can even result in economies of scale (for example, targeting instruments and interface for safety nets), system papers often share and draw on lessons from other sectors of human development. While methodologically these analyses tend to be less robust as they do not establish causality, the benefit of this approach is that it aims to unpack the role and effect of system-level factors between crises (macro level) and health outcomes (micro level). In addition they specifically explore how the system conducts or buffers shocks.

a. Global Evidence on Pro-poor Health Services: As an example, Gottret et al. (2009) focused on how governments can protect pro-poor health services in the face of the GEC. The authors studied the nature of past crises, their health impacts, including intermediate indicators and final outcomes, and government responses to crises to draw lessons on how to positively impact health outcomes and reduce financial risk. Contrary to the literature that has a narrower focus on final health outcomes, they put more emphasis on understanding the linkages between intermediary mechanisms such as deteriorating fiscal position, reduction in government revenues, public expenditures on health, and development assistance for health (DAH), and health. Negative changes in these intermediaries affected both the supply of health care and demand by households. The paper concluded that broad-brush strategies to maintain overall levels of government health spending have failed to protect access to quality care for the poor. Focused efforts to sustain the supply of lower-level services, combined with targeted demand-side approaches such as conditional cash transfers, may be more effective.

b. Health Policy Responses to the GEC in Europe: In a policy overview paper Mladovsky et al. (2012) claimed that there is relatively little understanding of how economic downturns influence health systems. To contribute to the health system vulnerability literature, they presented evidence on health policy responses to the current crisis from the European region. The paper discussed the possible effects of these policies on health system performance and draws tentative conclusions about the implications for government responses to health system shocks. The main focus was on responses to the financial crises that started in 2007 and to other shocks to the health system to identify cases in which countries used crisis as a "window of opportunity" to undertake reforms that could mitigate short-, medium-, and long-term effects. One contribution of the paper is a survey-based systematic assessment of policy responses by governments to health system shocks. The results summarized responses from 45 of the targeted 53 countries. Based on this evidence, the authors provided a list of policy tools that are likely to promote health system goals. Another important list contained policy responses that presented a risk to access, financial protection, and equity principles, such as increasing user charges and reducing population coverage.

c. Effects of the GEC on Health in Europe: The World Health Organization (WHO 2013) published a document that summarizes preliminary findings from a new study that analyzes the effects of the crisis on health and health systems in Europe. The study focuses on macro and fiscal trends, trends in health expenditures, health system responses to the crisis, the impact of the crisis on health system performance, and on policy implications. This investigation adds a second wave of key informant interviews from 47 countries to the work cited in the paper by Mladovsky et al. (2012), which drew on information from key informants in 45 countries.

d. World Bank Financial Crisis Monitoring in the ECA Region: As part of the World Bank's financial crisis monitoring exercise, the Bank's ECA region has undertaken a survey on the financial situation of health insurance funds (HIFs) in the fall of 2009. The survey included detailed questions on revenues, expenditures, the insured population, utilization, and waiting lists. Based on responses from 10 countries[9] that participated in the survey, Koettl and Schneider (2010) found that because of overreliance on tax financing, HIFs faced a substantial drop in revenues in 2009. Most HIFs tried to protect core expenditures like primary care and prescription drugs, while cutting hospital expenditures. Further, HIFs also applied reduced reimbursement rates to providers to balance their budgets. The economic crisis caused a major shift in membership profiles from actively contributing members to those whose contributions are paid by the state. With unemployment increasing, the number of uninsured increased in several countries. There have been cases of reduction in the depth and/or breadth of statutory insurance coverage.

e. Increasing Interest in Lessons and Solutions on How to Manage Risk at the Sector Level: As the GEC, combined with the impact of aging populations, continues to strain country budgets in Europe, increasing attention is being paid by policy makers and researchers to the impact of the current crisis and to lessons on policy responses to identify effective strategies that help manage risk at the system level. *Health Policy* published a series of studies on the impact of the financial crises on health sector reform in Europe. Some of the most battered countries of the European Union (EU) in terms of fiscal and macro effects that were included in the studies are: Italy (de Belvis et al. 2012; Ferrè, Cuccurullo, and Lega 2012), Spain (Gené-Badia et al. 2012), and Portugal (Barros 2012b). Similarly, an organized panel at the European Conference on Health Economics (ECHE 2012) presented qualitative and quantitative evidence on the macroeconomic context and health system performance and reform efforts of Portugal (Barros 2012a), Ireland (Thomas 2012), and Greece (Yfantopoulos 2012). The panel discussed the economic and political economy context, health policy responses, and their consequent effects on the system and the population to draw on these lessons when designing the next generation of responses and reforms.

f. Country- and Regional-Level System Response Assessments: A review by Brenzel (2012) reveals increasing interest in establishing links between macro shocks and health sector performance, including a number of country-specific rapid assessments of the impact of the current GEC on health spending and health budgets (for example, in Mongolia, Tajikistan, and Jamaica) (Bredenkamp, Sølve Sande Lie, and Brenzel 2011; Chuma 2010; Gordon-Strachan and Brenzel 2010), regional studies by WHO in Africa (Kirigia et al. 2011), and a 26-country comparative study in Europe (Cylus, Mladovsky, and McKee 2012).

g. Global Macro Evidence: At the global level, although not with a focus on crises and health, two papers presented findings on the income elasticity of public and private health expenditures (Fleisher, Leive, and Schieber 2013; Xu, Saksena, and Holly 2011). Both analyzed macro panel data and applied simple elasticity calculation or more advanced methods, such as fixed effects model or dynamic panel data analysis. The estimated elasticities are important because they could serve as proxy measures for the vulnerability of public or private expenditures to fluctuations in GDP, representing the system's exposure to macro shocks. Using panel data from the Fiscal Health Database, constructed by the World Bank (2012) and covering 183 countries over 16 years (1995–2010), two papers explored the relationship between crisis and the health sector, with a focus on the transmission between the macrofiscal context and health sector responses to better understand the extent, nature, and drivers of counter- or pro-cyclical sector policies (Liang and Velényi 2013; Velényi and Smitz 2013).

h. Pro- vs. Countercyclical Sector Policy, and the Role of Targeting and Research to Contribute to Designing More Countercyclical Sector Policies: A common challenge for development has been that social outlays and fiscal contractions happen in concert during crises (pro-cyclical movement) (Alderman and Haque 2006; see box 2.1), straining the ability of governments to operate critical programs especially when the number of vulnerable populations increases. In a paper on the impact of the 2008–09 financial crises, Lewis and Verhoeven (2010) found that crises have a strong effect on government and household spending. These effects are highly variable depending on the severity of the downturn, and the cyclicality of government spending. Countercyclical spending is positively related to income. As countries become richer, they protect more social spending. On the other hand, it is the lowest-income countries that are most likely to curtail spending in a crisis. Comparing sectoral outlays, they found that during crises, health expenditures suffer more as compared to education spending. The authors concluded that countercyclical spending has taken root and countries are temporarily expanding safety nets by borrowing to protect social sector spending and redirecting fiscal resources to retain social services. However, this improvement is not uniform within regions or income groups, and there is space for improvement. Both papers emphasize the importance of targeting to make countercyclical policies more viable and highlight the importance of research[10] to inform the design of social programs and sector policies that aim to reduce vulnerability. An important practical consideration is whether and how governments can move from pro-cyclical to more countercyclical policies, including LICs that do not have fiscal space to finance year-round annual transfer programs to the needy (Alderman and Haque 2006).

Box 2.1 Why Is Government Health Expenditure More Pro-cyclical in Some Countries than in Others?

Countercyclical government spending has been found to be essential in fostering long-term economic and human development objectives (Brahmbhatt and Canuto 2012; Braun and di Gresia 2003; Darby and Melitz 2008; Doytch, Hu, and Mendoza 2010). Standard neo-classical and Keynesian theories suggest that fiscal policy should be countercyclical, with fiscal deficits declining when the economy is expanding and increasing during downturns (Akitoby et al. 2004). One component of countercyclical fiscal policy is countercyclical social policy, which includes unemployment benefits and other social transfers, as well as public expenditures on health and education (Darby and Melitz 2008; del Granado, Gupta, and Hajdenberg 2013; Doytch, Hu, and Mendoza 2010; Essama-Nssah and Moreno-Dodson 2013; Thornton 2008).

Despite the theoretical agreement on the benefits of countercyclical policies, evidence shows that in low- and lower-middle-income countries protecting public investments in health and maintaining public expenditures on health have not been the norm (Abbas and Hiemenz 2011; Brahmbhatt and Canuto 2012; del Granado, Gupta, and Hajdenberg 2013; Doytch, Hu, and Mendoza 2010; Lewis and Verhoeven 2010). The consequence of pro-cyclical behavior in less developed countries is that rather than mitigating, it amplifies economic fluctuations, with adverse effect on government revenues, poverty levels, long-term growth, and human capital formation (Thornton 2008).

Thus, it has been a vexing question for experts and policy makers to understand what the binding constraints are to attaining countercyclical policy making and, consequently, what the policy options are to break pro-cyclical fiscal and public health spending reflexes.

For example, in the context of Latin America, Braun and di Gresia note that while the adverse effects of economic volatility on safety nets and poverty are well known (Braun and di Gresia 2003; Wodon and Ayres 2000), social spending tended to be pro-cyclical. There are several factors that might lead to pro-cyclical responses of fiscal policy (Akitoby et al. 2004; Braun 2001; Gavin and Perotti 1997); among them, the most cited drivers are (a) political economy and (b) constraints to accessing credit markets (Akitoby et al. 2004; Calderon and Schmidt-Hebbel 2008; Doytch, Hu, and Mendoza 2010; Thornton 2008).

How to prepare (analytically) for the next crisis in terms of fiscal responses has become an important question (Cuesta and Martinez-Vazquez 2013). In the context of the recent global economic downturn and food price volatility (Doytch, Hu, and Mendoza 2010), the issue of undertaking social policies as part of the countercyclical response to crises has become ever so urgent. However, the empirical evidence on the relationship between business cycles and public expenditures on health is thin. In particular, little emphasis has been placed on studying specific ways of reducing pro-cyclicality in government health spending. There are only a handful of papers that empirically explore the relationship between business cycles and social spending (for example, Braun and di Gresia 2003), and only the most recent ones have global coverage to allow for comparison across regions and income groups. From this already thin set, only a few specifically discuss

box continues next page

Box 2.1 Why Is Government Health Expenditure More Pro-cyclical in Some Countries than in Others? *(continued)*

the relationship between business cycles and health spending (del Granado, Gupta, and Hajdenberg 2013; Doytch, Hu, and Mendoza 2010; Liang and Velényi 2013; Velényi and Smitz 2013).

Note: This review shows that economic crises and the health sector is a topic that has been receiving attention. Although mirroring the nature of the trigger itself, assessment, tracking, and mitigation efforts seem to be correlated with the proximity of crisis, data availability, and sensitivity to social sector needs.

Evidence Gap

Notwithstanding the growth in the crises-and-health literature, there are notable gaps. First, it is hard to find definitions for "health system shock" or "health system vulnerability." Mladovsky et al. (2012) define health system shock as *"an unexpected occurrence originating outside the health system which has a large negative effect on the availability of health system resources or a large positive effect on the demand for health services."* Second, to our knowledge, there has been no systematic effort to develop a conceptual framework and tools that could enable assessing the vulnerability of health systems to macro shocks.

Indisputably, compared to the fields of social protection, food security and nutrition (Cuesta, Tiwari, and Htenas 2012; FAO 2003, 2012[11]; Messier et al. 2012), and environmental vulnerability, the health sector lags behind in defining vulnerability; developing, piloting, and applying standardized tools to assess and benchmark vulnerability; developing, piloting, and applying country-specific vulnerability assessment tools to inform customized responses; and hence providing a systematic framework and assessment approach that would help policy makers link vulnerability to policy options.

Objectives of the Vulnerability Assessment Tool

The gaps identified in the literature in this area emphasize the need to develop a health system vulnerability assessment framework to guide analytical work and policy discussions, coupled with a pilot version of a global health system vulnerability assessment tool. The tool will facilitate performance benchmarking against peers and over time that can be easily applied by countries and practitioners, and serve as the foundation of country-specific vulnerability assessment tools.

The objective of a vulnerability assessment framework and tool package is to help identify areas for policy intervention, which could address problems in the supply and demand side of the system both separately or jointly. By identifying areas for policy intervention and matching gaps with policy options, the proposed health system vulnerability assessment framework and tools could contribute to reducing the sector's vulnerability to crises and better maintain system performance, including on key final outcomes, such as access to care, health status, and illness-related financial protection.

Health system vulnerability is multidimensional and, as such, it is necessary to examine factors outside of the health sector to better understand the likelihood and expected depth of vulnerability. The goal of the proposed assessment framework and tool is to help policy makers better understand the dimensions of vulnerability. This understanding, along with actionable data, can inform reform and policy processes aimed at increasing system resilience and countercyclical responses.

Vulnerability assessment considers three dimensions, which jointly determine overall system resilience. The first dimension, risk exposure, examines to what extent the health system is exposed to crisis. This dimension is largely beyond the control of the health sector. It includes external factors, such as macroeconomic and political stability. The second dimension, intrinsic vulnerability, examines the strengths and weaknesses of the system. This dimension captures innate, structural system fragility or natural resilience to shocks. The third dimension, extrinsic vulnerability, explores how reform policies position the health sector to withstand crises. This dimension examines preparedness, whether governments and policy makers have (rapid) reaction capacity to respond to crises.

A user-friendly framework and empirical tool should facilitate identifying weak spots and help policy formulation in the health sector, as well as technical discussions with other social sectors and ministries of finance and development.

Methodology of Health System Vulnerability Assessment

There are a number of general concepts and approaches to vulnerability assessment. Vulnerability assessment tools must be field and context specific to be meaningful. The challenges include: an agreed upon working definition of vulnerability in the context of the health sector; agreed upon methods to quantify vulnerability; ability to find appropriate data to pilot the proposed global and domestic assessment tools; application of these tools on a regular basis; and last, identifying a way to feed the results to policy making. The remaining section of this chapter explores these challenges and proposes some solutions.

Proposing a Vulnerability Assessment Framework
Properties of Vulnerability Assessment Frameworks
In general, the role of any vulnerability assessment framework is to identify the main relationships and "trigger variables" that can help predict the vulnerability of certain main outcomes to shocks. There are two key words in this general concept that we need to operationalize—vulnerability and shock.

a. Vulnerability: As there is no standard definition of health system vulnerability to crises, we first need to agree on what we mean by "crisis-related vulnerability of the health sector" and propose a working definition. For this, we draw on the vulnerability literature in other areas, such as food security and environmental vulnerability, which are more advanced both conceptually and in terms of empirical application of frameworks using quantitative and qualitative measurement techniques (Capaldo et al. 2010; Dercon 2001; Ligon and Schechter 2004; Lybbert et al. 2004; Sen 1983).

b. Shock: Because economic crises are heterogeneous in their triggers and magnitudes, vulnerability assessment is sensitive to the definition and measurement of crises. Therefore, crisis definition and measurement also need to be standardized for the purpose of system vulnerability assessment.

Defining Health System Vulnerability

The literature review showed that when it comes to vulnerability assessment, food security is an advanced field because it has standardized definitions, measures, frameworks, and tools for vulnerability assessment. While there is no authoritative approach, this field offers a number of robust approaches which can serve as an example for health system vulnerability assessment.

a. Defining Vulnerability: In the food security literature "vulnerability"[12] is referred to as "the full range of factors that place people at risk of becoming food insecure. This is determined by the exposure of an individual, household, or group to the risk factors and their ability to cope with or withstand stressful situations" (see FAO 2002 reference in Capaldo et al. 2010). Food security has been defined as universal and permanent access to sufficient, safe, and nutritious food (see FAO 1996 reference in Capaldo et al. 2010).

b. Quantification: Consequently, the dependent variable for modeling food vulnerability is not contentious. At its core, food vulnerability analysis provides a quantitative estimate of the probability that a given household will lose access to sufficient and quality food in the near future. A standard model has not arisen yet and different analytical methods coexist for food security analysis. These methods draw on data from various levels, including: national and subnational indicators (demography, macroeconomics, environmental, political, etc.); indicators specific to the subject (food economic indicators, such as food access, availability, and stability); household indicators (household characteristics, feeding practices, health and sanitation); and individual outcome indicators (food consumption, health and nutrition status) (FAO/FIVIMS 2002).

c. Vulnerability Framework and Monitoring: There are some evolving possible best-practice examples of how vulnerability frameworks and monitoring can help. A multisectoral effort led and coordinated by the World Bank's Poverty Reduction Groups has developed a proposal under the Crisis Response Window (CRW) for a framework to monitor food crises, which defines, identifies, and monitors food security crises at the national level (Cuesta, Tiwari, and Htenas 2012). The proposed monitoring system aims to contribute to the early detection of unfolding food security crises in most vulnerable IDA (International Development Association) countries. Vulnerability is defined in terms of degree of exposure to domestic food price spikes and limited macroeconomic capacity to mitigate their effects. The framework consists of two components: global and domestic monitoring. The proposal discusses and calibrates several indicators and triggers that can identify and predict crises. The two-pronged approach enables the activation of the CRW both "top-down" (as a result of changes in global food and fuel prices) and "bottom-up" (as a result of changes in domestic staple prices and macroeconomic variables for IDA countries).

d. Policy Feedback: Messier et al. (2012) have developed a maternal and child nutrition protection toolkit for stable, crisis, and emergency situations that offers practical guidance for policy makers and helps with the transmission between measurement, monitoring, and policy making.

But what is crisis-related health system vulnerability? Drawing on the definitions above and adapting them to our context, crisis-related vulnerability in the health system could be framed as the *full range of factors that place people at risk of becoming "health insecure" and factors that threaten universal and permanent access to adequate quality health care services*. That is, it can be understood as the population's exposure to health risks and illness-related financial shocks that would not have taken place without the economic shock.

a. Dependent Variable: There are several alternatives for selecting the outcome variable of interest. System performance, with respect to crisis-related vulnerability, could be quantified by a measure of access; an input that influences access, such as public or private expenditures on health care; or a final outcome measure. However, each of these has limitations. Finding reliable access data at the global level is not without challenge. The relationship between inputs, such as health care expenditures, and health outcomes is complex. Evidence shows that the level of health expenditures is not necessarily a good measure of health outcomes. System efficiency, choices in resource allocations, and the institutional context are some of the recognized reasons behind the variation in health outcomes for a given level of health expenditures. Final health outcome measures vary in the extent of responsiveness to crises. Some, such as mental health, suicide, and being underweight or wasted (weight for height) respond faster and can be early warning type variables. Others, such as child or maternal mortality and stunting (height for age), respond with a lag and tend to be more sensitive in a low-income context. Some of these measures also capture chronic system-level challenges. Last, among the final-outcome measures, household-level illness-related financial protection is an important measure of crisis-related system performance because it is an established proxy for the breakdown of safety nets and the poverty effects of crises via the health sector.

b. Multidimensionality: As health outcomes are multidimensional, it is important to understand that some of the inputs that influence outcomes are not directly within the control of the health sector.

These technical considerations have led us to two responses during the development process. First, we need to select and test alternative dependent variables. Second, the assessment framework and tool should be designed in a way that facilitates understanding and, to the extent it is possible and practical, the isolation of forces beyond the system that determine health outcomes. To be practical and trigger policy responses, it is important for the tool to distinguish between external and system-level factors and help identify actionable bottlenecks.

Crisis Typology and Measurement

A number of empirical studies and policy papers that focus on vulnerability assessment emphasize that the magnitude of the crisis matters in terms of its expected effect on the outcome variable of interest. Thus, in order to create an empirical tool, in addition to our attempt in the previous section to define and measure health system vulnerability, it is important to propose an operational definition and measures for crisis.

a. Defining Crisis: There is no consensus on definitions of different types of crises despite their frequency in development economics. One of the most important common features of crises is an *abrupt* change in economic indicators. Operational definitions require an indicator and a threshold.

b. Crisis Typology and Crisis Indicators: In a crisis typology, Ishihara (2005) identifies seven types of crises.[13] Crisis classification matters because different types of crises affect systems and population outcomes through different pathways. For example, the effect of a deep recession (characterized by continuous negative growth rates over consecutive periods), which directly affects revenues and budgets, is different from currency deflation, which can exert its effect through changes in relative prices, including food and medical inputs. Differences in the pathways, scope, and expected magnitudes have implications on the choice of response mechanisms and overall strategy for reform. Crisis heterogeneity can be complex and, therefore, this analysis will focus on a few selected measures that are most relevant to health sector vulnerability. The indicator selection is based on empirical evidence from the crisis and health literature, which will be discussed in more depth under the section on variable selection.

c. Measuring Crisis—Depth and Length: With respect to the magnitude of crises, the literature discusses two dimensions that are relevant for quantification; depth and length. In simplified terms, a country experiences a crisis as soon as the selected crisis indicator exceeds an agreed upon threshold value.[14] The deviation from the defined threshold, or with respect to a trend if the measurement is longitudinal, is the depth of the crisis. The start of the crisis is indicated when the variable exceeds the threshold value. The end of the crisis is represented when the indicator returns to the normal zone relative to the defined threshold. The length of the crisis is defined by the beginning and the end. In reality it is difficult to be precise regarding the length of the crisis, which emphasizes the need for crisis preparedness. In general, the severity of a crisis is determined by its length and distance from the normal zone, which is measured in standardized Z scores. To test the different response by governments during crises, empirical papers in the context of public expenditures on health have applied the concept of "output gap," which is measured in terms of standard deviation from the Hodrick-Prescott filtered trend line for GDP per capita. "Good" time is defined as economic output 1.5 standard deviations above the trend line (economic output potential), and "bad" time is when the economic performance is at least 1.5 standard deviations below the filtered trend line (del Granado, Gupta, and Hajdenberg 2013; Velényi and Smitz 2013).[15]

d. Policy and Impact Implications of Improved Understanding of Crisis Typology and Measurement: Intuitively, shorter crises may be easier to absorb but they leave little time for adjustment. On the other hand, longer crises provide ample time for policy makers to institute system reform through structural or "transformative" change. A better understanding of the dimensions and pathways of a given crisis can lead policy makers and system designers to focus on building reserves, increasing system efficiency, devising automatic stabilizers, and improving targeting mechanisms. This is particularly important because a population's ability to withstand shocks is directly related to the amount of buffer possessed by a government or system.

The Three Vectors of Health System Vulnerability

From theory and empirical evidence we know that crisis-related vulnerability depends on a number of factors, the interaction of those factors, and their relative weight on vulnerability. Therefore, in the proposed vulnerability assessment framework we break down crisis-related health system vulnerability into three main components: external factors, system-level factors, and household-level factors. These components, which jointly determine health sector resilience and health outcomes during crisis, are illustrated in figure 2.1.

The rationale behind this three-level breakdown illustrates the importance of structural factors in the economy, as well as crisis depth in terms of the expected impact of the crisis. Systems that are inherently more resilient and pro-poor are more likely to mitigate crisis effects on populations. However, where external

Figure 2.1 Three Main Components of the Vulnerability Assessment Framework for Vulnerability Scoring and Zoning: External, System, and Household Factors

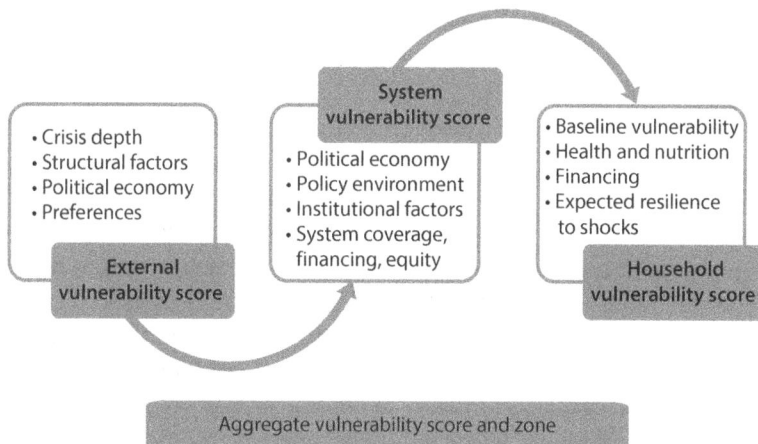

factors show higher levels of instability and these couple with weak system-level factors, the residual claimant of the crisis effect will ultimately be the household. If households have little buffer to cope with shocks, the crisis can have spillover effects beyond the current time horizon, including intergenerational poverty effects through pathways such as maternal and child health, and nutrition during the first 1,000 days (*The Lancet* 2008; Messier et al. 2012; SUN 2011).

The scope and limitations of each of the three vectors that determine aggregate-level system vulnerability are described here:

a. External Factors: This level focuses on selected key indicators of macro and fiscal performance and structural factors that affect the economic performance with the objective to identify risk factors, crisis pathways, and help measuring crisis depth and length (for example, using Z scores). To manage expectations and to provide information for intrasectoral and budget discussions, it is important to note that, by definition, external-level factors are beyond the scope of health sector policy making. However, these factors are critical components of the framework because they can offer information and points for discussion regarding revenue sources, as well as general and intersectoral budget allocation decisions. Many of the related policy instruments, however, cannot be directly and immediately influenced by health sector policy makers.

b. Health System–Level Factors: At this level, the framework and tools are designed to assess the robustness of the health system, by examining policy context and orientation, institutional aspects, health care financing, population coverage, system equity, as well as some basic dynamics of the political economy that contribute to defining the system's exposure to crises. This level is of critical importance because resolving the identified weaknesses, except for political economic dynamics that emanate from general country preferences and institutional development, is directly within the scope of the sector. Therefore, policy options regarding sector-level risk management are at the center of vulnerability assessment and consequent reform agendas that aim to improve the system's capacity to respond to and withstand shocks.

c. Household-Level Factors: At the household level, the assessment framework aims to capture increased household exposure to health risks due to the economic shock. The measures include change in access to care (individual and household-level coverage and utilization), health outcomes (infant and maternal mortality rates and nutrition measures), and illness-induced financial loss (catastrophic expenditures and their concentration) and poverty implications. It is somewhat artificial to distinguish some factors that could fit under both the system and household levels. For example, coverage can be both a system-level proxy and a household-level factor. Because our data are macro, this overlap will constrain our ambition to select variables for the household level. We are limited to data that are aggregated from household surveys. It is important to note that given the multisectoral determinants of health outcomes, risk at this level is a function of the performance of other sectors as well. Therefore, when assessing household-level vulnerability, beyond understanding the health-specific measures, ideally, data would need to be collected on enabling variables that fall under the responsibility of other sectors, such as social protection, education, and water and sanitation. Given the data limitations, the variables in this vector are limited to health and nutrition outcome measures that show where the given country is on that dimension compared to others or its performance over time. The data do not necessarily allow for predicting factors such as household savings that would help us project the country's future vulnerability.

It is important to consider the relationship and interactions among the three levels and the respective influence of the selected indicators in each vector on the aggregate measure of health system vulnerability (figure 2.1).

The next aggregation challenge is obtaining an "overall vulnerability measure," the combination of the performance under each vector. Because some of the vectors are beyond the health sector's capacity, two options are available. If aggregation is equally weighted, this would simply provide a measure of what risk the population faces and, largely, capture structural characteristics. On the other hand, if one wanted to emphasize the role of sector-level risk management responsibilities and the capacity of the sector to shape the institutions and policies to respond to crises, then this vector would be assigned a higher weight. The different weighting methods can serve as incentives, depending on whether the task team's primary objective is to inform general government, health sector policy, or household-level performance issues and attitudes.

The following examples highlight the relations and interactions between the external, system, and household levels:

- Health sector outcomes are heavily affected by social preferences. Some governments and systems place more weight on social safety nets, equity, and pro-poor financing and service delivery. These result in higher structural preparedness and resilience (Tandon et al. 2013).
- The political economy and relationships between the Ministry of Finance (MOF) and Ministry of Health (MOH) and also within the sector are important because these dynamics influence resource allocation decisions, the design of targeting mechanisms, and program placement. These dynamics strongly affect the extent of crisis responsiveness.
- If the system is structurally sound and more resilient to crises, it will absorb the majority of the shock and mitigate the impact on households. Beyond structural preparedness, if policy makers respond to early warning signals then systems, once again, can absorb more of the shock and alleviate pressure on households thereby mitigating the depth of impact.

Therefore, it is important to quantify the performance of countries on each of the three main areas based on selected variables and to understand the consequences of methodological choices regarding the construction of the aggregate vulnerability measure, which, beyond the raw vulnerability zones, also captures the interplay among the three vectors.

Developing a Global Health System Vulnerability Assessment Tool

Criteria for Data Sources for Health System Vulnerability Assessment

The vulnerability assessment tool is proposed to be used for benchmarking across countries and over time, and it aims to be a practical and user-friendly instrument that can be applied by client countries and sector teams. To this end, data sources that are relevant for the three vectors of health system vulnerability as proposed in the conceptual framework were identified. Additional criteria included the following: that the sources are annually available, internationally comparable and consistent over time, have global coverage, and do not involve material additional collection efforts and expenditures from client countries.

To meet these criteria, the analysis draws on rich and diverse pieces of information that are currently found in multiple databases. A new synthetic database, referred to as the Fiscal Health Database, which was developed by the World Bank (2012), includes, among other things, data on health expenditures, health outcomes, government revenue, spending and debt, as well as other measures of fiscal and financial sustainability related to the health sector and the overall macroeconomy.

This macro database combines several sources of data produced by different organizations and authors, including for instance WHO National Health Accounts (NHA) data, the World Bank's World Development Indicators (WDI) and HNP Stats (Health, Nutrition, and Population), International Monetary Fund (IMF) data (including Article IV and other datasets), episodes of financial crises (Laeven and Valencia 2012), labor statistics from the International Labour Organization (ILO), data on official development assistance (ODA), Health Equity and Financial Protection (HEFPro), data on political economy from the Polity Project and from the International Country Risk Guide (ICRG) Political Risk Rating Index,[16] and others (see annex 2A).

Using this macro panel, which covers 2,500 variables, 183 countries, and 50 years for some variables, we focused on the series between 1995 and 2010. Both external and system-level measures are available for this period. The NHA data series, developed and maintained by the WHO, starts from 1995. A brief overview of the database, including metadata and descriptive statistics of key variables, as well as some limitations, will be presented under the section that discusses the empirical application and results (also see annex 2B).

Rationale for Variable Selection

To operationalize the concept of the proposed system vulnerability assessment framework and tool, it is necessary to select indicators that can help quantify vulnerability. Because of the large number of variables in the database, the following criteria were applied to develop a parsimonious tool: (a) ensure theoretical and empirical relevance; (b) ensure data availability; and (c) avoid ambiguity or bimodality, and redundancy. Basic statistical robustness checks were performed during the variable selection process including standard descriptive analyses and correlation tests.

For the tool to be useful, applied, and cost effective, it must rely on data that are annually updated, comparable and consistent, of acceptable quality, and publicly accessible. Table 2B.1 provides the full list of variables considered for health system vulnerability analysis. During the data mining process two main challenges were identified, which led to the reduction of the variable set in each of the three vectors:

a. Data Inconsistency and Standardization: Data inconsistencies between major sources of global data required the comparison of variable definitions; data collection and construction processes; and the performance of sensitivity analyses in order to identify a selected standardized set that can be used for vulnerability analysis.

b. Data Gaps and Global Public Good: There are significant data gaps in the global dataset at all three levels of the analysis. Because of missing data (see table 2C.3), the number of variables (dimension) in each of the three vectors was reduced. At the external level the equity proxy variables (Gini Coefficient and Poverty Gap at $1.25) and the variable for country policy and institutional assessment (CPIA) were dropped due to missing observations. At the system level, due to missing or unreliable data, some proxy variables for coverage and system equity (for example, access to antenatal care and its concentration index) as well as for development assistance for health (DAH) were dropped, and an immunization index of the various immunization measures was constructed to collapse these into one dimension. Serious data challenges on system equity were identified. While there are valuable efforts—for example, the series provided by the HEFPro database of the World Bank—such data are not mainstream or regularly updated. The data are only available for selected countries at most for three data points between 2001 and 2010 and not available in a time series format that would allow analysts and policy makers to track changes continuously over time. Last, although it is recognized that institutions and system-level political economic dynamics are critical in terms of vulnerability outcomes, there has been little empirical work done in this domain that would help fill the identified data gaps. The collection and integration of data on system-level political economy and institutional dynamics will be more feasible in country-specific analyses rather than in the context of global assessment where the compilation and dynamic update and validation of country-level data would require major efforts. Nevertheless, some precursors of systematic assessment in the European context can be found in the work by Mladovsky et al. (2012). Such efforts should be encouraged and broadened beyond Europe to strengthen understanding of the role of these system-level factors in vulnerability assessment. Given that the data are a macro panel, the most data limitations were found at the household-level vector. There are missing data for important household-level variables, including health and nutrition outcomes such as maternal mortality ratio, height for age, and weight for age; measures of financial protection such as catastrophic expenditures as share of nonfood household expenditures; equity of access and financial protection such as concentration index for access or utilization and catastrophic expenditures; and household savings, which could be used as a proxy for financial buffer at this level and which could potentially be a predictive not a descriptive factor, such as the health outcome measures listed above.

These basic data mining efforts have resulted in critical observations and questions. Should vulnerability assessment be considered important and become a mainstreamed tool, findings from the data mining process could feed high-level discussions on data collection, standardization, and financing. For example, if additional indicators were to be of interest to make the tool more relevant and practical, would data collection efforts fall under the "global public good" category and be financed by the development community, or is there a role for governments to play, perhaps by matching funds, as it is a joint responsibility to manage risks at the level of the health system?

The outcome of the data selection process for health system vulnerability assessment that meets the described criteria—relevance, consistency, reliability, and availability—is captured in table 2.1.

Table 2.1 Reduced Set of Variables at the Three Levels for Health System Vulnerability Assessment

Levels	Dimension type	Variable (dimension)	Data source	Unit
External	Macro	GDP growth (PPP per capita)	WB WDI	% growth
	Fiscal space	Debt-to-GDP ratio	IMF	% of GDP
	Fiscal space *LICs/LMICs	Official development assistance (ODA)	WB WDI	% of GNI
	Structural *UMICs/HICs	Unemployment rate	WB WDI & IMF	% of population
	Demography	Senior age dependency (65+)	WB WDI	% of working-age population
	Political economy and governance	ICRG index	ICRG	Score
Health system	Commitment to health from budget	GHE/GGE	WB WDI	GHE % of GHE
	Health financing level (log)	Log THE PPP per capita	WB WDI	2005 int dollars
	Health financing trend	THE PPP per capita growth	WB WDI	% growth
	Role of government in health	GHE/THE	WB WDI	PHE % of THE
	Trend of public expenditures on health	GHE PPP per capita growth	WHO	% growth
	Proxy for coverage	Vaccination index	WB (WDI & HNP Stats)	% of 1-year-old children
Household	Maternal and child health outcomes	Infant mortality rate (IMR)	WB (WDI & HEFPro)	IMR by 1,000 live births
		Maternal mortality rate (MMR)	WB WDI	MMR per 100,000 births
	Nutrition (chronic and crises)	Height for age (H4A)	WB (WDI & HEFPro)	% of children < 5
		Weight for age (W4A)	WB (WDI & HEFPro)	% of children < 5

Note: * = Variables customized based on income level; GDP = gross domestic product; GGE = general government expenditures; GHE = government health expenditures; GNI = gross national income; HEFPro = Health Equity and Financial Protection; HIC = high-income country; HNP = Health, Nutrition, and Population; ICRG = International Country Risk Guide; IMF = International Monetary Fund; LIC = low-income country; LMIC = lower-middle-income country; ODA = official development assistance; PHE = public health expenditure; PPP = purchasing power parity; THE = total health expenditure; UMIC = upper-middle-income country; WB = World Bank; WB WDI = World Bank World Development Indicators; WHO = World Health Organization.

Although descriptive analyses are performed beyond the variables that comprise these reduced dimensions, the vulnerability zoning and vulnerability assessment radar plots will draw on the dimensions presented in table 2.1. A brief rationale for the selected variables is discussed here.

1. External Factors: This vector includes six dimensions that span macro, fiscal, structural, demographic, and political economic domains. Out of these, there are two that have relevance tied to the level of development (official development assistance [ODA] as share of gross national income [GNI], and unemployment rate). Among the fiscal space dimensions, ODA as share of GNI is relevant for low- and lower-middle-income countries because it is primarily these countries that benefit from foreign assistance. ODA increases fiscal space but also vulnerability if aid flows are volatile.[17] The other fiscal space proxy, debt-to-GDP ratio, is relevant for all income levels. In fact, a number of advanced economies have high debt-to-GDP ratios, which has been a cause for concern especially during the recent global economic crisis. Unemployment rate as a structural parameter of the economy is more relevant for upper-middle- and high-income countries where the share of formal sector is higher in the economy. Further, with respect to the system implications, where funding is through social insurance, employment is especially relevant as employment-based contributions will be the function of unemployment rate (Koettl and Schneider 2010). For descriptive statistics income level is explored but not included in the reduced set for two reasons. First, the analyses will be presented by income groups. It would be duplicative to include this as one of the dimensions. Second, although income is one driver of health expenditures, it is well known that income alone cannot explain the variation in health expenditures across countries. A number of other factors matter, among them demography, technology, political economy, and government social preferences.[18] Hence, the remaining dimensions aim to proxy some of the variables that are expected to drive the dynamics between the external context and system financing and coverage. Senior dependency ratio is included because aging societies face a common challenge. As the ratio of working-age population declines, so does the revenue base, while at the same time the pressures on social expenditures, such as pension and health expenditures, increase. Together, these conditions can slow economic growth. Last, the ICRG index— a combined measure of political, economic, and financial risk—is included to proxy for political economy and governance.
2. Health System–Level Factors: This vector consists of six dimensions, of which four are measures of health financing, one is a measure of government commitment to the health sector from general budget allocations, and one is a proxy measure of system coverage. Among the health care financing measures, the level of total health expenditures (in log to compact the distribution), the growth rate of total health expenditures, public expenditures on health as share of total health expenditures (the role or size of the government in the health sector), and the growth rate of public expenditures on health were

included. These variables help capture how these dimensions change over time, especially before, during, and after crises. For example, government response to a decline in GDP growth or an increase in the debt-to-GDP ratio can be tracked. Does the government increase its commitment to health? Do public expenditures on health increase? These responses will be influenced by preferences and structural characteristics, such as more social sensitivity in expenditures and the presence of automatic stabilizers in countries. Only one coverage proxy on immunization rates was included. Unfortunately, there are no sufficient data on the equity dimension of either health care financing or on coverage. System equity and political economy measures are lacking and will require future research to expand on these critical dimensions.

3. Household-Level Factors: There are only four dimensions at the household level and these focus solely on health and nutrition outcomes. Maternal and child health measures show large variation both across and within income groups, which makes these indicators relevant measures to benchmark performance. The literature also suggests differential effect by income group and the depth of the crisis. The nutrition measures are relevant because, for example, the transmission from food prices through nutrition vulnerability can affect households in profound ways, contributing to maternal and child mortality or, through the cognitive channel, to reduced life-time potentials. The two nutrition measures capture a chronic aspect—height for age (H4A)—and a measure that is more responsive to rapid changes in economic and nutrition context—weight for age (W4A). Unfortunately, nutrition measures are more problematic because there are more missing observations in the global dataset. One cross-sectional year (2003) is relatively more populated while other years suffer from more missing observations (see table 2C.3). This requires averaging data over two to three years and prevents analysts and policy makers from tracking performance over time. Last, due to missing data, measures for financial protection or for household savings were not included.

Methodology

Two empirical approaches can be applied to put the assessment tool to practical use: vulnerability zoning and vulnerability radar plots.

Vulnerability Zoning

Objective and Use of Vulnerability Zoning: Vulnerability zoning focuses on the development of system vulnerability zones, based on standardized vulnerability Z scores, which are calculated for the selected variables. Vulnerability zoning is designed to help identify performance issues with respect to high/low performers that managed/failed to push system resilience frontiers. The zoning method was chosen over explicit ranking as the objective of the tool is not "naming and shaming." Instead, this tool is designed to help countries and their development partners assess the country's performance position in the global or reference group (see more in box 2.2) distribution on a given vulnerability dimension,

Box 2.2 Reference Groups for Descriptive Analyses

Various reference groups have been defined for comparison, including the full global list (G), World Bank–defined income groups (WB-IG), closest 30 income grouping (C30-IG), and regional classification (R) (table B2.2.1).

Table B2.2.1 Reference Groups for Calculating System Vulnerability Z Scores and Zones

Reference groups	External factors (EF)	System factors (SF)	Household factors (HHF)
Global (G)	Z score for X_i for all dimensions of EF	Z score for X_i for all dimensions of SF	Z score for X_i for all dimensions of HHF
Income group (WB or C30)	Z score for X_i for all dimensions of EF	Z score for X_i for all dimensions of SF	Z score for X_i for all dimensions of HHF
Region (R)	Z score for X_i for all dimensions of EF	Z score for X_i for all dimensions of SF	Z score for X_i for all dimensions of HHF

Note: X_i = selected variables.

These groups were created to respond to questions that vary depending on the focus of the analysis. For each income group, two alternatives are tested. One is the World Bank Group's standard income classification (WB-IG), which changes by year as countries transition from one income class to another. To be internally consistent for comparison in the cross section, scoring is done by the classification for the target year. Another income group classification, called closest thirty (C30), is tested. This classification may be more informative because there is large deviation in income within the World Bank income groups. Comparing two countries at the upper and lower cutoff points of the World Bank income group on all dimensions of health system vulnerability to crises may not make sense. Hence, how the Z scores change using the alternative income group classification, which compares the country to its closest 30 peers in terms of economic output (real GDP per capita), is explored. This is a robustness check to better understand how sensitive the Z scores are to the classification and to see how this affects scoring and zoning results. Such a test is useful to be more confident with respect to policy implications of findings.

vector, or on overall system vulnerability to crises. The dimension-by-dimension vulnerability scoring and zoning approach is to help analysts and policy makers assess which areas are actionable and merit policy responses. Given the panel data context, this approach should enable both comparison across countries for a cross-sectional data point (relative performance to reference group or other countries), as well as measuring changes over time between data points (performance of a country relative to its past performance).

Overview of Method for Vulnerability Assessment: Implementing health system vulnerability assessment comprises three basic steps:

a. Calculating Vulnerability Z Scores: First, the standardized Z scores[19] for the selected variables (X_i) (also referred to as "dimensions") under each of the three vulnerability vectors (see a schematic illustration in table 2.2) is calculated.

Table 2.2 Vulnerability-Resilience Scale for "Vulnerability Zoning"

Standard deviation range Z_s	Vulnerability zones	Vulnerability class	Vulnerable vs. resilient
Z score < −3sd	−4	Extreme	Vulnerable
−3 <= Z_s < −2	−3	High	
−2 <= Z_s < −1	−2	Moderate	
−1 <= Z_s < 0	−1	Low	
Z_s = 0	0	Neutral	
1 >= Z_s > 0	1	Low	Resilient
2 >= Z_s > 1	2	Moderate	
3 >= Z_s > 2	3	High	
Z score > 3sd	4	Extreme	

This method is widely applied in the vulnerability assessment literature, for example, in fiscal and environmental vulnerability assessment. The Z score shows how many standard deviations the value for the given country and dimension is away from the mean of the reference group. The interpretation of the Z scores has been homogenized for all dimensions so that variables that improve resilience are positive and variables that increase vulnerability are negative. Standardization has required inverting the scale for a number of dimensions, such as debt-to-GDP ratio, senior dependency ratio, infant mortality, and aid dependency (ODA/GNI).

b. Mapping Z Scores to Vulnerability Zones: Second, the Z scores (that is, the standard deviation of the standardized Z scores for which the ranges are shown in the first column of table 2.2) are mapped into vulnerability zones. The proposed vulnerability and resilience scale ranges between minus 4 and plus 4 (see second column of table 2.2), where minus 4 indicates that the country's performance on the given indicator deviates more than 3 standard deviations from the reference group. In order to visually capture the extent of vulnerability for the country on the given dimension, color-coded vulnerability zoning was applied as illustrated in the table below, ranging from dark orange to dark blue at the two extremes of vulnerability and resilience.

c. Aggregating Vulnerability Dimensions: Third, an effort is made to aggregate the results for all vulnerability dimensions across the three levels and identify an overall vulnerability zone. As a prior, there are reservations regarding the method to construct such aggregates because of the noted data limitations. Therefore, it is important to recognize that this exercise is primarily diagnostic and descriptive and does not aim to serve as a predictive tool. Conceptually, there are two choices. The implementation and benefits/limitations of these choices are discussed below.

- Diagnostic approach: This approach recommends first calculating the Z scores, mapping these into vulnerability zones for each dimension,[20] and then averaging these zones for each vector, thereby constructing vulnerability zone results for each of the three vectors (external, system, and household-level factor) and, finally, averaging these into a total vulnerability zone for the country in a given year (see schematic in table 2.3). For convenience,

Table 2.3 Schematic for Constructing the Vulnerability Zones for Each Level and the Aggregate Vulnerability Zone

	Total score for external factors (EF)					Total EF	Total score for system factors (SF)						Total SF	Total score for household-level factors (HHF)				Total HHF	Total VZ
	Macro	Fiscal space	Structural	Demography	Political-economy and governance		Commitment to health	Health financing level	Health financing trend	Government in health	Government health trend	Coverage		Health outcomes		Nutrition outcomes			Aggregate vulnerability zone
Country	GDP growth	Debt-to-GDP	Unemployment	SR dependency	ICRG index	Average for external	GHE/GGE	Log THE PC	THE growth	GHE/THE	GHE growth	Vaccination	Average for system	IMR	MMR	H4A	W4A	Average for household	
1	—	—	—	—	—	—	—	—	—	—	—	—	—	—	—	—	—	—	—
2	—	—	—	—	—	—	—	—	—	—	—	—	—	—	—	—	—	—	—
3	—	—	—	—	—	—	—	—	—	—	—	—	—	—	—	—	—	—	—
n	—	—	—	—	—	—	—	—	—	—	—	—	—	—	—	—	—	—	—

Note: GDP = gross domestic product; GGE = general government expenditures; GHE = government health expenditures; H4A = height for age; ICRG = International Country Risk Guide; IMR = infant mortality rate; MMR = maternal mortality rate; SR = senior; THE PC = total health expenditure per capita; VZ = vulnerability zone; W4A = weight for age.

equal weights for all dimensions and vectors are used. However, the users of this tool can access the variables in the three vulnerability vectors and can practice their own judgment to assign weights to each dimension and vector. Assessing the proper weights for the proposed tool is beyond the scope of this book as it would require further empirical evidence and normative discussions. The drawback of the diagnostic approach is that it compromises comparability. As an example, if the number of dimensions within a vector changes over time for the same country, claims that the comparison is meaningful would lose validity because we would be comparing performance of a vector with changing composition. Assume that the weight-for-age dimension is present in t_0 and it has negative value but that it is missing in t_1. In this case one might erroneously conclude an observed improvement over time. With respect to the benefits, this approach is useful as diagnostic analytic work to explore which countries suffer from most missing observations, for which dimensions, and in which years the gaps are more acute. This diagnostic approach is important to inform future efforts that aim to improve vulnerability assessment. Because data limitations are not negligible, and are important to draw attention to, results will be presented using this approach. The alternative approach, presented below, would lead to constraining the sample and dimensions to an extent that a global vulnerability assessment would not be possible. Thus, the reader must bear in mind that comparisons, at times, may be artifacts of the data.

- Statistical approach: This approach, which focuses on statistical comparability, would require dropping all dimensions where there is significant missing data for the global set, as well as countries where observations are missing. Analysts would likely choose this second option as it enables comparing performance between countries and over time using the same number of dimensions; that is, using true statistical comparators and benchmarks. However, the downside is that—cognizant of the data gaps—this method would result in a reduced set of variables and countries and undermine the original aim for vulnerability assessment at a global scale.

Vulnerability Radar Plots

Vulnerability radar plots are proposed because they help comparisons undertaken for a small group of countries and provide a quick visual overview of vulnerability exposures on all dimensions of the proposed 3-vector vulnerability tool. These radar plots also facilitate comparison over time, for example, vulnerability performance before and after crises.

The radar plots rely on an alternative method for scoring, range standardization, which uses a simple formula[21] to standardize numerical values to fall between the range of 0 and 1 (Kaly et al. 1999). In range standardization the minimum value for the indictor for the group (Min X_i) is subtracted from the numerical value of the selected indicator for the country under assessment (X_i); then this (X_i − Min X_i) value is divided by the range of the variable (Max X_i − Min X_i).

While this is conceptually comparable to the Z score calculation, one advantage of the range-standardized vulnerability score (also referred to as "V score") is that this constrains the data to fall between 0 and 1, which can easily be plotted for comparison on a standardized scale. During the applied analysis, this range is scaled to be between 0 and 100 for easier visual interpretation.

The proposed empirical application of the vulnerability radar plot is captured in figure 2.2. To construct vulnerability radar plots, the variables (dimensions) for each of the three major vectors discussed were selected, which include five dimensions[22] under the external, six dimensions under the system-level, and one dimension under the household-level vector (see figure 2.2). Second, the interpretation of the constructed V scores was standardized so that the center of the radar plot means that the country's performance on the given variable is low (that is, high vulnerability to crisis), and as the value approaches toward the outside ring of the radar plot, its performance on the given dimension improves (that is, more resilient to crises). The plots between pre- and postcrisis years can illustrate whether the crisis erodes resilience and to what extent, and which dimension and vector are the most affected and require policy attention and action.

To sum up the methodological discussion, the development of the proposed assessment framework and tool so far has been primarily based on theory, empirical evidence, and basic statistical analyses. Therefore, the framework in its

Figure 2.2 Illustration of the Dimensions of System Vulnerability Radar Plot and Its Interpretation

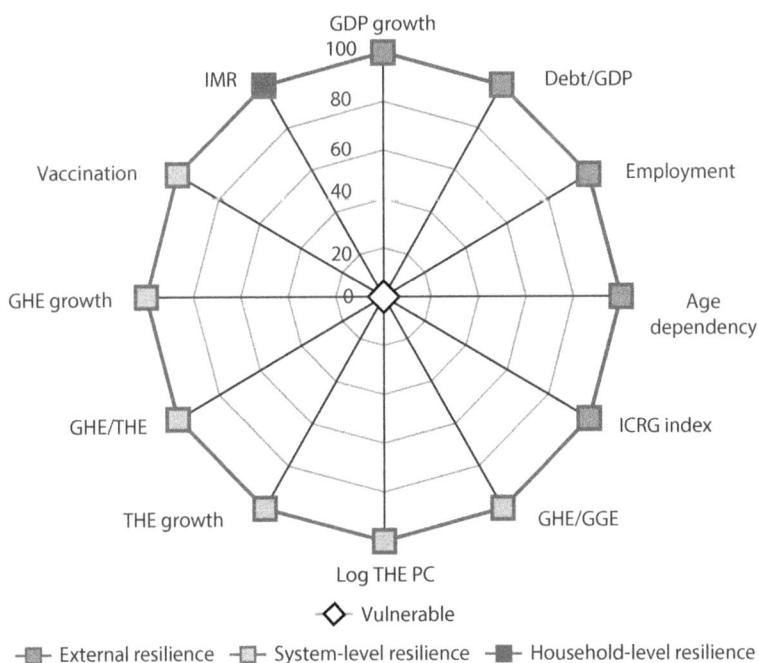

Note: GDP = gross domestic product; GGE = general government expenditures; GHE = government health expenditures; ICRG = International Country Risk Guide; IMR = infant mortality rate; THE PC = total health expenditure per capita.

current format is a descriptive and not predictive tool. To develop a predictive tool or a robust aggregated score, which would consist of sub-indices from the three major components, further analytical work would be required to test the criteria. Further, data gaps would need to be addressed to give countries equal opportunity to enter vulnerability assessment.

Empirical Application of Global Tool

The EU countries of Estonia, Greece, Ireland, and Portugal were chosen to illustrate the empirical application of the global tool through the use of radar plots. Radar plots provide an easy visual introduction to the applied use and interpretation of the tool. All four of the selected countries are HICs that have been experiencing crisis-related pressures on their health systems.

Applying the Radar Plots to Selected EU Countries

The radar plots are constructed for three years: 2003, 2005, and 2010. These years were chosen to include observations prior to the current global economic crisis, which started in 2007, and during the crisis in order to see changes before and after the crisis. Needless to say, these simple descriptive graphs do not enable causal analysis, so their interpretation is correlational. We tested a number of reference groups to construct the radar plots, including the World Bank income group classification, closest 30 income group peers, regional, and global. Using a different reference group changes the performance of the country as the dimension is measured relative to the mean and range of the reference group. Which reference group is used depends on the interest of the analyst or policy maker. Ultimately, they decide whether the objective is to compare a country to its region, income group peers, or benchmark on a global league table. To focus the discussion, radar plots applying two of these analytical filter options are presented: closest 30 income group peers and region.

In general, it is important to note that country performance in radar plots that use the closest-30-peer reference group is relative to these comparator countries and not necessarily to the countries that are captured by the same radar plot. In this case we chose this presentation and not the World Bank group's income classification because the selected OECD countries are close to each other in terms of per capita economic output (see log[23] real GDP per capita in table 2.4). Therefore, using the narrower income distribution is superior.

The figures that capture pre- and postcrisis performance show that with respect to the external factors, GDP growth significantly dropped for Greece (around zero in figure 2.3b), Ireland (around 30 percent mark on the plot), and Estonia (around 70 percent mark). The relative performance on the fiscal space dimension (measured by debt-to-GDP ratio) also deteriorated between 2005 and 2010, except for Estonia. Ireland and Portugal are around the 55 percent mark and Greece is around the 35 percent mark. Likewise, employment declined from around the 75 percent mark in 2005 to below 55 for Portugal and below 35 for Ireland and Estonia by 2010, affecting the revenue base, social security

Table 2.4 Log Real GDP per Capita for Selected European Union Countries, 1995–2010

IG	R	Country	1995	1996	1997	1998	1999	2000	2001	2002	2003	2004	2005	2006	2007	2008	2009	2010
H	ECS	Estonia	9.0	9.1	9.2	9.2	9.3	9.4	9.4	9.5	9.6	9.6	9.7	9.8	9.9	9.8	9.7	9.7
H	ECS	Greece	9.8	9.8	9.8	9.8	9.9	9.9	10.0	10.0	10.0	10.1	10.1	10.2	10.2	10.2	10.1	10.1
H	ECS	Ireland	—	—	—	—	—	10.4	10.4	10.5	10.5	10.5	10.6	10.6	10.6	10.6	10.5	10.5
H	ECS	Portugal	9.8	9.8	9.8	9.9	9.9	10.0	10.0	10.0	10.0	10.0	10.0	10.0	10.0	10.0	10.0	10.0

Note: ECS = Europe and Central Asia (now ECA); GDP = gross domestic product; H = high-income country; IG = income group; R = region; — = not available.

contributions, and demand for transfer payments (automatic stabilizers). While age dependency is a relatively static dimension, as it does not change quickly in a short time frame, the drop in the lines for Greece and Portugal to around the 75 percent mark and for Ireland to below 50 suggest that this factor is expected to lead to increasing revenue and expenditure pressures. In addition to the economic and financial turmoil, the drop in the ICRG index indicates that the crisis was accompanied by rising political risk, especially for Greece but also notable in Ireland and Portugal.

Regarding the system-level indicators, while performance on log total per capita health expenditures and health expenditure growth increased from 2005 to 2010 for Ireland and Portugal, the relative performance for Estonia and Greece has deteriorated. These total health expenditure patterns, however, cannot solely be attributed to the economic shock. As discussed in the literature, age and technology pressures contribute to the increases in the levels of health expenditures (Tandon et al. 2013). It is interesting to see how these governments respond to the shock. In Portugal, in 2010 the growth rate of public expenditures on health (government health expenditures [GHE] growth) increased relative to its performance in 2005, while the growth rates for the other three countries declined. Estonia nearly reached the 25 percent mark on the plot (figure 2.3b). In general, the pre- and postcrisis plots show a reduction in commitments to health from general expenditures (GHE/GGE) as well as in the share of public financing for the sector (GHE/THE [total health expenditure]). The time series data in table 2.5 verify the stagnation (slight decline) in public expenditures in all of the case countries, except Portugal.

Notwithstanding the relative decline in commitment to health and public financing of health care, the selected service delivery and health outcome indicators improved, implying that essential services, such as vaccination coverage, and infant mortality rate (IMR) outcomes have not been significantly affected by the crisis. The EU case studies presented in this book illustrate that efficiency enhancement in the health systems of these countries has been a positive impact of the crisis. The crisis inflicted a value-for-money squeeze and catalyzed some needed changes in these health sectors.

To put the radar plots into context, the performance of these countries was explored over the period of 1995 and 2010 for three variables of interest: GDP growth, general government expenditures (GGE), and government expenditures on health (GHE) (Velényi and Smitz 2013). Table 2.6 shows the "output

Figure 2.3 Vulnerability Radar Plot for European Union Set Using Closest 30 Reference Group, 2005 and 2010

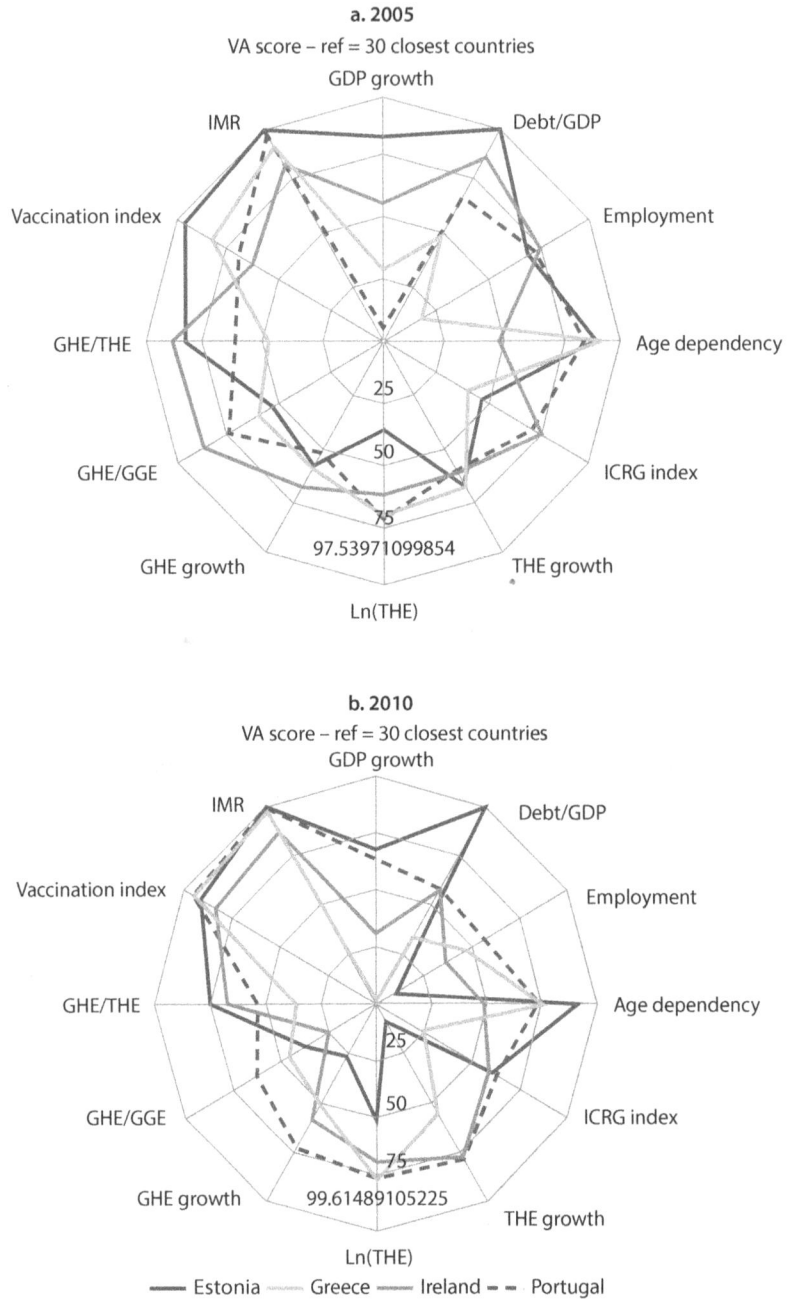

a. 2005

VA score – ref = 30 closest countries

b. 2010

VA score – ref = 30 closest countries

——— Estonia ········ Greece ——— Ireland – – Portugal

Note: GDP = gross domestic product; GGE = general government expenditures; GHE = government health expenditures; ICRG = International Country Risk Guide; IMR = infant mortality rate; Ln = logarithm; THE = total health expenditure; VA = vulnerability assessment.

Table 2.5 Log Real GHE per Capita for Selected European Union Countries, 1995–2010

IG	R	Country	1995	1996	1997	1998	1999	2000	2001	2002	2003	2004	2005	2006	2007	2008	2009	2010
H	ECS	Estonia	5.9	6.0	6.1	6.0	6.0	6.0	6.0	6.1	6.2	6.4	6.5	6.6	6.7	6.9	7.0	6.9
H	ECS	Greece	6.5	6.5	6.6	6.6	6.7	6.8	7.0	7.0	7.1	7.1	7.3	7.4	7.4	7.5	7.5	7.4
H	ECS	Ireland	6.8	6.8	6.9	7.0	7.1	7.2	7.4	7.5	7.6	7.7	7.7	7.8	7.9	8.0	7.9	7.8
H	ECS	Portugal	6.5	6.6	6.6	6.7	6.8	7.0	7.0	7.1	7.2	7.2	7.3	7.3	7.4	7.4	7.5	7.6

Note: ECS = Europe and Central Asia (now ECA); GHE = government health expenditures; H = high-income county; IG = income group; R = region.

Table 2.6 GDP, GGE, and GHE Output Gaps for Selected European Union Countries, 1996–2010

IG	R	Country	1996	1997	1998	1999	2000	2001	2002	2003	2004	2005	2006	2007	2008	2009	2010
GDP output gap																	
H	ECS	Estonia	−0.41	0.75	0.84	−0.79	−0.06	−0.23	−0.40	−0.35	−0.64	−0.18	0.98	2.18	1.30	−2.05	−0.72
H	ECS	Greece	−0.18	−0.04	−0.21	−0.47	−0.12	−0.15	−0.89	0.16	0.25	−0.80	1.08	1.98	1.54	−0.48	−2.26
H	ECS	Ireland	0.00	0.00	0.00	0.00	−0.19	−0.38	0.02	−0.40	−0.54	−0.05	0.89	2.68	0.97	−2.17	−0.84
H	ECS	Portugal	−0.78	−0.68	0.25	0.63	1.47	1.20	0.44	−1.48	−0.85	−0.90	−0.26	1.44	1.25	−1.49	−0.01
GGE output gap																	
H	ECS	Estonia	−0.65	−0.35	1.31	0.74	−0.70	−1.10	0.48	0.09	−0.69	−0.63	0.00	0.46	2.10	0.76	−2.04
H	ECS	Greece	−0.63	0.05	−0.44	−0.58	1.05	0.11	−0.26	−0.03	0.48	−1.16	−0.77	0.41	1.40	1.83	−2.17
H	ECS	Ireland	0.33	0.28	−0.61	0.38	−0.86	0.51	0.81	0.25	0.14	−0.18	−0.73	−0.43	−0.30	−2.11	2.69
H	ECS	Portugal	0.54	−0.63	−0.48	−0.06	0.28	1.48	−0.31	−0.41	0.51	1.33	−0.86	−1.01	−2.31	0.93	1.22
GHE output gap																	
H	ECS	Estonia	0.48	1.67	−0.04	0.25	−0.56	−1.09	−0.66	0.16	0.12	−0.16	−0.65	0.35	2.10	0.84	−1.83
H	ECS	Greece	0.43	0.13	−1.19	−1.01	−0.77	1.54	0.82	0.13	−1.43	−0.28	1.04	−0.10	0.83	1.16	−1.79
H	ECS	Ireland	−0.44	0.61	−0.21	−1.10	−1.12	0.36	0.88	0.25	0.26	−0.55	−0.40	0.65	1.95	0.66	−2.34
H	ECS	Portugal	0.75	−0.26	−1.46	−1.36	2.45	0.54	0.08	0.00	−0.76	1.00	−0.04	−0.31	−1.40	0.62	0.27

Note: ECS = Europe and Central Asia (now ECA); GDP = gross domestic product; GGE = general government expenditures; GHE = government health expenditures; H = high-income country; IG = income group; R = region. The color code represents the sign and size of the output gap. Blue/orange corresponds to higher/lower performance in the given year relative to the values on the filtered trend line for the variable of interest (also referred to as "good"/"bad" times). The three shades (light, medium, and dark) show the depth of the output gap, which is mapped from the calculated Z scores. For example, the corresponding Z score values for "good" times are: light = Z score < 1.5 standard deviations; medium = Z score between 1.5 and 2 standard deviations; and dark = Z score above 2 standard deviations.

gap" for these variables for the selected countries. Negative/positive output gap ("bad" and "good" times) is defined when the cyclical component of the given variable is at least 1.5 standard deviations below/above the filtered trend line.[24] The statistics in this table are color coded to distinguish between low (below 1.5 standard deviations), moderate (between 1.5 and 2 standard deviations), and high (above 2 standard deviations) output gap values. Orange/blue shading signals negative/positive output gap. The statistics show that output gap was the highest in 2009 and 2010, and show a lagged effect from GDP to GGE and GHE. In Ireland fiscal expansion is indicated in 2010 relative to the trend line. On the other hand, the government expenditures on health are well below the trend line, suggesting a consolidation in the sector. In contrast, despite the mild GDP output gap for Portugal, government health spending is above the trend line, implying countercyclical behavior.

Table 2.7 Mean Correlation over 15 Years between Cycles during "Average" and "Bad" Times

Country	Correlation between cycles			Cycle correlation when output gap < 0		
	GDP_GGE	GDP_GHE	GGE_GHE	GDP_GGE	GDP_GHE	GGE_GHE
Estonia	0.31	0.26	0.62	−0.38	−0.47	0.63
Greece	0.55	0.38	0.42	0.65	0.45	0.56
Ireland	0.00	0.25	−0.44	0.39	−0.26	−0.66
Portugal	−0.31	−0.05	0.55	−0.10	−0.20	0.58

Note: GDP = gross domestic product; GGE = general government expenditures; GHE = government health expenditures. Blue represents pro-cyclical relationship between the variables of interest; for example, co-movement of GDP and general government expenditures, or GDP and government health expenditures. Orange represents countercyclical relationship between the variables of interest.

The cyclical correlations between the growth (GDP), fiscal (GGE), and government health expenditure (GHE) cycles for the case countries over the 15-year time horizon show that, on average, Portugal has practiced countercyclical fiscal and health policies (respectively −0.31 and −0.05), and health sector expenditures have been more countercyclical during negative output gaps (−0.2). Ireland also stands out in its countercyclical health policy during output gaps (−0.25), and this seems to have taken place in the face of fiscal adjustment (0.39) (table 2.7) (see more in Velényi and Smitz 2013).

Note that changing the reference group to region (figure 2.4) and world (figure 2.5) renders a different picture, showing that performance relative to these groups has deteriorated especially on the fiscal and structural dimensions and health prioritization. However, on the positive side, system coverage and IMR outcomes are unaffected.

Vulnerability Zoning: EU and Global Sets

The objectives of the tool are to construct the vectors that are expected to influence health system vulnerability to crises and propose a way to quantify vulnerability along the selected dimensions. Ideally, if the variables account for a large variation in the outcome variable, and if the data are consistent over time, this would allow the analyst or policy maker to compare changes over time and the relative performance of countries. Table 2.8 shows the zoning results for the three vectors and the overall zoning for health system vulnerability. The zones, as described earlier, span between minus and plus four, which respectively stand for extreme vulnerability or resilience. The results suggest that health systems in the selected countries have become more vulnerable over time, between the three data points, except for Portugal, which shows mild resilience despite the prolonged shock. Further, the table enables the analyst or policy maker to see which vector drives the overall vulnerability zone, and determine whether this is actionable. Last, because of the data limitations, it is possible that comparing longitudinal performance may not be meaningful if the dimensions change over time. In order to understand how the data affect our findings the full set of selected dimensions, including their zoning result (table 2.9), is presented. This unpacking of the data allows for better identification of the challenges and

**Figure 2.4 Vulnerability Radar Plot for European Union Set Using Regional Reference Group,
2005 and 2010**

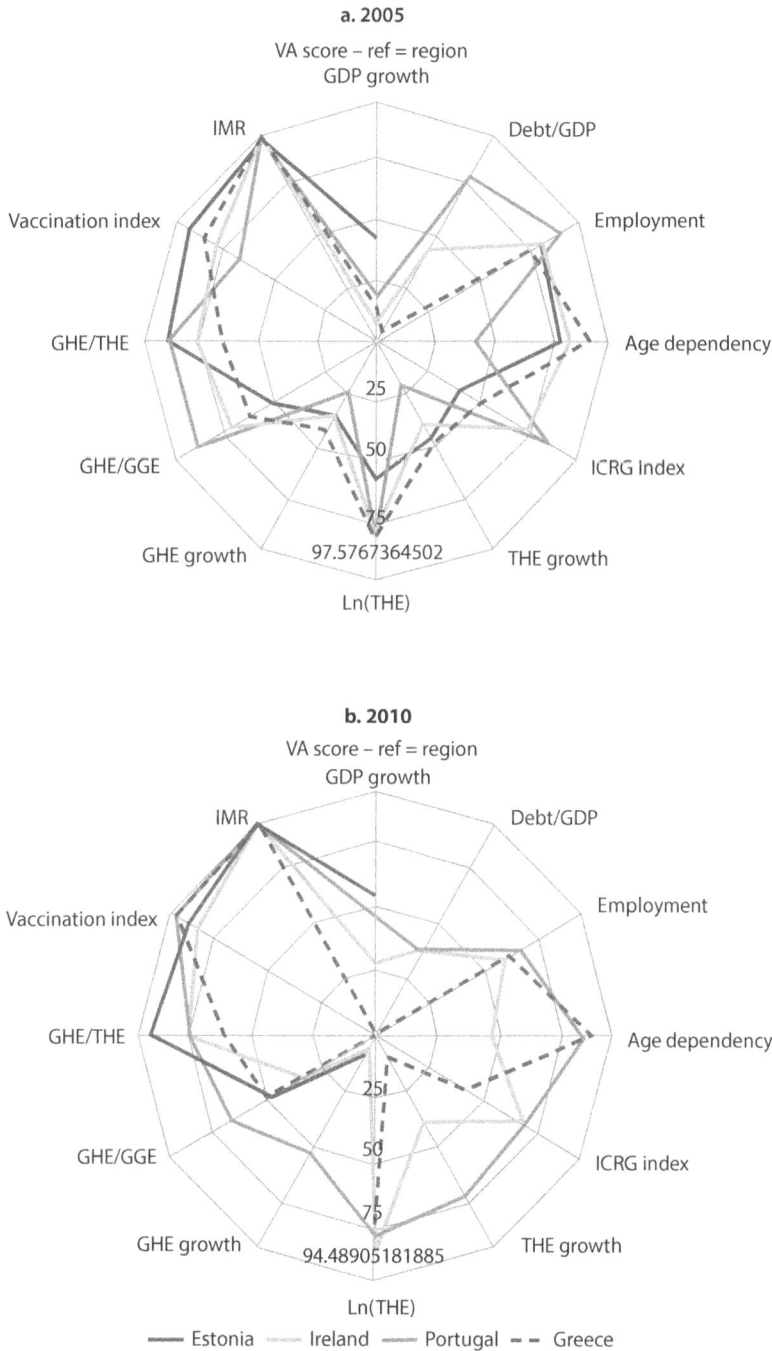

a. 2005

b. 2010

—— Estonia   ········ Ireland   —— Portugal   – – Greece

Note: GDP = gross domestic product; GGE = general government expenditures; GHE = government health
expenditures; ICRG = International Country Risk Guide; IMR = infant mortality rate; Ln = logarithm; THE = total
health expenditure; VA = vulnerability assessment.

Figure 2.5 Vulnerability Radar Plot for European Union Set Using Global Reference Group, 2005 and 2010

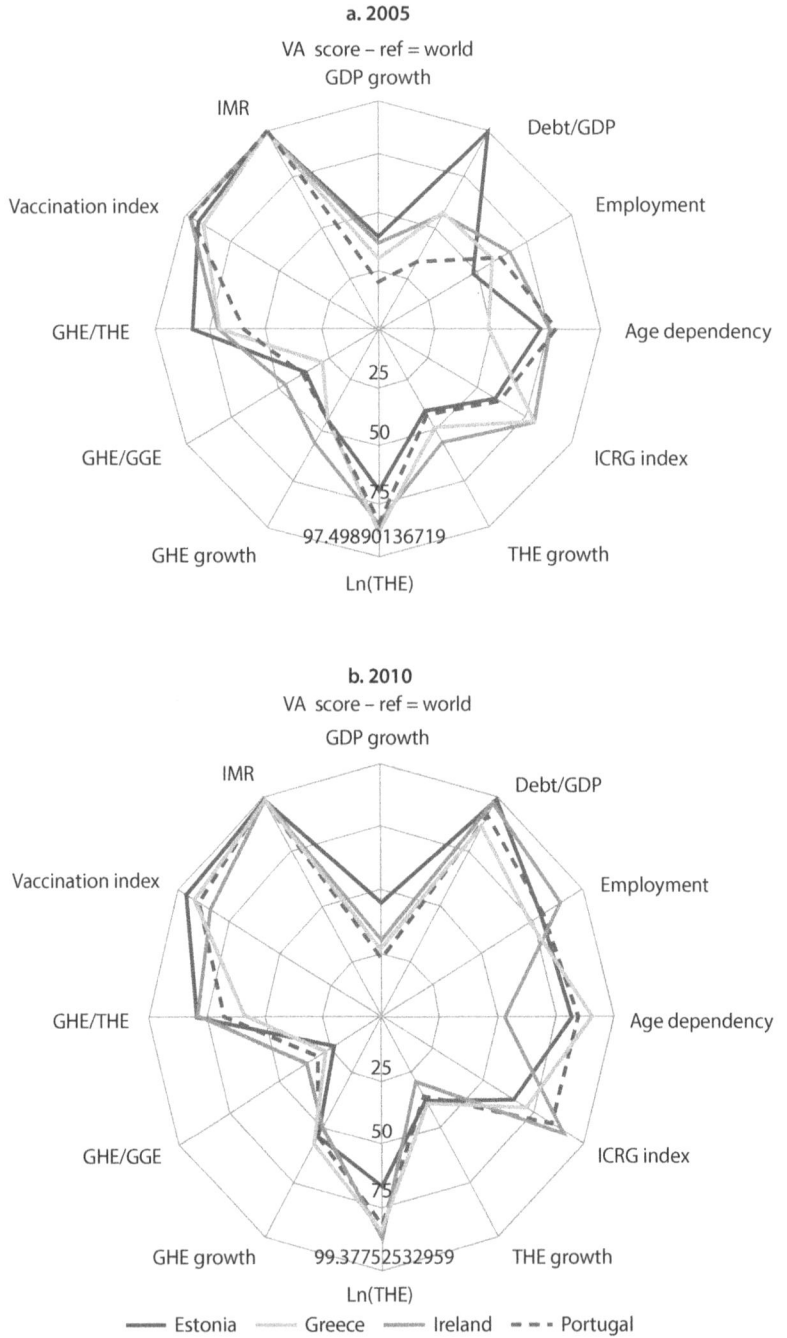

Note: GDP = gross domestic product; GGE = general government expenditures; GHE = government health expenditures; ICRG = International Country Risk Guide; IMR = infant mortality rate; Ln = logarithm; THE = total health expenditure; VA = vulnerability assessment.

Table 2.8 Change in Vulnerability Zone for the Three Vectors and Overall, 2003–05 and 2005–10

Country	IG-C30 difference	Vector mean for external	Vector mean for system	Vector mean for household	Total vulnerability score
Difference IG-C30, 2003–05					
Estonia	UM	0.00	−0.17	0.00	−0.06
Greece	H	−0.80	0.67	0.00	−0.04
Ireland	H	−0.20	0.00	0.00	−0.07
Portugal	H	−0.40	−0.33	0.00	−0.24
Difference IG-C30, 2005–10					
Estonia	H	−0.80	−0.83	0.00	−0.54
Greece	H	−0.40	−1.50	0.00	−0.63
Ireland	H	−1.40	−0.83	0.00	−0.74
Portugal	H	0.20	0.33	0.00	0.18

Note: H = high-income country; IG-C30 = income group closest 30; UM = upper-middle-income country. The color code corresponds to the direction of the change in the vulnerability score between the selected reference years (2003, 2005, and 2010). Orange/blue represents a deterioration/improvement in the vulnerability score between the most recent and previous reference year. The changes are relative to the scale presented in table 2.2.

design of policy responses. The unpacked data are especially relevant for the global data as a number of countries and variables could bias the interpretation. The global results for 2003, 2005, and 2010 are presented by income group classification in the statistical annex (2C).

Conclusions, Limitations, and Linkages

This chapter mapped out and tested a new way of assessing the vulnerability of health sectors to economic downturns. An extensive literature review within and outside the health sector on the topic of vulnerability to economic downturns found the following:

1. There is increasing evidence and research on the impact of downturns on health outcomes. This impact is different for LICs, MICs, and HICs, and not surprisingly the strongest links appear to be in LICs whereas the weakest links were in HICs.
2. There is limited evidence and research on the impact of downturns on health systems, beyond general findings on health spending. This "evidence gap" is the strong motivation for the need to develop and test robust methods and tools for assessing vulnerability.
3. Health appears to be far behind other sectors, such as social protection, nutrition, and environment, in systematically assessing risks and vulnerabilities to downturns.

Not only is health far behind other sectors in assessing vulnerabilities, but more important it is not typically seen as being part of a safety net function.

Table 2.9 Vulnerability Zones for the Selected Dimensions of the Vulnerability Vectors and Total Vulnerability for OECD Set, 2003, 2005, and 2010

Vulnerability zoning			Total score for external factors					Subtotal	Total score for system factors						Sub-total	Total score for household factors		Subtotal	Total
			Macro	Fiscal space	Struc-tural	Demog-raphy	Political econ and governance		Commit-ment to health	Health financing level	Health financ-ing trend	Govern-ment in health	Govern-ment HF trend	Cover-age		Health outcome			Total vulnera-bility score
Year and country	Region	IG-C30	GDP growth	Debt-to-GDP	Unem-ploy-ment	SR depen-dency	ICRG politi-cal risk index	Vector mean for external	GHE/GGE	Log THE PC	THE growth	GHE/THE	GHE growth	Vacci-nation	Vector mean for sys-tem	IMR	MMR	Vector mean for house-hold	
2003																			
Estonia	ECS	UM	2	2	−1	−2	1	0.40	1	−1	2	1	1	1	0.83	1	1	1.00	0.74
Greece	ECS	H	2	−1	−2	−2		−0.80	−1	1	−1	−1	1	1	0.00	1	—	1.00	0.07
Ireland	ECS	H	1	1	1	1	2	1.20	1	1	1	1	1	−1	0.67	1	—	1.00	0.96
Portugal	ECS	H	−2	1	1	−1	1	0.00	1	1	1	−1	1	1	0.67	1	—	1.00	0.56
2005																			
Estonia	ECS	UM	2	2	1	−2		0.40	−1	−1	1	1	1	1	0.67	1	1	1.00	0.69
Greece	ECS	H	−1	−2	−2	−2	−1	−1.60	−1	1	2	−1	2	1	0.67	1	—	1.00	0.02
Ireland	ECS	H	1	1	1	1	−1	1.00	1	1	1	1	1	−1	0.67	1	—	1.00	0.89
Portugal	ECS	H	−2	−1	1	1	1	−0.40	1	1	1	−1	1	1	0.33	1	—	1.00	0.31
2010																			
Estonia	ECS	H	−1	2	−2	−2	1	−0.40	−1	1	−2	1	−1	1	−0.17	1	—	1.00	0.14
Greece	ECS	H	−3	−2	−2	−1	−2	−2.00	−1	1	−2	−2	−2	1	−0.83	1	—	1.00	−0.61
Ireland	ECS	H	−1	−1	−2	1	1	−0.40	−2	1	1	−1	−1	1	−0.17	1	—	1.00	0.14
Portugal	ECS	H	−1	−1	1	1	1	−0.20	1	1	1	−1	1	1	0.67	1	—	1.00	0.49

Note: ECS = Europe and Central Asia (now ECA); GDP = gross domestic product; GGE = general government expenditures; GHE = government health expenditures; H = high-income country; HF = health financing; ICRG = International Country Risk Guide; IG-C30 = income group closest 30; IMR = infant mortality rate; MMR = maternal mortality rate; OECD = Organisation for Economic Co-operation and Development; SR = senior; THE PC = total health expenditure per capita; UM = upper-middle-income country; — = not available. The color code is as explained in table 2.2.

Consistent with the A.T.M. approach outlined in chapter 1, this chapter tackled the "A" by developing a framework and an instrument that can be used at the global level for country comparison using vulnerability zoning, and by providing the foundations for an assessment tool that can be applied at the national level. The assessment instrument can capture relative vulnerability by using available data sets from leading institutions. This is an important step in engaging the health sector more deeply in risk management initiatives and connecting it to broader social safety net programs.

By learning from the literature from other sectors, the assessment framework and tool piloted and reviewed in this chapter examines three vectors of vulnerability: external to the health system, internal within the health system, and related to the households that rely on, or are impacted by, the health system. Within each of the vectors, indicators were selected and tested. A number of factors were considered in selecting the indicators, which included relevance to the topic, availability for a large number of countries, and clarity in direction of impact. The data were then used and presented in two ways: vulnerability zoning and vulnerability radar plots. Radar plots are more visually effective in placing a few countries relative to each other, and the zoning presents more in-depth information of how each country is placed on a number of dimensions relative to different reference groups like income level or region. Examples from Europe were used to show how the methodology and tool can be used.

The objective of this work on assessment of vulnerability is not to "name and shame" countries but to provide a catalytic and empirical input into decision making and longer-term planning within the health sectors of countries. This is especially important as the health sector continues to grow in relative importance as an economic sector and one that impacts the population in a number of ways. The health sector as a share of the economy has consistently grown relative to most other sectors in the overwhelming majority of high- and middle-income emerging countries. This typically reflects the importance the population places on their health needs and on health care services. Moreover, the increasing size of the health sector gives it a larger fiscal footprint both on the public sector side and on the private spending side. This larger footprint makes it more vulnerable to economic downturn and financial crises. Failure to assess the risks associated with unexpected downturns is likely to leave the sector, and consequently the population, vulnerable.

The approach described in this chapter is but a first attempt at quantifying risks and vulnerabilities from economic downturns through the health sector. As such, the approach is a start of a process that may produce more refined instruments and increasingly more relevant data. At the current stage, data selection was limited to available and not customized databases, and it is hoped that future iterations will bring more attention to other factors in health sector vulnerability that do not currently have existing indicators. This will require more dedicated data collection efforts and a global push that can motivate funding such a global public good.

Another limitation of this first attempt relates to the methodology used. The current tool is purely descriptive. Without principal component and regression analyses, it is not possible to assess the weight of the selected variables with respect to their impact on overall vulnerability. Therefore, ranking interpretation was omitted. This limitation is also important as analysts and policy makers cannot focus policy reactions as strategically and precisely in the absence of such information. This emphasizes a need for further development of the tool using more robust statistical techniques and robustness checks.

Another important next step relates to the development of country-specific assessment tools to make the analysis more customized and valued. This requires additional data sources at the national, subnational, and possibly household levels. In addition to the quantitative approach, for country-specific assessment, the application of mixed methods is encouraged as unobservable factors, such as political, economic, and institutional dynamics, may not be easily quantifiable. These tools would need to be piloted.

Despite these constraints, this first attempt at vulnerability assessment can be used to identify: (a) countries that have fragile macrofiscal conditions, which make health systems more prone to contraction; (b) how the health system performs on financing and coverage; (c) how countries perform on final outcomes measures; and (d) where the combination of the results in these vectors places the country in overall system vulnerability and which vector—if any—dominates the aggregate vulnerability zone result. The identification of dominant vectors or factors is to inform the government where policy formulation is missing and will help to build more resilient health systems.

Moreover, country reports can be quickly prepared from the existing data that show where the vulnerabilities are the largest. Such data can inform policy discussions about the range of policies that can be applied to reduce vulnerability and at the same time bring the health sector more forcefully into the overall social safety net.

The work on assessment of vulnerability is naturally linked to tracking of the impact of downturns on the health sector as well as to the critical policies that can be developed to mitigate downturn.

Annex 2A The Fiscal Health Database

The Fiscal Health Database[25] is a macro panel database containing information on 183 countries for more than 2,500 variables related to macroeconomics and fiscal space. The data are organized by country (using the World Bank's three-letter code nomenclature) and year, and include data only from publicly available databases as of November 1, 2012. The database was created to assist with empirical analyses linked to health sector fiscal capacity and sustainability.

The database combines information from seven publically available databases which have country-level data on a broad range of determinants of health spending including revenues, health outcomes, development outcomes, equity outcomes, political climate, and labor force participation.

Table 2A.1 Overview of the Fiscal Health Database

Number of variables	2,581			
Number of observations	14,684		Time horizon	
Organization	Dataset	Type of data	Year start	Year end
1. WHO	WHO NHA	Health expenditure, services	1995	2011
2. World Bank	HNP Stats	Health outcomes; equity outcomes	1990	2009
3. World Bank	World Development Indicators (WDI)	Health outcomes	1960	2011
4. IMF	World Economic Outlook (WEO)	Revenue data	1980	2017
5. ILO	Labor Stats	Labor force participation	1990	2020
6. Polity Project	Polity Project	Political regime	1950	2010
7. HEFPro	Health Equity and Financial Protection	Health outcomes data by income quintiles	1995	2010

Note: HEFPro = Health Equity and Financial Protection; HNP = Health, Nutrition, and Population; ILO = International Labour Organization; IMF = International Monetary Fund; NHA = National Health Accounts; WHO = World Health Organization.

Annex 2B Variables Used for Vulnerability Assessment

Table 2B.1 Variables Selected to Implement the Health System Vulnerability Assessment

Levels	Variable (dimension)	Data source	Unit	Variable name
External	GDP PPP per capita	WB WDI	2005 int dollars	NY_GDP_PCAP_PP_KD
	LN(GDP PPP per capita)	WB WDI	Score	ln(NY_GDP_PCAP_PP_KD)
	GDP PPP per capita growth	WB WDI	% growth	ln(NY_GDP_PCAP_PP_KD) y0 - ln(NY_GDP_PCAP_PP_KD) y-1
	Debt/GDP	IMF	% of GDP	IM_GGXWDG / IM_NGDP
	Primary surplus	WB WDI	% of GDP	GC_BAL_CASH_GD_ZS
	Unemployment rate	WB WDI & IMF	% of population	SL_UEM_TOTL_ZS & IM_LUR
	Age dependency	WB WDI	% of working-age population	SP_POP_DPND_OL
	ICRG index	ICRG	Score	Political risk index
	ODA	WB WDI	% of GNI	DT_ODA_ODAT_GN_ZS
Health system	THE PPP per capita	WB WDI	2005 int dollars	SH_XPD_PCAP_PP_KD
	THE PPP per capita growth	WB WDI	% growth	ln(SH_XPD_PCAP_PP_KD) y0 - ln(SH_XPD_PCAP_PP_KD) y-1
	GHE PPP per capita	WHO	Int dollars	NHA_GGEH_capPPP
	GHE PPP per capita growth	WHO	% growth	ln(GHE_PPP_PC) y0 - ln(GHE_PPP_PC) y-1

table continues next page

Table 2B.1 **Variables Selected to Implement the Health System Vulnerability Assessment** *(continued)*

Levels	Variable (dimension)	Data source	Unit	Variable name
Health system (*cont.*)	GHE/GGE	WB WDI	PHE % of GHE	SH_XPD_PUBL_GX_ZS
	GHE/THE	WB WDI	PHE % of THE	SH_XPD_PUBL
	OOP/THE	WB WDI	OOP % of THE	SH_XPD_OOPC_TO_ZS
	Vaccination index	WB (WDI & HNP Stats)	% of 1-year-old children	Unweighted mean of SH_IMM_IDPT
				SH_IMM_MEAS
				hnpstats_SH_IMM_ HEPB
				hnpstats_SH_IMM_ IBCG
				hnpstats_SH_IMM_ POL3
	Vaccination CI	WB HEFPro	Score	HFPro_immu_all_CI
Household	IMR	WB (WDI & HEFPro)	IMR by 1,000 live births	SP_DYN_IMRT_IN HFPro_IMR_all
	IMR CI	WB HEFPro	Score	HFPro_IMR_CI
	Height for age	WB (WDI & HEFPro)	% of children < 5	Mean between: SH_STA_STNT_ZS
				HFPro_stunting_all
	Height for age CI	WB HEFPro	Score	HFPro_stunting_CI
	Weight for age	WB (WDI & HEFPro)	% of children < 5	Mean between: SH_STA_MALN_ZS HFPro_Uweight_all
	Weight for age CI	WB HEFPro	Score	HFPro_Uweight_CI
	MMR	WB WDI	MMR per 100,000 births	SH_STA_MMRT_NE
	Catastrophic health expenditures	WB HEFPro	% of population	HFPro_fp_hc_25
	Catastrophic health expenditures CI	WB HEFPro	Score	HFPro_fp_ci_25

Note: For technical analysis, see Wagstaff et al. 2011.[26] CI = concentration index; GDP = gross domestic product; GGE = general government expenditures; GHE = government health expenditures; GNI = gross national income; HEFPro = Health Equity and Financial Protection; HNP = Health, Nutrition, and Population; ICRG = International Country Risk Guide; IMF = International Monetary Fund; IMR = infant mortality rate; LN = logarithm; MMR = maternal mortality rate; ODA = official development assistance; OOP = out-of-pocket payment; PHE = public health expenditure; PPP = purchasing power parity; THE = total health expenditures; WB WDI = World Bank *World Development Indicators*; WHO = World Health Organization.

Table 2B.2 Data Availability for Vulnerability Dimensions, 2003, 2005, and 2010

Variable	2003	2005	2010
Log GDP	183	183	178
GDP growth	183	183	178
Debt-to-GDP ratio	164	169	169
Primary surplus	106	111	101
Unemployment	115	123	105
Age dependency	177	177	177
ICRG index	134	134	134
ODA/GNI	131	136	130
Log THE per capita	180	180	180
THE growth	180	180	180
GHE growth	179	179	176
Log GHE per capita	179	179	176
GHE/THE	180	180	180
GHE/GGE	180	180	178
OOP/THE	180	180	180
Vaccination index	179	179	180
IMR	181	181	181
W4A	47	87	42
H4A	50	87	44
MMR	69	94	60
Catastrophic health expenditures headcount	41	0	0
Catastrophic health expenditures CI	42	0	0

Note: CI = concentration index; GDP = gross domestic product; GGE = general government expenditures; GHE = government health expenditures; GNI = gross national income; H4A = height for age; ICRG = International Country Risk Guide; MMR = maternal mortality rate; ODA = official development assistance; OOP = out-of-pocket payment; THE = total health expenditure; W4A = weight for age.

Annex 2C Health System Vulnerability Zoning for Global Set Using Closest-30 Income Peer Referencing

Table 2C.1 Vulnerability Zoning Using Closest-30-Peer Referencing for High-Income Countries (HICs), 2010

Country	Region	IG-C30 H 2010	Macro GDP growth	Macro Debt-to-GDP	Fiscal space ODA/GNI	Structural Unemployment	Demography SR dependency	Political economy and governance ICRG political risk index	Subtotal Vector mean for external	Commitment to health GHE/GGE	Health financing level Log THE PC	Health financing trend THE growth	Government in health GHE/THE	Government HF trend GHE growth	Coverage Vaccination	Subtotal Vector mean for system	Health outcome IMR	MMR	H4A	W4A	Subtotal Vector mean for household	Total Total vulnerability score
Australia	EAS	H	−1	1	—	1	1	1	0.60	1	1	1	−1	1	−1	0.33	1	—	—	—	1.00	0.64
Brunei Darussalam	EAS	H	−1	2	—	2	2	−1	0.80	−2	−2	−1	1	−1	1	−0.67	−1	—	—	—	−1.00	−0.29
Hong Kong SAR, China	EAS	H	1	1	—	1	1	−1	0.60	—	—	—	—	—	—	—	—	—	—	—	—	0.60
Japan	EAS	H	2	−4	—	1	−2	1	−0.40	2	2	1	—	1	—	1.17	1	—	—	—	1.00	0.59
Korea, Rep.	EAS	H	2	1	—	2	1	−1	1.00	−1	−1	2	−2	2	1	0.17	1	—	—	—	1.00	0.72
Macao SAR, China	EAS	H	—	—	—	—	—	—	—	—	—	—	—	—	—	—	—	—	—	—	—	—
New Zealand	EAS	H	−1	1	—	1	1	2	0.80	2	—	1	—	1	1	1.17	1	—	—	—	1.00	0.99
Singapore	EAS	H	2	−2	—	2	1	−1	0.40	−2	—	1	−4	1	—	−0.67	2	—	—	—	2.00	0.58
Austria	ECS	H	1	−1	—	1	−1	2	0.40	1	—	1	—	1	−2	0.50	1	—	—	—	1.00	0.63
Belgium	ECS	H	1	−1	—	−1	−1	1	−0.20	—	—	1	—	1	—	1.00	1	—	—	—	1.00	0.60
Croatia	ECS	H	−1	1	1	−1	−2	1	−0.17	2	—	−1	2	1	—	1.00	—	1	—	—	1.00	0.61
Cyprus	ECS	H	−1	1	—	1	1	−1	0.20	−3	—	−1	−3	−1	—	−1.33	1	—	—	—	1.00	−0.04

table continues next page

Table 2C.1 Vulnerability Zoning Using Closest-30-Peer Referencing for High-Income Countries (HICs), 2010 *(continued)*

Vulnerability zoning			Total score for external factors						Subtotal	Total score for system factors						Subtotal	Total score for household factors				Subtotal	Total
			Macro		Fiscal space	Struc-tural	Demog-raphy	Politi-cal econ-omy and gover-nance		Com-mit-ment to health	Health financ-ing level	Health financ-ing trend	Gov-ern-ment in health	Gov-ern-ment HF trend	Cover-age		Health outcome					
Country	Region	IG-C30 H 2010	GDP growth	Debt-to-GDP	ODA/GNI	Unem-ploy-ment	SR depen-dency	ICRG politi-cal risk index	Vector mean for external	GHE/GGE	Log THE PC	THE growth	GHE/THE	GHE growth	Vacci-nation	Vector mean for sys-tem	IMR	MMR	H4A	W4A	Vector mean for house-hold	Total vulnerability score
Czech Republic	ECS	H	1	1	—	1	−1	−1	0.20	1	−1	−1	2	−1	1	0.17	—	—	—	—	1.00	0.46
Denmark	ECS	H	−1	1	—	1	−1	−1	0.20	1		1	2	−1	−1	0.83	—	—	—	—	1.00	0.68
Estonia	ECS	H	−1	2	—	−2	−2		−0.40	−1		−2	1	−1	1	−0.17	—	—	—	—	1.00	0.14
Finland	ECS	H	1	1	—	−1	−1	2	0.40	−1		1	1	1	1	0.67	—	—	—	—	1.00	0.69
France	ECS	H	−1	−1	—	−1	−1	−1	−1.00	1		1	1	1	−2	0.50	—	—	—	—	1.00	0.17
Germany	ECS	H	2	−1	—	1	−2		0.20	2		1	1	1	1	1.17	—	—	—	—	1.00	0.79
Greece	ECS	H	−3	−2	—	−2	−1	−2	−2.00	−1		−2	−2	−2	1	−0.83	—	—	—	—	1.00	−0.61
Hungary	ECS	H	−1	−1	—	−1	−2		−0.80	1		1		−1	1	0.00		1	—	—	1.00	0.07
Iceland	ECS	H	−2	−1	—	−1	1		−0.40	−2		−1	1	−1	1	0.33	—	—	—	—	1.00	0.31
Ireland	ECS	H	−1	−1	—	−2	1		−0.40	−2		−1		−1	1	−0.17	—	—	—	—	1.00	0.14
Italy	ECS	H	−1	−2	—	−1	−2	−1	−1.40	1		1	1	−1	1	0.33	—	—	—	—	1.00	−0.02
Luxembourg	ECS	H	—	—	—	—	—	—				—			—		—	—	—	—		
Netherlands	ECS	H	−1	−1	—	−1	−1	−1	−0.20	2	2	1	1	1	1	1.33	—	—	—	—	1.00	0.71
Norway	ECS	H	−1	−1	—	1	−1		0.20	1		1	1	1	1	1.00	—	—	—	—	1.00	0.73
Portugal	ECS	H	1	−1	—	−1	−1	−1	−0.20	1		1	−1	1	1	0.67	—	—	—	—	1.00	0.49
Slovak Republic	ECS	H	1	1	—	−2	1	−1	0.00	1		−1	−1	1	1	0.00		1	—	—	1.00	0.33

table continues next page

Table 2C.1 Vulnerability Zoning Using Closest-30-Peer Referencing for High-Income Countries (HICs), 2010 (continued)

Vulnerability zoning			Total score for external factors								Total score for system factors							Total score for household factors					Total
			Macro		Fiscal space		Structural	Demography	Political economy and governance	Subtotal	Commitment to health	Health financing level	Health financing trend	Government in health	Government HF trend	Coverage	Subtotal	Health outcome				Subtotal	Total
Country	Region	IG-C30 H 2010	GDP growth	Debt-to-GDP	ODA/GNI	Fiscal space	Unemployment	SR dependency	ICRG political risk index	Vector mean for external	GHE/GGE	Log THE PC	THE growth	GHE/THE	GHE growth	Vaccination	Vector mean for system	IMR	MMR	H4A	W4A	Vector mean for household	Total vulnerability score
Slovenia	ECS	H	-1	1	—	—	1	-1	-1	-0.20	1	1	-1	1	1	1	0.67	1	—	—	—	1.00	0.49
Spain	ECS	H	-1	1	—	—	-4	-1	-1	-1.20	1	1	-1	1	-1	1	0.33	1	—	—	—	1.00	0.04
Sweden	ECS	H	2	1	—	—	-1	-1	2	0.60	2	1	1	1	1	-3	0.33	1	—	—	—	1.00	0.64
Switzerland	ECS	H	-1	1	—	—	-1	-1	1	0.20	2	2	1	-1	1	1	1.00	1	—	—	—	1.00	0.73
United Kingdom	ECS	H	1	-1	—	—	-1	-1	1	-0.20	1	1	1	2	1	1	1.17	1	—	—	—	1.00	0.66
Antigua and Barbuda	LCN	H	-4	-2	—	1	—	—	—	-1.67	1	-1	2	1	2	1	1.00	1	—	—	—	1.00	0.11
Bahamas, The	LCN	H	-1	1	—	—	-2	2	1	0.20	1	-1	-1	-3	-1	-2	-0.67	-2	—	—	—	-2.00	-0.82
Barbados	LCN	H	—	—	—	—	—	—	—	—	—	—	—	—	—	—	—	—	—	—	—	—	—
Bahrain	MEA	H	-2	1	—	—	—	3	-2	0.00	-1	-2	1	1	1	1	0.17	-1	—	—	—	-1.00	-0.28
Israel	MEA	H	1	-1	—	—	1	1	-3	-0.20	-1	-1	1	-2	1	1	-0.17	1	—	—	—	1.00	0.21
Kuwait	MEA	H	-1	2	—	—	2	2	-3	0.40	-2	-3	-4	2	-4	1	-1.83	-2	—	—	—	-2.00	-1.14
Malta	MEA	H	1	-1	—	—	1	1	—	0.60	1	—	—	-1	—	-2	0.17	1	—	—	—	1.00	0.59
Oman	MEA	H	-1	2	—	—	—	2	-2	0.25	-2	-3	-4	-1	-4	1	-1.83	-1	—	—	—	-1.00	-0.86
Qatar	MEA	H	—	—	—	—	—	—	—	—	—	—	—	—	—	—	—	—	—	—	—	—	—
Saudi Arabia	MEA	H	1	2	—	—	-1	2	-2	0.40	-2	-2	-1	-1	1	1	-0.67	1	1	—	—	1.00	0.24

table continues next page

Table 2C.1 Vulnerability Zoning Using Closest-30-Peer Referencing for High-Income Countries (HICs), 2010 (*continued*)

Country	Region	IG-C30 H 2010	Macro GDP growth	Fiscal space Debt-to-GDP	Fiscal space ODA/GNI	Structural Unemployment	Demography SR dependency	Political economy and governance ICRG political risk index	Subtotal Vector mean for external	Commitment to health Health financing level	Health financing GHE/GGE	Health financing Log THE PC	Health financing trend THE growth	Health financing trend GHE/THE	Government in health GHE growth	Government HF trend GHE growth	Coverage Vaccination	Subtotal Vector mean for system	IMR	MMR	H4A	W4A	Subtotal Vector mean for household	Total vulnerability score
United Arab Emirates	MEA	H	−2	2	—	—	3	−1	0.50	−2	−2	−2	−3	1	−3		1	−1.33	−1	—	—	—	−1.00	−0.61
Canada	NAC	H	1	−1	—	−1	−1	1	−0.20	—	—	1	1	−1	1	1	−4	−0.40	−1	—	—	—	−1.00	−0.53
United States	NAC	H	−1	−1	—	−1	1	−1	−0.60	2	2	2	1	−2	2	2	1	1.00	−1	—	—	—	−1.00	−0.20
Equatorial Guinea	SSF	H	−2	2	1	—	2	—	0.75	−2	−2	1	−1	−1	−1	−1	−4	−1.00	−4	—	—	—	−4.00	−1.42

Note: EAS = East Asia (now EAP); ECS = Europe and Central Asia (now ECA); GDP = gross domestic product; GGE = general government expenditures; GHE = government health expenditures; GNI = gross national income; H (and HIC) = high-income country; HF = health financing; H4A = height for age; ICRG = International Country Risk Guide; IG-C30 = income group closest 30; IMR = infant mortality rate; LCN = Latin America and the Caribbean (now LAC); MEA = Middle East and North Africa (now MNA or MENA); MMR = maternal mortality rate; NAC = North America; ODA = official development assistance; SAR = special administrative region; SR = senior; SSF = Sub-Saharan Africa (now SSA); THE PC = total health expenditure per capita; W4A = weight for age; — = not available. The color code in the table is based on the description presented in table 2.2.

Table 2C.2 Vulnerability Zoning Using Closest-30-Peer Referencing for Upper-Middle-Income Countries (UMICs), 2010

Country	Region	IG-C30 UM 2010	Macro space	Fiscal space: GDP growth	Fiscal space: Debt-to-GDP	ODA/GNI	Structural: Unemployment	Demography: SR dependency	Political economy and governance: ICRG political risk index	Sub-total: Vector mean for external	Commitment to health: GHE/GGE	Health financing level: Log THE PC	Health financing trend: THE growth	Government in health: GHE/THE	Government health trend: GHE/THE growth	Coverage: Vaccination	Sub-total: Vector mean for system	IMR	MMR	H4A	W4A	Sub-total: Vector mean for household	Total vulnerability score
Fiji	EAS	UM		−2	−1		1	1	—	0.00	−1	−1	1	1	1	1	0.00	1	1	—	—	1.00	0.33
Malaysia	EAS	UM		1	−1	1	2	2	1	1.00	−1	−2	1	−1	−1	1	−0.50	1	1	—	—	1.00	0.50
Palau	EAS	UM		−1	—	−4	—	—	—	−2.50	1	2	−1	2	−1	−3	0.00	−1	—	—	—	−1.00	−1.17
Belarus	ECS	UM		2	1		2	−1	−1	0.67	−1	−1	1	1	2	1	0.33	1	1	—	—	1.00	0.67
Bosnia and Herzegovina	ECS	UM		−1	1	−2	−3	−3		−1.60	2	2	1	1	1	−1	1.00	1	1	—	—	1.00	0.13
Bulgaria	ECS	UM		−1	1		1	−3	1	−0.20	1	1	−1	1	−1	−1	−0.33	1	1	—	—	1.00	0.16
Kazakhstan	ECS	UM		1	2		1	1	1	1.17	−1	−2	1	−1	1	1	0.17	−2	−1	—	—	−1.50	−0.06
Latvia	ECS	UM		−1	1		−2	−2	1	−0.60	−1	1	1	−1	−1	−1	−0.33	1	1	—	—	1.00	0.02
Lithuania	ECS	UM		1	1		−3	−2	1	−0.40	1	1	1	1	1	1	0.33	1	1	—	—	1.00	0.31
Macedonia, FYR	ECS	UM		−1	1		−4	−1		−1.20	1	2	1	1	−1	1	0.67	1	1	—	—	1.00	0.16
Montenegro	ECS	UM		−1	1		—	−1		−0.50	1	1	1	1	1	1	0.50	1	1	—	—	1.00	0.33
Poland	ECS	UM		1	−1		−1	−1	2	0.00	1	1	1	1	1	1	1.00	1	1	—	—	1.00	0.67
Romania	ECS	UM		−1	−1		1	−2	1	0.00	−1	−1	−1	2	−1	−1	−0.17	1	1	—	—	1.00	0.28
Russian Federation	ECS	UM		1	1		1	−1	1	0.20	−1	−1	−1	−1	−1	1	−0.67	1	1	—	—	1.00	0.18

table continues next page

Table 2C.2 Vulnerability Zoning Using Closest-30-Peer Referencing for Upper-Middle-Income Countries (UMICs), 2010 *(continued)*

Vulnerability zoning			Total score for external factors							Total score for system factors							Total score for household factors					Total
			Macro	Fiscal space	Fiscal space	Structural	Demography	Political economy and governance	Sub-total	Commitment to health	Health financing level	Health financing trend	Government in health	Government health trend	HF Coverage	Sub-total	Health outcome				Sub-total	
Country	Region	IG-C30 UM 2010	GDP growth	Debt-to-GDP	ODA/GNI	Unemployment	SR dependency	ICRG political risk index	Vector mean for external	GHE/GGE	Log THE PC	THE growth	GHE/THE	GHE growth	Vaccination	Vector mean for system	IMR	MMR	H4A	W4A	Vector mean for household	Total vulnerability score
Serbia	ECS	UM	−1	−1	1	−2	−2	−1	−1.00	1	2	−1	1	−1	1	0.50	1	1	—	—	1.00	0.17
Turkey	ECS	UM	2	1	1	−1	1	−2	0.33	1	1	1	1	1	1	1.00	1	1	—	—	1.00	0.78
Argentina	LCN	UM	2	−1	1	1	−1	−1	0.17	1	1	−2	−1	−2	1	−0.33	1	−1	—	—	0.00	−0.06
Brazil	LCN	UM	2	−1	1	1	1	1	0.83	−2	1	2	−1	2	1	0.50	−1	−1	—	—	−1.00	0.11
Chile	LCN	UM	1	2	1	1	1	2	1.33	1	1	−1	−1	−1	1	−0.17	1	1	—	—	1.00	0.72
Colombia	LCN	UM	−1	1	1	1	1	−1	0.00	2	1	1	2	1	−1	1.00	−1	1	—	—	−1.00	0.00
Costa Rica	LCN	UM	−1	1	1	1	1	2	0.83	4	2	1	1	1	−1	1.33	1	1	—	—	1.00	1.06
Dominica	LCN	UM	−1	−1	−2	—	—	—	−1.33	−1	−1	3	1	2	1	0.83	−1	—	—	—	−1.00	0.17
Dominican Republic	LCN	UM	2	−1	1	−1	1	1	0.83	−1	−1	2	−1	2	−1	0.33	−1	—	—	—	−1.00	0.06
Grenada	LCN	UM	−2	−3	−1	—	−1	—	−1.25	1	−1	−2	1	−2	1	−1.00	−1	—	—	—	1.00	−0.42
Jamaica	LCN	UM	−2	−4	1	−1	−1	2	−0.83	−2	1	−2	−2	−1	1	−0.83	1	—	—	—	1.00	−0.22
Mexico	LCN	UM	1	1	1	1	1	1	1.00		1		1		1	0.20	−1	−1	—	—	−1.00	0.07
Panama	LCN	UM	1	1	1	1	1	—	1.00		1			1	1	1.00	−1	—	—	—	−1.00	0.33
Peru	LCN	UM	2	1	1	1	1	−1	0.83	−1	−1	1	−1	−1	1	0.00	1	−2	—	—	−0.50	0.11
St. Kitts and Nevis	LCN	UM	−2	−4	−1	—	—	—	−2.33	−1	1	3	−1	3	1	0.67	1	—	—	—	1.00	−0.22
St. Lucia	LCN	UM	1	−1	−2	1	1	—	−0.25	1	1	−1	1	−1	1	0.33	1	—	—	—	1.00	0.36

table continues next page

Table 2C.2 Vulnerability Zoning Using Closest-30-Peer Referencing for Upper-Middle-Income Countries (UMICs), 2010 (continued)

Country	Region	IG-C30 UM 2010	Macro (GDP growth 2010)	Fiscal space (Debt-to-GDP)	Fiscal space (ODA/GNI)	Structural (Unemployment)	Demography (SR dependency)	Political economy and governance (ICRG political risk index)	Sub-total (Vector mean for external)	Commitment to health (GHE/GGE)	Health financing level (Log THE PC)	Health financing trend (THE growth)	Government in health (GHE/THE)	Government trend in HF (GHE growth)	Coverage (Vaccination)	Sub-total (Vector mean for system)	Health outcome (IMR)	MMR	H4A	W4A	Sub-total (Vector mean for household)	Vector Sub-total	Total vulnerability score
St. Vincent and the Grenadines	LCN	UM	-2	-1	—	—	1	—	-0.75	-1	-2	-1	2	-1	1	-0.33	-1	—	—	—	-1.00	-1.00	-0.69
Suriname	LCN	UM	1	1	-1	—	1	1	0.60	1	1	-1	-1	-1	-1	-0.33	-1	—	—	—	-1.00	-1.00	-0.24
Uruguay	LCN	UM	2	-1	-1	—	—	1	0.50	2	1	1	1	—	—	1.17	1	-1	—	—	0.00	0.00	0.56
Venezuela, RB	LCN	UM	-2	1	1	1	1	-3	-0.17	—	-2	-3	-2	-3	-1	-2.20	1	—	—	—	1.00	1.00	-0.46
Algeria	MEA	UM	-1	2	—	-1	1	-1	0.17	-1	-2	-2	2	—	—	-0.50	-1	—	—	—	-1.00	-1.00	-0.44
Lebanon	MEA	UM	1	-3	—	—	1	-2	-0.40	-1	-1	-1	-2	—	-3	-1.17	1	—	—	—	1.00	1.00	-0.19
Libya	MEA	UM	—	—	—	—	—	—	—	—	—	—	—	—	—	—	—	—	—	—	—	—	—
Botswana	SSF	UM	1	1	—	—	2	1	1.20	1	1	-2	1	-2	—	0.00	-1	-4	—	—	-2.50	-2.50	-0.43
Gabon	SSF	UM	1	1	—	1	2	-2	0.60	-2	-3	-1	-1	—	-3	-1.50	-3	—	—	—	-3.00	-3.00	-1.30
Mauritius	SSF	UM	1	-1	1	1	1	—	0.60	-1	-1	2	-2	2	—	0.17	1	—	—	—	1.00	1.00	0.59
Namibia	SSF	UM	1	1	—	—	1	3	1.40	1	1	-1	1	—	-3	0.00	-1	—	—	—	-1.00	-1.00	0.13
Seychelles	SSF	UM	2	-1	2	—	—	1	1.00	-2	2	2	2	—	1	0.50	-1	—	—	—	-1.00	-1.00	0.17
South Africa	SSF	UM	-1	—	-2	-2	1	1	0.17	-1	-1	-1	-1	—	-3	-0.67	-2	—	—	—	-2.00	-2.00	-0.83

Note: EAS = East Asia and Pacific (now EAP); ECS = Europe and Central Asia (now ECA); GDP = gross domestic product; GGE = general government expenditures; GHE = government health expenditures; GNI = gross national income; HF = health financing; H4A = height for age; ICRG = International Country Risk Guide; IG-C30 = income group closest 30; IMR = infant mortality rate; LCN = Latin America and the Caribbean (now LAC); MEA = Middle East and North Africa (now MNA or MENA); MMR = maternal mortality rate; ODA = official development assistance; SR = senior; SSF = Sub-Saharan Africa; THE PC = total health expenditure per capita; UM (and UMIC) = upper-middle-income country; W4A = weight for age; — = not available. The color code in the table is based on the description presented in table 2.2.

Table 2C.3 Vulnerability Zoning Using Closest-30-Peer Referencing for Lower-Middle-Income Countries (LMICs), 2010

| | | | Total score for external factors | | | | | | Sub-total | Total score for system factors | | | | | | Sub-total | Total score for household factors | | | | Sub-total | Total |
| | | | | Fiscal space | Fiscal space | Struc-tural | Demog-raphy | Political economy and governance | | Com-mit-ment to health | Health financing level | Health financing trend | Gov-ern-ment in health | Gov-ern-ment HF trend | Cover-age | | Health outcome | | | | | |
Country	Region	IG-C30 LM 2010	GDP growth	Debt-to-GDP	ODA/GNI	Unem-ploy-ment	SR depen-dency	ICRG politi-cal risk index	Vector mean for exter-nal	GHE/GGE	Log THE PC	THE growth	GHE/THE	GHE growth	Vacci-nation	Vector mean for system	IMR	MMR	H4A	W4A	Vector mean for house-hold	Total vul-nera-bility score
China	EAS	LM	3	1	1	2	−1	−1	0.83	1	−1	2	−1	2	1	0.67	1	1	1	1	1.00	0.83
Indonesia	EAS	LM	1	1	1	1	1	−1	0.67	−1	−2	−2	−1	2	−1	−0.33	1	−1	—	—	1.00	0.44
Kiribati	EAS	LM	−2	—	−1	—	—	—	−1.50	1	2	−2	2	−2	1	0.33	1	—	—	—	1.00	−0.06
Micronesia, Fed. Sts.	EAS	LM	−1	—	−3	—	1	—	−1.00	2	2	—	2	1	−1	1.17	1	—	—	—	1.00	0.39
Mongolia	EAS	LM	1	—	—	−1	1	2	0.80	−1	−1	1	−1	1	1	−0.33	1	—	—	—	1.00	0.49
Papua New Guinea	EAS	LM	—	—	—	—	—	1	1.00	−1	−1	1	1	1	−3	−0.33	−1	—	—	—	−1.00	−0.11
Philippines	EAS	LM	—	1	1	1	1	1	1.00	1	−1	−2	−2	1	−1	−0.50	1	—	—	—	1.00	0.50
Samoa	EAS	LM	−1	—	−3	—	−1	—	−1.67	3	2	2	2	2	−1	1.50	−1	—	—	—	1.00	0.28
Solomon Islands	EAS	LM	1	1	−4	—	1	—	−0.25	3	1	−1	3	−1	−1	0.67	1	—	—	—	1.00	0.47
Thailand	EAS	LM	2	1	1	2	−1	−2	0.50	1	−2	−1	2	2	−1	0.33	1	—	—	—	1.00	0.61
Tonga	EAS	LM	−2	—	−2	—	−1	—	−1.67	1	−1	1	2	1	1	0.83	1	—	—	—	1.00	0.06

table continues next page

Table 2C.3 Vulnerability Zoning Using Closest-30-Peer Referencing for Lower-Middle-Income Countries (LMICs), 2010 *(continued)*

Vulnerability zoning			Total score for external factors						Sub-total	Total score for system factors						Sub-total	Total score for household factors				Sub-total	Total
			Macro space	Fiscal space	Fiscal space	Structural	Demography	Political economy and governance	Vector mean for external	Commitment to financing health	Health financing level	THE growth	Government in health trend	Government HF trend	Coverage	Vector mean for system	Health outcome				Vector mean for household	Total vulnerability score
Country	Region	IG-C30 LM	GDP growth 2010	Debt-to-GDP	ODA/GNI	Unemployment	SR dependency	ICRG political risk index external		GHE/GGE	Log THE PC	THE growth	GHE/THE	GHE growth	Vaccination system		IMR	MMR	H4A	W4A		Total score
Vanuatu	EAS	LM	-1	—	-2	—	1	—	-0.67	2	1	2	2	2	-3	1.00	1	—	—	—	1.00	0.44
Albania	ECS	LM	1	-1	-1	-1	-1	1	-0.33	-1	—	-1	-2	-1	1	-0.50	2	1	-1	1	0.75	-0.03
Armenia	ECS	LM	-1	1	1	-2	-2	1	-0.67	1	—	-1	-1	-1	1	-0.67	1	1	1	1	1.00	-0.11
Azerbaijan	ECS	LM	1	2	1	1	1	-1	0.83	-2	—	1	-3	—	-3	-1.50	-3	1	—	—	-1.00	-0.56
Georgia	ECS	LM	1	1	1	-2	-3	—	-0.40	-1	2	—	-2	1	1	0.33	1	1	2	2	1.50	0.48
Moldova	ECS	LM	2	1	1	1	-4	1	0.33	1	2	—	—	1	1	0.17	2	1	—	—	1.50	0.67
Turkmenistan	ECS	LM	2	2	1	—	2	—	1.75	1	-3	2	—	2	1	0.33	-2	1	—	—	-0.50	0.53
Ukraine	ECS	LM	1	1	1	1	-3	1	0.33	-1	—	—	—	—	-1	0.33	1	1	—	—	1.00	0.56
Belize	LCN	LM	-2	-2	-1	1	1	—	-0.60	1	—	1	—	1	1	0.33	1	1	—	—	1.00	0.24
Bolivia	LCN	LM	-1	1	1	1	-1	1	0.20	-1	—	—	—	1	-1	-0.67	-1	-4	—	—	-1.25	-0.57
Ecuador	LCN	LM	-1	1	1	1	1	-2	0.17	1	—	-2	—	—	1	-0.17	—	1	—	—	1.00	0.33
El Salvador	LCN	LM	-1	-1	1	1	1	-1	0.00	—	—	1	-2	—	1	0.67	-1	1	1	1	0.50	0.39
Guatemala	LCN	LM	-1	1	1	—	1	-1	0.20	2	—	—	-1	-1	—	0.00	—	—	-3	-1	-1.00	-0.27
Guyana	LCN	LM	1	-1	1	1	1	—	0.60	2	—	—	1	-2	2	0.50	2	1	—	—	1.50	0.87
Honduras	LCN	LM	-1	1	1	1	1	1	0.67	2	—	—	1	1	1	0.80	1	1	—	—	1.00	0.82
Nicaragua	LCN	LM	-1	-2	1	—	-1	1	-0.40	2	2	—	1	1	2	1.20	1	1	—	—	1.00	0.60

table continues next page

Table 2C.3 Vulnerability Zoning Using Closest-30-Peer Referencing for Lower-Middle-Income Countries (LMICs), 2010 *(continued)*

Country	Region	IG-C30 LM 2010	Macro GDP growth	Fiscal space Debt-to-GDP	Fiscal space ODA/GNI	Structural Unemployment	Demography SR dependency	Political economy and governance ICRG political risk index	Sub-total Vector mean for external	Commitment to health GHE/GGE	Health financing level Log THE PC	Health financing THE growth	Government in health GHE/THE	Government health trend GHE growth	Coverage Vaccination	Sub-total Vector mean for system	IMR	MMR	H4A	W4A	Sub-total Vector mean for household	Total Total vulnerability score
Paraguay	LCN	LM	3	2	1	1	1	−1	1.17	1	1	1	−2	−1	1	0.17	1	−1	—	—	0.00	0.44
Djibouti	MEA	LM	—	—	—	—	—	—	—	—	—	—	—	—	—	—	—	—	—	—	—	—
Egypt, Arab Rep.	MEA	LM	1	−2	1	1	1	−1	0.17	−2	−1	−1	−2	−1	1	−0.67	1	1	1	1	0.50	0.00
Iran, Islamic Rep.	MEA	LM	—	—	—	—	—	—	—	—	—	—	—	—	—	—	—	—	—	—	—	—
Iraq	MEA	LM	−2	−3	1	1	1	−3	−1.20	−1	2	−1	2	1	−2	0.17	−1	1	—	—	−1.00	−0.68
Jordan	MEA	LM	−1	−1	1	−1	—	1	0.00	2	1	1	1	1	1	0.50	1	2	2	—	1.50	0.67
Morocco	MEA	LM	−1	−1	1	−1	—	2	0.17	−1	−1	−1	−2	—	1	−0.17	−1	−1	—	—	−1.00	−0.33
Syrian Arab Republic	MEA	LM	−1	1	1	1	—	−1	0.33	−2	−1	−1	−1	−1	−1	−1.17	−1	−1	—	—	−0.33	−0.39
Tunisia	MEA	LM	−1	1	1	−1	—	1	0.33	−1	−1	−1	−1	−1	1	−0.67	1	—	—	—	1.00	0.22
West Bank and Gaza	MEA	LM	—	—	—	—	—	—	—	—	—	—	—	—	—	—	—	—	—	—	—	—
Bhutan	SAS	LM	1	−1	1	2	—	—	0.40	1	1	1	2	1	1	0.83	−1	1	—	—	−1.00	0.08
India	SAS	LM	2	−1	1	—	—	1	0.80	−2	−1	−1	−2	—	−2	−1.17	−1	—	—	—	−1.00	−0.46
Maldives	SAS	LM	1	−1	−3	1	—	—	−0.50	−1	—	—	—	—	1	0.33	2	1	−2	—	0.33	0.06
Pakistan	SAS	LM	−1	−1	1	—	—	−2	−0.80	−2	−2	−1	−1	2	1	−0.17	−1	—	—	—	−1.00	−0.66
Sri Lanka	SAS	LM	2	—	1	1	−1	−1	0.40	−1	−2	−1	−1	−1	1	−0.83	1	—	—	−2	0.00	−0.14

table continues next page

67

Table 2C.3 Vulnerability Zoning Using Closest-30-Peer Referencing for Lower-Middle-Income Countries (LMICs), 2010 *(continued)*

Country	Region	IG-C30 LM	Macro: GDP growth 2010	Fiscal space: Debt-to-GDP	Fiscal space: ODA/GNI	Structural: Unemployment	Demography: SR dependency	Political economy and governance: ICRG political risk index	Sub-total: Vector mean for external	Commitment to health: GHE/GGE	Health financing level: Log THE PC	Health financing: THE growth	Government in health financing: GHE/THE growth	Government health financing trend: GHE/THE	Coverage: Vaccination	Sub-total: Vector mean for nation system	IMR	MMR	H4A	W4A	Sub-total: Vector mean for household	Total vulnerability score
Angola	SSF	LM	−1	1	1	—	2	−1	0.40	−1	−2	−4	−4	2	−1	−1.67	−4	—	—	—	−4.00	−1.76
Cameroon	SSF	LM	−1	2	1	—	1	1	0.80	−1	−1	1	2	−1	1	0.17	−2	—	—	—	−2.00	−0.34
Cape Verde	SSF	LM	1	−2	−1	−1	−1	—	−0.80	−1	−1	1	1	1	1	0.33	1	—	1	—	1.00	0.18
Congo, Rep.	SSF	LM	1	1	−1	—	1	−2	0.00	−2	−3	−1	−1	−1	−1	−1.50	−2	—	—	—	−2.00	−1.17
Côte d'Ivoire	SSF	LM	−2	−2	−1	—	1	−2	−1.20	−1	−1	−1	−2	1	1	−0.50	−2	—	—	—	−2.00	−1.23
Lesotho	SSF	LM	1	2	1	—	−2	—	0.50	1	2	2	2	2	1	1.67	3	—	—	—	3.00	1.72
Nigeria	SSF	LM	1	2	1	—	1	−2	0.60	−2	−1	−2	−1	−1	−2	−1.50	−2	—	—	—	−2.00	−0.97
São Tomé and Príncipe	SSF	LM	−1	−2	−2	—	−1	—	−1.50	1	1	−1	−1	−1	2	0.17	2	—	—	—	2.00	0.22
Sudan	SSF	LM	−1	−1	1	—	1	−2	−0.40	−1	−1	−2	−1	1	1	−0.50	−1	—	—	—	−1.00	−0.63
Swaziland	SSF	LM	−1	1	1	—	1	—	0.50	−1	−1	−1	−1	1	1	−0.33	−3	—	−2	1	−1.33	−0.39

Note: EAS = East Asia and Pacific (now EAP); ECS = Europe and Central Asia (now ECA); GDP = gross domestic product; GGE = general government expenditures; GHE = government health expenditures; GNI = gross national income; HF = health financing; H4A = height for age; ICRG = International Country Risk Guide; IG-C30 = income group closest 30; IMR = infant mortality rate; LCN = Latin America and the Caribbean (now LAC); LM (and LMIC) = lower-middle-income; LMIC = lower-middle-income country; MEA = Middle East and North Africa (now MNA or MENA); MMR = maternal mortality rate; ODA = official development assistance; SAS = South Asia; SR = senior; SSF = Sub-Saharan Africa; THE PC = total health expenditure per capita; W4A = weight for age; — = not available. The color code in the table is based on the description presented in table 2.2.

Table 2C.4 Vulnerability Zoning Using Closest-30-Peer Referencing for Low-Income Countries (LICs), 2010

Country	Region	IG-C30 L 2010	Macro: GDP growth	Fiscal space: Debt-to-GDP	Fiscal space: ODA/GNI	Structural: Unemployment	Demography: SR dependency	Political economy and governance: ICRG political risk index	Subtotal: Vector mean for external	Commitment to health: GHE/GGE	Health financing level: Log THE PC	Health financing trend: THE growth	Government in health: GHE/THE	Government HF trend: GHE growth	Coverage: Vaccination	Subtotal: Vector mean for system	Health outcome: IMR	MMR	H4A	W4A	Subtotal: Vector mean for household	Total vulnerability score
Cambodia	EAS	L	1	1	1	—	1	—	1.00	1	-1	2	1	1	1	0.50	-1	-1	—	—	-1.00	0.17
Lao PDR	EAS	L	2	-1	1	—	1	—	0.75	-1	-1	1	-1	2	-2	-0.33	-1	—	—	—	1.00	0.47
Timor-Leste	EAS	L	2	—	1	—	1	—	1.33	-2	-3	-3	1	-3	-1	-1.17	1	—	-3	—	-1.00	-0.28
Vietnam	EAS	L	1	-1	1	1	-1	1	0.33	-1	1	1	-1	1	1	0.33	1	1	1	—	1.00	0.56
Kyrgyz Republic	ECS	L	-3	-1	1	—	-1	—	-1.00	-1	-1	-1	1	-1	1	0.33	1	1	1	—	1.00	0.11
Tajikistan	ECS	L	1	1	1	—	1	—	1.00	-1	1	1	-2	1	—	0.17	-1	—	1	—	0.00	0.39
Uzbekistan	ECS	L	1	2	1	2	1	—	1.40	-1	1	1	-1	2	2	0.50	-1	-1	—	—	-1.00	0.30
Haiti	LCN	L	-4	2	-4	—	-2	-2	-2.00	-2	1	1	-2	1	-2	-0.50	-1	—	—	—	-1.00	-1.17
Yemen, Rep.	MEA	L	1	1	1	—	-2	1	1.00	-2	-1	-3	-2	-3	-1	-2.00	-1	—	—	—	-1.00	-0.67
Afghanistan	SAS	L	1	—	-3	—	2	—	0.00	-2	-2	-1	-2	-1	-2	-1.67	-1	—	—	—	-1.00	-0.89
Bangladesh	SAS	L	1	—	1	—	-2	1	0.25	-1	-1	1	-1	-1	2	0.00	1	—	—	—	1.00	0.42
Nepal	SAS	L	1	—	1	—	-2	1	0.25	-1	-1	1	-1	1	2	0.00	1	—	—	—	1.00	0.42
Benin	SSF	L	-1	1	1	—	1	—	0.50	-1	-1	-1	-1	-2	1	-0.17	-1	—	—	—	-1.00	-0.22
Burkina Faso	SSF	L	1	1	1	—	2	1	1.20	1	1	1	1	1	2	0.83	-1	—	1	—	0.00	0.68
Burundi	SSF	L	—	—	—	—	—	—	—	—	—	—	—	—	—	—	—	—	—	—	—	—
Central African Republic	SSF	L	-1	1	1	—	-2	—	-0.25	-1	-2	-1	-1	1	-2	-1.00	-2	—	—	—	-2.00	-1.08
Chad	SSF	L	3	1	1	—	1	—	1.50	-2	-1	-1	-1	2	-3	-1.00	-2	—	—	—	-2.00	-0.50

table continues next page

Table 2C.4 Vulnerability Zoning Using Closest-30-Peer Referencing for Low-Income Countries (LICs), 2010 (continued)

Vulnerability zoning			Total score for external factors						Sub-total	Total score for system factors						Sub-total	Total score for household factors				Sub-total	Total
			Macro	Fiscal space	Fiscal space	Structural	Demography	Political economy and governance		Commitment to health	Health financing level	Health financing trend	Government in health	Government health trend	Coverage		Health outcome					Total vulnerability score
Country	Region	IG-C30 L 2010	GDP growth	Debt-to-GDP	ODA/GNI	Unemployment	SR dependency	ICRG political risk index	Vector mean for external	GHE/GGE	Log THE PC	THE growth	GHE/THE	GHE growth	Vaccination	Vector mean for system	IMR	MMR	H4A	W4A	Vector mean for household	Total score
Comoros	SSF	L	-2	-1	1	—	1	—	-0.25	1	-1	4	2	4	-1	1.50	1	—	—	—	1.00	0.75
Congo, Dem. Rep.	SSF	L	—	—	—	—	—	—	—	—	—	—	—	—	—	—	—	—	—	—	—	—
Eritrea	SSF	L	—	—	—	—	—	—	—	—	—	—	—	—	—	—	—	—	—	—	—	—
Ethiopia	SSF	L	2	-1	1	—	—	-1	0.40	-1	-1	2	1	1	1	0.83	1	—	—	—	1.00	0.74
Gambia, The	SSF	L	-1	-2	-1	—	2	-1	-0.20	—	-1	1	1	1	-1	0.00	-1	—	—	—	-1.00	-0.40
Ghana	SSF	L	1	-1	-1	—	-1	2	0.40	—	1	1	1	1	2	0.83	1	—	—	—	1.00	0.74
Guinea	SSF	L	-2	-3	-1	—	-1	-2	-1.40	-2	—	-1	-2	-1	-2	-1.17	-1	—	—	—	-1.00	-1.19
Guinea-Bissau	SSF	L	-1	-1	-1	—	—	-1	-0.60	-2	—	-1	-2	-1	-1	-0.67	-2	—	—	—	-2.00	-1.09
Kenya	SSF	L	-1	-1	1	—	1	1	0.20	—	-1	—	—	-1	1	0.00	3	—	—	—	3.00	1.07
Liberia	SSF	L	—	—	—	—	—	—	—	—	—	—	—	—	—	—	—	—	—	—	—	—
Madagascar	SSF	L	-2	-2	1	—	-1	-1	-1.00	1	-2	-2	1	-2	1	-0.83	3	—	—	—	3.00	0.39
Malawi	SSF	L	1	-1	-1	—	-1	—	0.00	1	1	—	—	—	2	0.50	1	—	—	—	1.00	0.50
Mali	SSF	L	-1	1	1	—	2	1	0.80	1	-1	-1	1	-1	-2	-0.33	-2	—	—	—	-2.00	-0.51
Mauritania	SSF	L	-1	-2	1	—	—	—	-0.75	-1	-2	-1	1	-1	-2	-1.00	-2	—	—	—	-2.00	-1.25
Mozambique	SSF	L	1	-1	-1	—	-1	—	-0.50	1	1	-1	2	-1	-1	-0.17	-1	—	—	—	-1.00	-0.56
Niger	SSF	L	1	1	1	—	1	—	1.00	1	1	-1	—	-1	-1	-0.33	1	—	—	—	1.00	0.56
Rwanda	SSF	L	1	1	1	—	1	—	0.50	3	2	1	1	1	1	1.50	1	—	—	—	1.00	1.00

table continues next page

Table 2C.4 Vulnerability Zoning Using Closest-30-Peer Referencing for Low-Income Countries (LICs), 2010 *(continued)*

Country	Region	IG-C30	GDP 2010 (Macro)	GDP growth (Macro)	Fiscal space	Debt-to-GDP (Fiscal space)	ODA/GNI (Fiscal space)	Unemployment (Structural)	SR dependency (Demography)	ICRG political risk index (Political economy and governance)	Vector mean for external (Sub-total)	GHE/GGE (Commitment to health)	Log THE PC (Health financing level)	THE growth (Health financing trend)	GHE/THE (Government in health)	GHE growth (Government health trend)	Vaccination (HF Coverage)	Vector mean for system (Sub-total)	IMR	MMR	H4A	W4A	Vector mean for household (Sub-total)	Total vulnerability score
Senegal	SSF	L	−1	1	—	—	1	—	1	−1	0.20	1	1	1	1	1	−2	0.50	1	—	—	—	1.00	0.57
Sierra Leone	SSF	L	1	−1	—	—	1	—	2	—	0.75	−1	2	−1	−2	−1	1	−0.33	−2	—	—	—	−2.00	−0.53
Tanzania	SSF	L	1	−1	—	—	−1	—	−1	1	−0.20	2	1	1	2	1	1	1.33	1	—	−1	—	0.00	0.38
Togo	SSF	L	−1	−1	—	—	1	—	−1	−1	−0.60	2	1	−1	1	1	2	1.00	−1	—	—	—	−1.00	−0.20
Uganda	SSF	L	−1	1	—	—	1	—	1	−1	0.20	1	2	1	−2	−1	−2	−0.17	1	—	—	—	1.00	0.34
Zambia	SSF	L	1	1	—	—	1	—	−1	2	0.80	2	1	−1	1	−1	1	0.50	1	—	—	—	1.00	0.77

Note: EAS = East Asia and Pacific (now EAP); ECS = Europe and Central Asia (now ECA); GDP = gross domestic product; GGE = general government expenditures; GHE = government health expenditures; GNI = gross national income; HF = health financing; H4A = height for age; ICRG = International Country Risk Guide; IG-C30 = income group closest 30; IMR = infant mortality rate; L (and LIC) = low-income country; LCN = Latin America and the Caribbean (now LAC); MEA = Middle East and North Africa (now MNA or MENA); MMR = maternal mortality rate; ODA = official development assistance; SAS = South Asia; SR = senior; SSF = Sub-Saharan Africa; THE PC = total health expenditure per capita; W4A = weight for age; — = not available. The color code in the table is based on the description presented in table 2.2.

Table 2C.5 Vulnerability Zoning Using Closest-30-Peer Referencing for High-Income Countries (HICs), 2005

Country	Region	IG-C30 H 2005	GDP growth (Macro)	Fiscal space GDP	Fiscal space Debt-to-GDP	Structural ODA/GNI	Unemployment	Demography SR dependency	ICRG political risk index	Vector mean for external (Sub-total)	Commitment to health GHE/GGE	Health financing level Log THE PC	Health financing trend THE growth	Government in health GHE/THE	Government health trend GHE growth	Coverage Vaccination	Vector mean for system (Sub-total)	Health outcome IMR	MMR	H4A	W4A	Vector mean for household (Sub-total)	Total vulnerability score
Australia	EAS	H	-1	2	—	—	1	-1	1	0.40	1	1	-1	-1	-1	1	0.00	1	—	—	—	1.00	0.47
Brunei Darussalam	EAS	H	-2	2	—	—	1	2	-2	0.20	-2	-2	-2	2	-2	1	-0.83	-1	—	—	—	-1.00	-0.54
Hong Kong SAR, China	EAS	H	3	1	—	—	1	1	-1	1.00	—	—	—	—	—	—	—	—	—	—	—	—	1.00
Japan	EAS	H	-1	-4	—	—	1	-2	1	-1.00	1	1	2	1	1	1	1.00	1	—	—	—	1.00	0.33
Korea, Rep.	EAS	H	1	1	—	—	2	1	-1	0.80	-1	2	2	-2	2	1	0.17	1	—	—	—	1.00	0.66
Macao SAR, China	EAS	H	2	—	—	—	2	2	—	1.67	—	—	—	—	—	—	—	—	—	—	—	—	1.67
New Zealand	EAS	H	-1	1	—	—	2	—	2	1.00	2	1	1	1	1	-1	0.83	1	—	—	—	1.00	0.94
Singapore	EAS	H	2	-2	—	—	1	—	-1	0.20	-2	2	2	-4	2	2	-0.50	2	—	—	—	2.00	0.57
Austria	ECS	H	-1	-1	—	—	1	-1	1	-0.20	-1	1	1	-1	-1	1	-0.17	1	—	—	—	1.00	0.21
Belgium	ECS	H	-1	-2	—	—	1	-1	1	-0.80	1	-1	1	-1	-1	1	0.00	1	—	—	—	1.00	0.07
Cyprus	ECS	H	-1	-1	—	—	1	-1	1	-0.20	-3	1	1	-3	1	1	-1.00	1	—	—	—	1.00	-0.07
Denmark	ECS	H	-1	1	—	—	1	-1	1	0.20	1	1	-1	1	-1	1	0.33	1	—	—	—	1.00	0.51
Finland	ECS	H	1	1	—	—	-1	-1	2	0.40	1	1	1	1	1	1	0.67	1	—	—	—	1.00	0.69
France	ECS	H	-1	-1	—	—	—	-1	-1	-1.00	-1	1	1	1	1	1	0.33	1	—	—	—	1.00	0.11
Germany	ECS	H	-2	-1	—	—	-3	-2	1	-1.40	1	1	1	1	1	1	1.00	1	—	—	—	1.00	0.20

table continues next page

Table 2C.5 Vulnerability Zoning Using Closest-30-Peer Referencing for High-Income Countries (HICs), 2005 *(continued)*

Vulnerability zoning

Country	Region	IG-C30 H 2005	Macro: GDP growth	Fiscal space: Debt-to-GDP	Fiscal space: ODA/GNI	Structural: Unemployment	Demography: SR dependency	Political economy and governance: ICRG political risk index	Sub-total: Vector mean for external	Commitment to health: GHE/GGE	Health financing level: Log THE PC	Health financing trend: THE growth	Gov in health: GHE/THE	Government HF trend: GHE growth	Coverage: Vaccination	Sub-total: Vector mean for system	IMR	MMR	H4A	W4A	Sub-total: Vector mean for household	Total vulnerability score
Greece	ECS	H	-1	-2	—	-2	-2	-1	-1.60	-1	2	2	-1	2	1	0.67	1	—	—	—	1.00	0.02
Iceland	ECS	H	2	1	—	2	1	2	1.60	2	-2	-1	—	-1	1	0.33	2	—	—	—	2.00	1.31
Ireland	ECS	H	1	1	—	1	1	1	1.00	1	1	1	1	1	-1	0.67	1	—	—	—	1.00	0.89
Italy	ECS	H	-2	-2	—	-1	-2	-1	-1.60	-1	1	1	1	1	1	0.33	1	—	—	—	1.00	-0.09
Luxembourg	ECS	H	—	—	—	—	—	—	—	—	—	—	—	—	—	—	—	—	—	—	—	—
Netherlands	ECS	H	-1	1	—	1	1	1	0.20	-1	1	1	-1	1	1	0.33	1	—	—	—	1.00	0.51
Norway	ECS	H	-1	1	—	1	1	1	0.20	1	1	1	-1	1	-1	0.67	1	—	—	—	1.00	0.62
Portugal	ECS	H	-2	-1	—	1	1	1	-0.40	1	1	1	-1	1	-1	0.33	1	—	—	—	1.00	0.31
Slovenia	ECS	H	1	1	—	1	1	-1	0.20	1	1	1	-1	1	1	0.67	1	—	—	—	1.00	0.62
Spain	ECS	H	-1	1	—	-2	-1	-1	-0.80	1	1	1	-1	1	1	0.67	1	—	—	—	1.00	0.29
Sweden	ECS	H	1	1	—	-1	-1	2	0.40	-1	2	-1	-1	-1	-3	-0.67	1	—	—	—	1.00	0.24
Switzerland	ECS	H	-1	1	—	1	1	1	-0.20	2	2	-1	-1	-1	1	0.33	1	—	—	—	1.00	0.38
United Kingdom	ECS	H	-1	1	—	1	-1	1	0.20	1	1	1	2	1	-1	0.83	-1	—	—	—	-1.00	0.01

table continues next page

Table 2C.5 Vulnerability Zoning Using Closest-30-Peer Referencing for High-Income Countries (HICs), 2005 *(continued)*

Vulnerability zoning			Total score for external factors						Sub-total	Total score for system factors						Sub-total	Health outcome				Sub-total	Total
			Macro	Fiscal space	Fiscal space	Struc-tural	Demog-raphy	Political economy and governance		Commit-ment to health	Health financing level	Health financing trend	Govern-ment health	Govern-ment health trend	Cover-age						Total score for household factors	
Country	Region	IG-C30 H 2005	GDP growth	Debt-to-GDP	ODA/GNI	Unem-ployment	SR depen-dency	ICRG political risk index	Vector mean for external	GHE/GGE	Log THE PC	THE growth	GHE/THE	GHE growth	Vacci-nation	Vector mean for system	IMR	MMR	H4A	W4A	Vector mean for household	Total vulner-ability score
Bahamas, The	LCN	H	−1	1	—	−2	2	1	0.20	1	−2	−1	−2	−2	−1	−1.17	−4	—	—	—	−4.00	−1.66
Bahrain	MEA	H	−2	1	—	—	3	−2	0.00	−2	−2	−1	−1	−1	2	−0.83	−1	—	—	—	−1.00	−0.61
Israel	MEA	H	1	−1	—	−1	1	−3	−0.60	−2	1	−1	−1	−1	1	−0.50	1	—	—	—	1.00	−0.03
Kuwait	MEA	H	2	1	—	2	2	−2	1.00	−2	−3	−2	−1	−1	2	−0.83	−2	—	—	—	−2.00	−0.61
Malta	MEA	H	−1	−1	—	1	1	1	0.20	1	2	1	1	1	−2	0.67	1	—	—	—	1.00	0.62
Qatar	MEA	H	—	—	—	—	—	—	—	—	—	—	—	—	—	—	—	—	—	—	—	—
United Arab Emirates	MEA	H	—	—	—	—	—	—	—	—	—	—	—	—	—	—	—	—	—	—	—	—
Canada	NAC	H	−1	−1	—	−1	1	1	−0.20	1	1	−1	1	1	−4	−0.17	−1	—	—	—	−1.00	−0.46
United States	NAC	H	1	−1	—	1	−1	−1	−0.20	2	2	1	−3	1	1	0.67	−1	—	—	—	−1.00	−0.18

Note: EAS = East Asia and Pacific (now EAP); ECS = Europe and Central Asia (now ECA); GDP = gross domestic product; GGE = general government expenditures; GHE = government health expenditures; GNI = gross national income; H (and HIC) = high-income country; HF = health financing; H4A = height for age; ICRG = International Country Risk Guide; IG-C30 = income group closest 30; IMR = infant mortality rate; LCN = Latin America and the Caribbean (now LAC); MEA = Middle East and North Africa (now MNA or MENA); MMR = maternal mortality rate; NAC = North America; ODA = official development assistance; SAR = special administrative region; SR = senior; THE PC = total health expenditure per capita; W4A = weight for age; — = not available. The color code in the table is based on the description presented in table 2.2.

Table 2C.6 Vulnerability Zoning Using Closest-30-Peer Referencing for Upper-Middle-Income Countries (UMICs), 2005

Vulnerability zoning			Total score for external factors						Sub-total	Total score for system factors						Sub-total	Total score for household factors				Sub-total	Total
			Macro space	Fiscal space	Fiscal space	Structural	Demography	Political economy and governance	Vector mean for external	Commitment to health	Health financing level	Health financing trend	Government in health	Government health trend	Coverage	Vector mean for system	Health outcome				Vector mean for household	Total vulnerability score
Country	Region	IG-C30 UM 2005	GDP growth	Debt-to-GDP	ODA/GNI	Unemployment	SR dependency	ICRG political risk index		GHE/GGE	Log THE PC	THE growth	GHE/THE	GHE growth	Vaccination		IMR	MMR	H4A	W4A		
Malaysia	EAS	UM	−1	1	—	2	1	1	0.83	−2	−1	−2	−2	−2	1	−1.33	1	1	−1	−3	−0.50	−0.33
Palau	EAS	UM	−1	—	−4	2	—	—	−1.00	2	−1	−1	−1	−1	1	0.67	−1	—	—	—	−1.00	−0.44
Croatia	ECS	UM	−1	1	1	−2	−2	1	−0.33	2	1	1	2	—	1	1.40	1	1	—	—	1.00	0.69
Czech Republic	ECS	UM	2	1	—	1	−1	−1	0.40	−1	1	1	2	−1	1	0.83	1	—	1	—	1.00	0.74
Estonia	ECS	UM	2	2	—	1	−2	−1	0.40	—	−1	−1	1	—	1	0.67	1	1	1	—	1.00	0.69
Hungary	ECS	UM	−1	−1	—	1	−1	1	−0.20	—	1	1	1	1	1	1.00	1	1	1	—	1.00	0.60
Latvia	ECS	UM	2	1	—	1	−2	1	0.60	—	1	1	1	—	1	0.33	1	1	1	—	1.00	0.64
Lithuania	ECS	UM	2	1	—	1	−2	1	0.60	—	1	1	1	1	1	1.00	1	1	1	—	1.00	0.87
Poland	ECS	UM	−1	1	—	−2	−1	1	−0.40	−1	1	1	1	1	1	0.67	1	1	1	—	1.00	0.42
Slovak Republic	ECS	UM	1	1	—	−3	−1	1	−0.20	—	1	1	1	1	1	1.00	1	—	—	—	1.00	0.60
Antigua and Barbuda	LCN	UM	−1	−2	1	—	—	—	−0.67	−1	−1	−1	−1	—	1	0.00	1	2	—	—	1.50	0.28
Argentina	LCN	UM	1	−2	1	−1	−1	1	0.17	1	2	1	−1	2	1	1.00	1	−1	1	1	0.50	0.56

table continues next page

Table 2C.6 Vulnerability Zoning Using Closest-30-Peer Referencing for Upper-Middle-Income Countries (UMICs), 2005 *(continued)*

Vulnerability zoning

Country	Region	IG-C30 UM 2005	Total score for external factors							Total score for system factors							Total score for household factors					Total
			Macro	Fiscal space	Fiscal space	Structural	Demography	Political economy and governance	Sub-total	Commitment to health	Health financing level	Health financing trend	Government in health	Government HF trend	Coverage	Sub-total	Health outcome				Sub-total	Total
			GDP growth	Debt-to-GDP	ODA/GNI	Unemployment	SR dependency	ICRG political risk index	Vector mean for external	GHE/GGE	Log THE PC	THE growth	GHE/THE	GHE growth	Vaccination	Vector mean for system	IMR	MMR	H4A	W4A	Vector mean for household	Total vulnerability score
Barbados	LCN	UM	−1	−1	1	−1	−1	—	−0.60	1	1	−2	−1	−2	−1	−0.67	−1	—	—	—	−1.00	−0.76
Belize	LCN	UM	−1	−3	1	1	1	—	−0.20	−1	−2	1	1	1	1	0.17	−1	−1	−1	−1	−0.50	−0.18
Chile	LCN	UM	−1	2	1	1	1	2	1.00	1	1	1	−2	1	−1	0.17	1	1	2	2	1.50	0.89
Costa Rica	LCN	UM	−1	1	1	1	1	1	0.67	3	1	1	1	−1	−1	0.67	1	1	—	—	1.00	0.78
Dominica	LCN	UM	−2	−1	−2	—	—	—	−1.67	−1	−1	1	1	−1	1	−0.33	1	1	—	—	1.00	−0.33
Grenada	LCN	UM	2	−2	−2	1	1	—	−0.25	−1	−1	2	1	2	1	0.67	1	—	—	—	1.00	0.47
Mexico	LCN	UM	−1	1	1	2	1	1	0.83	2	−1	−1	−2	−1	1	0.00	−1	−1	1	—	−0.50	0.11
Panama	LCN	UM	1	1	1	1	1	1	0.67	1	1	−2	−2	−1	1	0.17	−1	−1	—	—	−1.00	−0.06
St. Kitts and Nevis	LCN	UM	−1	−4	1	—	—	—	−1.33	−2	−1	−1	−1	−1	1	−0.50	1	2	—	—	1.50	−0.11
St. Lucia	LCN	UM	−1	−1	−1	−1	1	—	−0.60	−1	−1	1	−1	−1	1	−0.67	1	1	—	—	1.00	−0.09
St. Vincent and the Grenadines	LCN	UM	−1	−1	—	—	1	—	−0.50	−1	1	1	1	1	1	−0.33	−1	1	—	—	0.00	−0.28

table continues next page

Table 2C.6 Vulnerability Zoning Using Closest-30-Peer Referencing for Upper-Middle-Income Countries (UMICs), 2005 (continued)

Country	Region	IG-C30 UM 2005	GDP growth	Debt-to-GDP	ODA/GNI	Unemployment	SR dependency	ICRG political risk index	Vector mean for external	GHE/GGE	Log THE PC	THE growth	GHE/THE	GHE growth	Govt HF trend	Vaccination	Vector mean for system	IMR	MMR	H4A	W4A	Vector mean for household	Total vulnerability score
			Macro	*Fiscal space*	*Fiscal space*	*Struc-tural*	*Demog-raphy*	*Political economy and governance*	*Sub-total*	*Com-mitment to health*	*Health financing level*	*Health financing trend*	*Health financing trend*	*Govern-ment in health*	*Govern-ment HF trend*	*Cover-age*	*Sub-total*	*Health outcome*				*Sub-total*	*Total*
Trinidad and Tobago	LCN	UM	1	1	—	1	2	−1	0.80	−1	−1	3		−2	3	1	0.50	−1	—	—	—	−1.00	0.10
Uruguay	LCN	UM	1	−1	1	−1	−2	1	−0.17	1	2	−1	1	1	1	1	0.50	1	1	1	−1	0.50	0.28
Venezuela, RB	LCN	UM	2	1	1	1	1	−3	0.50	−1	−1	−1		−2	1	−1	−0.50	1	−1	—	—	0.00	0.00
Lebanon	MEA	UM	−2	−4	1	1	1	−2	−1.20	1	2	−1		−1	1	−3	−0.33	1	—	—	1	0.33	−0.40
Libya	MEA	UM	1	2	—	—	2	−2	0.80	−2	−2	−2		−1	−2		−1.33	−1	—	−1	—	−1.00	−0.51
Oman	MEA	UM	−1	2	—	—	2	−1	0.50	−2	−2	−2		2	−2		−0.83	−1	—	—	—	−1.00	−0.44
Saudi Arabia	MEA	UM	−1	1	—	−2	2	−2	−0.40	−1	−1	−1		−1	−1		−0.33	−1	—	−1	—	−1.00	−0.58
Botswana	SSF	UM	−2	1	1	—	2	1	0.60	2	2	−2		2	−2	1	0.50	−1	—	—	—	−1.00	0.03
Gabon	SSF	UM	−2	−1	1	—	1	−2	−0.60	−2	−3	−2		−2	−3	−4	−2.67	−3	—	—	—	−3.00	−2.09
Mauritius	SSF	UM	−2	−1	1	1	1	—	0.00	−1	−1	−1		−1	−1		−0.33	1	—	—	—	1.00	0.22
Seychelles	SSF	UM	1	−3	−1	—	—	—	−0.50	−1	−2	−2		2	−2	1	−0.50	1	—	—	−3	−1.00	−0.67

Note: EAS = East Asia and Pacific (now EAP); ECS = Europe and Central Asia (now ECA); GDP = gross domestic product; GGE = general government expenditures; GHE = government health expenditures; GNI = gross national income; HF = health financing; H4A = height for age; ICRG = International Country Risk Guide; IG-C30 = income group closest 30; IMR = infant mortality rate; LCN = Latin America and the Caribbean (now LAC); MEA = Middle East and North Africa (now MNA or MENA); MMR = maternal mortality rate; ODA = official development assistance; SR = senior; SSF = Sub-Saharan Africa; THE PC = total health expenditure per capita; UM (and UMIC) = upper-middle-income country; W4A = weight for age; — = not available. The color code in the table is based on the description presented in table 2.2.

Table 2C.7 Vulnerability Zoning Using Closest-30-Peer Referencing for Lower-Middle-Income Countries (LMICs), 2005

Vulnerability zoning

Country	Region	IG-C30 LM 2005	Total score for external factors							Total score for system factors							Total score for household factors					Total
			Macro	Fiscal space	Fiscal space	Struc-tural	Demog-raphy	Politi-cal econ-omy and gover-nance	Sub-total	Com-mit-ment to health	Health financ-ing level	Health financ-ing trend	Gov-ern-ment health	Govern-ment health trend	Cover-age	Sub-total	Health outcome				Sub-total	
			GDP growth	Debt-to-GDP	ODA/ GNI	Unem-ploy-ment	SR depen-dency	ICRG politi-cal risk index	Vector mean for exter-nal	GHE/ GGE	Log THE PC growth	THE growth	GHE/ THE	GHE/ THE growth	Vacci-nation	Vector mean for sys-tem	IMR	MMR	H4A	W4A	Vector mean for house-hold	Total vulner-ability score
China	EAS	LM	2	1	1	1	−1	1	0.83	−1	−1	1	−1	−1	−1	−0.33	1	1	2	1	1.25	0.58
Fiji	EAS	LM	−1	1	1	1	1	—	0.60	−1	−1	−2	2	−1	−1	−0.33	1	1	—	—	1.00	0.42
Indonesia	EAS	LM	1	1	—	−1	1	−1	0.33	−1	−2	−2	−1	1	1	−1.33	1	—	−1	−2	−0.67	−0.56
Kiribati	EAS	LM	−2	—	−1	—	—	—	−1.50	2	2	1	2	−1	−1	0.83	1	—	—	—	1.00	0.11
Micronesia, Fed. Sts.	EAS	LM	−1	—	−2	—	1	—	−0.67	2	2	2	2	1	1	1.67	−1	—	—	—	−1.00	0.00
Philippines	EAS	LM	−1	1	1	1	1	1	0.67	−1	2	2	−1	1	−1	−0.33	1	1	—	—	1.00	0.44
Samoa	EAS	LM	−1	—	1	—	1	—	−0.33	−1	2	2	1	−1	−2	0.50	1	1	—	—	1.00	0.39
Thailand	EAS	LM	−1	−1	1	2	1	−1	0.17	1	−2	−1	1	3	1	−0.17	1	1	1	−1	0.50	0.17
Tonga	EAS	LM	−2	—	−1	—	−1	—	−1.33	1	1	−2	−1	−1	1	0.50	−1	−1	—	—	0.00	−0.28
Vanuatu	EAS	LM	−1	—	1	—	1	—	−0.33	−1	−1	−1	1	−1	−2	−0.17	−1	−1	—	—	0.00	−0.17
Albania	ECS	LM	1	−1	1	−1	−1	1	−0.33	−1	1	−1	−1	−1	1	−0.33	1	1	−2	1	−0.25	−0.31
Armenia	ECS	LM	2	1	1	−3	−1	−1	−0.50	−1	−1	−1	−2	−1	1	−0.17	1	1	1	1	1.00	0.11
Azerbaijan	ECS	LM	4	2	2	—	−1	1	1.33	−2	3	−3	1	−1	−2	−0.67	−1	−1	−1	−1	−0.50	0.06
Belarus	ECS	LM	2	2	1	2	−2	−2	0.50	−1	1	1	2	1	1	0.83	2	1	2	2	1.75	1.03

table continues next page

Table 2C.7 Vulnerability Zoning Using Closest-30-Peer Referencing for Lower-Middle-Income Countries (LMICs), 2005 *(continued)*

Country	Region	IG-C30 LM 2005	Macro space: GDP growth	Debt-to-GDP	Fiscal space: ODA/GNI	Fiscal structural: Unemployment	Demography: SR dependency	Political economy and governance: ICRG political risk index	Sub-total: Vector mean for external	Commitment to health: GHE/GGE	Health financing level: Log THE PC	Health financing trend: THE growth	Government in health: GHE/THE	Government health trend: GHE growth	HF trend	Coverage: Vaccination	Sub-total: Vector mean for system	Health outcome: IMR	MMR	H4A	W4A	Sub-total: Vector mean for household	Total: Total vulnerability score
Bosnia and Herzegovina	ECS	LM	1	−2		−3	−2	—	−1.00	1	1	−1	−1	−1		1	0.00	2	1	1	2	1.50	0.17
Bulgaria	ECS	LM	1	1	—	1	−3	1	0.20	1	1	1	1	−1		1	1.00	1	1	1	2	1.25	0.82
Georgia	ECS	LM	1	1	1	−1	−4	—	−0.40	−1	2	1	−2	3		−1	0.33	1	1	2	1	1.25	0.39
Kazakhstan	ECS	LM	2	2	1	1	1	1	1.33	−1	−2	2	1	2		1	0.17	−2	1	−1	−1	−1.25	0.08
Macedonia, FYR	ECS	LM	−1	−2	1	−3	−1	—	−1.20	2	1	−1	−1				0.50	1	1	1	2	1.25	0.18
Montenegro	ECS	LM	−1	1	1	−3	−2	—	−0.80	1	1	1	2				0.40	1	1	—	1	1.00	0.20
Romania	ECS	LM	1	1	—	1	−2	1	0.40	1	−1	−1	1			1	0.50	−1	1	1	—	0.00	0.30
Russian Federation	ECS	LM	1	1	—	1	−1	−1	0.20	−1	1	2	1	2		1	1.00	1	1	1	1	1.00	0.73
Serbia	ECS	LM	1	−1	−2	−1	−2	−1	−1.00	2	1	1	1			−1	0.67	2	1	1	1	1.25	0.31
Turkey	ECS	LM	1	1	1	1	1	−1	0.33	1	1	1	1			−1	0.67	1	1	−1	1	0.50	0.50
Turkmenistan	ECS	LM	2	2	1	—	1	—	1.50	−2	−2	1	−2			1	−0.67	−2	—	—	—	−2.00	−0.39
Ukraine	ECS	LM	−1	1	1	1	−3	1	0.00	1	1	1	1	−1		1	0.33	1	1	—	—	1.00	0.44
Bolivia	LCN	LM	−1	−1	1	1	1	−1	0.00	1	1	1	1			1	0.67	−1	—	−2	1	−0.67	0.00
Brazil	LCN	LM	−1	−1	1	1	1	−1	0.00	−2	2	2	−2	−1		−1	−0.17	−1	−1	—	—	−1.00	−0.39
Colombia	LCN	LM	−1	1	1	1	1	−2	0.17	2	−1	−1	3	−1		1	0.50	−1	−1	−1	−1	−1.00	−0.11

table continues next page

Table 2C.7 Vulnerability Zoning Using Closest-30-Peer Referencing for Lower-Middle-Income Countries (LMICs), 2005 (continued)

			Total score for external factors						Sub-total	Total score for system factors						Sub-total	Total score for household factors				Sub-total	Total
			Macro	Fiscal space	Fiscal space	Structural	Demography	Political economy and governance		Commitment to health	Health financing level	Health financing trend	Government health	Government trend	Coverage		Health outcome					Total vulnerability score
Country	Region	IG-C30 LM 2005	GDP growth	Debt-to-GDP	ODA/GNI	Unemployment	SR dependency	ICRG political risk index	Vector mean for external	GHE/GGE	Log THE PC	THE growth	GHE/THE	GHE growth	Vaccination	Vector mean for system	IMR	MMR	H4A	W4A	Vector mean for household	Total
Dominican Republic	LCN	LM	1	1	1	-1		-1	0.33	-1	-1	1	-2	2	-1	-0.33	-1	-1	1	1	0.00	0.00
Ecuador	LCN	LM	1	1	1			-2	0.50	1	-1	1	-2	-1	-1	-0.50	-1	-2	-1	-1	-1.25	-0.42
El Salvador	LCN	LM	-1	1	1			1	0.67	2	-1	-1	-1	1	1	0.17	1	1	—	—	1.00	0.61
Guatemala	LCN	LM	-1	1	-1	-1		1	0.60	2	-1	-1	-2	1	-1	0.00	1	-1	—	—	0.00	0.20
Guyana	LCN	LM	-2	-1	-1			1	-0.40	1	1	1	2	1	1	1.17	1	1	—	—	1.00	0.59
Honduras	LCN	LM	-1	-1				1	0.33	2	1	1	1	-1	1	0.50	1	—	1	1	0.33	0.39
Jamaica	LCN	LM	-1	-3	1			1	-0.33	-3	-2	-4	-1	-4	1	-2.17	-1	2	1	1	0.67	-0.61
Paraguay	LCN	LM	-1	1	1		-1	-1	0.33	1	1	1	-1	1	1	0.33	1	1	1	1	1.00	0.56
Peru	LCN	LM	1	1	1			-1	0.67	2	-1	1	1	-1	1	0.50	1	-2	-1	-1	-0.67	0.17
Suriname	LCN	LM	-1		1	-1		-1	0.00	1	-1	-1	-1	1	-1	0.00	-1	1	—	-2	-0.67	-0.22
Algeria	MEA	LM	-1	1		-1	2	-1	0.17	-1	-2	-1	2	-1	-1	-0.67	-2	-1	1	1	-0.67	-0.39
Egypt, Arab Rep.	MEA	LM	-1	-3		-1		1	-0.67	-1	-1	-1	-1	1	1	-0.33	-1	—	1	1	-0.33	-0.44
Iran, Islamic Rep.	MEA	LM	-1	1	1	1		-1	0.33	-1	-1	3	-2	2	1	0.33	-2	1	1	1	0.25	0.31

table continues next page

Table 2C.7 Vulnerability Zoning Using Closest-30-Peer Referencing for Lower-Middle-Income Countries (LMICs), 2005 *(continued)*

			Total score for external factors								Total score for system factors							Total score for household factors					Total
Country	Region	IG-C30 LM 2005	Macro space	GDP growth 2005	Debt-to-GDP	ODA/GNI	Unemployment	SR dependency	ICRG political risk index	Vector mean for external (Sub-total)	GHE/GGE	Log THE PC growth	THE growth	GHE/THE	GHE growth	Vaccination	Vector mean for system (Sub-total)	IMR	MMR	H4A	W4A	Vector mean for household (Sub-total)	Total vulnerability score
Iraq	MEA	LM	—	-2	-4	-4	-2	1	-3	-2.33	-2	-1	-3	1	-3	-2	-1.67	1	1	1	1	1.00	-1.00
Jordan	MEA	LM	—	1	-1	-1	-1	1	2	0.50	1	2	-1	-1	-1	1	0.17	1	1	—	—	1.00	0.56
Morocco	MEA	LM	—	-1	-1	1	-1	1	2	0.17	-2	-1	-1	-2	-1	1	-1.00	-1	—	1	1	0.33	-0.17
Syrian Arab Republic	MEA	LM	—	-1	1	1	1	1	-1	0.33	-1	-1	-1	-1	-1	-1	-1.00	-1	—	1	-1	-0.33	-0.33
Tunisia	MEA	LM	—	-1	1	-1	1	1	-1	0.00	-1	-1	-1	-1	-1	1	-0.67	-1	—	1	1	0.33	-0.11
Maldives	SAS	LM	—	-3	1	-2	—	1	—	-0.75	1	2	1	1	2	—	1.00	1	—	—	—	1.00	0.42
Sri Lanka	SAS	LM	—	1	1	—	1	-1	-2	0.00	-1	-1	-1	-1	-1	1	-0.67	1	—	1	1	1.00	0.11
Cape Verde	SSF	LM	—	1	-1	-1	-2	-1	—	-0.80	1	-1	-1	1	-1	1	0.00	1	—	1	1	1.00	0.07
Equatorial Guinea	SSF	LM	—	2	2	1	—	2	—	1.75	-2	-2	-2	-1	-2	-4	-2.17	-4	-3	-3	-2	-3.00	-1.14
Namibia	SSF	LM	—	-1	1	—	—	1	3	1.00	1	1	2	1	-1	-1	0.50	-2	—	—	-2	-2.00	-0.17
South Africa	SSF	LM	—	-1	1	1	-2	2	1	0.33	-1	2	-1	-2	1	-4	-0.83	-4	-4	-3	-3	-3.50	-1.33
Swaziland	SSF	LM	—	-1	-1	1	1	1	2	0.50	2	1	1	1	1	1	1.17	-4	-3	—	—	-3.50	-0.61

Note: EAS = East Asia and Pacific (now EAP); ECS = Europe and Central Asia (now ECA); GDP = gross domestic product; GGE = general government expenditures; GHE = government health expenditures; GNI = gross national income; HF = health financing; H4A = height for age; ICRG = International Country Risk Guide; IG-C30 = income group closest 30; IMR = infant mortality rate; LCN = Latin America and the Caribbean (now LAC); LM (and LMIC) = lower-middle-income country; MEA = Middle East and North Africa (now MNA or MENA); MMR = maternal mortality rate; ODA = official development assistance; SAS = South Asia; SR = senior; SSF = Sub-Saharan Africa; THE PC = total health expenditure per capita; W4A = weight for age; — = not available. The color code in the table is based on the description presented in table 2.2.

81

Table 2C.8 Vulnerability Zoning Using Closest-30-Peer Referencing for Low-Income Countries (LICs), 2005

Country	Region	IG-C30 L 2005	Total score for external factors — Macro space: GDP growth	Fiscal space	Debt-to-GDP	ODA/GNI	Structural: Unemployment	Demography: SR dependency	Political economy and governance: ICRG political risk index	Sub-total: Vector mean for external	Total score for system factors — Commitment to health: GHE/GGE	Health financing level: Log THE PC	Health financing trend: THE growth	Government commitment in health: GHE/THE	Government in health trend: GHE growth	Government HF trend: Vaccination / Coverage	Sub-total: Vector mean for system	Total score for household factors — Health outcome: IMR	MMR	H4A	W4A	Sub-total: Vector mean for household	Total vulnerability score
Cambodia	EAS	L	3	—	1	1	—	1	—	1.50	1	1	1	-1	-2	1	0.17	-1	-1	-1	-1	-1.00	0.22
Lao PDR	EAS	L	1	—	-1	1	2	-1	—	0.00	-2	-1	-1	-2	-2	-2	-1.67	-1	-1	-1	-1	-1.00	-0.89
Mongolia	EAS	L	1	—	—	1	1	1	2	1.20	2	-1	-2	2	-2	1	0.00	1	1	1	1	1.00	0.73
Papua New Guinea	EAS	L	-1	—	—	1	—	1	1	0.50	1	-1	-1	2	-2	-1	-0.33	1	-2	-1	1	-0.25	-0.03
Solomon Islands	EAS	L	-1	—	1	-3	—	1	—	-0.50	2	-1	-1	2	3	-1	0.67	2	—	—	—	2.00	0.72
Timor-Leste	EAS	L	1	—	1	-1	—	1	1	0.33	4	2	2	2	2	-2	1.67	1	—	—	—	1.00	1.00
Vietnam	EAS	L	2	—	1	1	1	-1	1	0.83	-1	2	2	-2	-1	2	0.33	2	1	-1	-1	0.25	0.47
Kyrgyz Republic	ECS	L	-2	—	-1	-1	1	-2	—	-1.00	1	-1	1	-1	1	2	0.50	2	2	2	1	1.75	0.42
Moldova	ECS	L	2	—	1	1	1	-4	1	0.33	1	2	2	-1	1	2	1.17	2	2	2	1	1.75	1.08
Tajikistan	ECS	L	2	—	-1	-1	1	1	1	0.25	-1	2	2	-2	1	-1	0.17	1	2	1	1	1.25	0.56
Uzbekistan	ECS	L	1	—	1	—	2	-1	1	0.80	-1	1	1	-1	-1	2	0.17	1	2	2	1	1.50	0.82
Haiti	LCN	L	-1	—	1	1	—	-2	-2	-0.60	-1	-1	-2	-2	-1	-1	-1.33	1	-1	2	1	0.75	-0.39
Nicaragua	LCN	L	-1	—	-2	1	1	1	1	-0.50	2	2	1	1	1	1	1.33	1	2	1	1	1.25	0.69

table continues next page

82

Table 2C.8 Vulnerability Zoning Using Closest-30-Peer Referencing for Low-Income Countries (LICs), 2005 *(continued)*

Country	Region	IG-C30 L 2005	Macro space GDP growth	Fiscal space Debt-to-GDP	Fiscal space ODA/GNI	Structural Unemployment	Demography SR dependency	Political economy and governance ICRG political risk index	Sub-total Vector mean for external	Commitment to health GHE/GGE	Health financing level Log THE PC	Health financing trend THE growth	Government in health GHE/THE	Government health trend GHE growth	Coverage Vaccination	Sub-total Vector mean for system	Health outcome IMR	Health outcome MMR	Health outcome H4A	Health outcome W4A	Sub-total Vector mean for household	Total Total vulnerability score
West Bank and Gaza	MEA	L	—1	—	—1	—	1	—	—0.33	—	—	—	—	—	—	—	1	—	—	—	1.00	0.33
Yemen, Rep.	MEA	L	—1	1	1	—2	—	1	0.17	—1	1	—	—1	—	1	—0.33	—1	—	—	—	—1.00	—0.39
Afghanistan	SAS	L	2	—	—3	—	2	—	0.33	—1	1	—	—2	—1	—2	—0.33	—1	—2	—1	—	—1.33	—0.44
Bangladesh	SAS	L	1	—	2	—	—1	—1	0.25	—1	—2	—	1	—1	1	—0.50	2	—1	—2	—	—0.33	—0.19
Bhutan	SAS	L	1	—1	—	2	1	—	0.40	1	1	1	1	1	1	0.67	—1	—	—	—	—1.00	0.02
India	SAS	L	2	1	—1	1	—1	1	0.83	—2	1	1	—2	1	—2	—0.83	—1	—2	1	—3	—1.25	—0.42
Nepal	SAS	L	—1	—1	1	1	—1	—	0.00	—2	—1	—1	—2	—1	—1	—0.83	2	2	—1	—2	0.25	—0.19
Pakistan	SAS	L	1	1	1	1	1	—2	0.17	—2	—2	—1	—2	—2	—1	—1.17	—1	—1	—	—	—1.00	—0.67
Angola	SSF	L	2	1	1	—	1	—1	0.80	—2	1	—	—3	—1	—3	—0.83	—4	—	—	—	—4.00	—1.34
Benin	SSF	L	—1	1	—	—	1	—	0.50	—1	—1	1	1	1	1	0.33	—1	—1	—1	1	0.00	0.28
Burkina Faso	SSF	L	1	1	1	—	2	1	1.20	2	2	2	1	1	2	1.50	—1	—1	—1	—2	—0.75	0.65
Burundi	SSF	L	—	—	—	—	—	—	—	—	—	—	—	—	—	—	—	—	—	—	—	—
Cameroon	SSF	L	—1	—1	—	—	1	1	0.67	—1	—1	—1	—2	—1	1	—0.83	—2	—1	—1	1	—0.75	—0.31
Central African Republic	SSF	L	—1	—1	2	—	—2	—	—0.50	—1	—2	—1	—1	—2	—2	—1.50	—2	1	—1	—1	—0.67	—0.89

table continues next page

Table 2C.8 Vulnerability Zoning Using Closest-30-Peer Referencing for Low-Income Countries (LICs), 2005 *(continued)*

Vulnerability zoning			Total score for external factors							Total score for system factors							Total score for household factors					Total
			Macro	Fiscal space	Fiscal space	Struc-tural	Demog-raphy	Political economy and gover-nance	Sub-total	Com-mit-ment to health	Health financ-ing level	Health financ-ing trend	Gov-ern-ment in health	Gov-ern-ment HF trend	Cover-age	Sub-total	Health outcome				Sub-total	Total vul-nera-bility
Country	Region	IG-C30 L 2005	GDP growth	Debt-to-GDP	ODA/GNI	Unem-ploy-ment	SR depen-dency	ICRG politi-cal risk index	Vector mean for exter-nal	GHE/GGE	Log THE PC	THE growth	GHE/THE	GHE growth	Vacci-nation	Vector mean for sys-tem	IMR	MMR	H4A	W4A	Vector mean for house-hold	Total score
Chad	SSF	L	2	1	1	—	1	—	1.25	—	−1	−1	−1	1	−3	−0.67	−2	−3	−1	−2	−2.00	−0.47
Comoros	SSF	L	−1	1	1	—	1	—	0.50	−1	−2	−1	−1	1	−1	−0.50	1	—	—	—	1.00	0.33
Congo, Dem. Rep.	SSF	L	—	—	—	—	—	—	—	—	—	—	—	—	—	—	—	—	—	—	—	—
Congo, Rep.	SSF	L	1	−1	−2	—	1	−1	−0.40	−1	−1	−1	−1	1	−2	−0.67	−3	−4	−1	−1	−2.25	−1.11
Côte d'Ivoire	SSF	L	−2	1	1	—	—	−2	−0.60	−2	−2	−2	−2	−1	−1	−1.17	−2	−1	—	1	−0.75	−0.84
Eritrea	SSF	L	−1	−2	−2	—	2	—	−0.75	−2	−2	−2	−1	1	2	−0.67	2	2	—	1	2.00	0.19
Ethiopia	SSF	L	1	1	1	—	−1	—	0.50	1	−2	−1	−1	1	−1	−0.83	1	—	−1	1	−0.33	−0.22
Gambia, The	SSF	L	−2	−1	−1	—	2	2	0.00	1	−1	2	1	1	2	0.17	—	—	—	—	0.33	0.17
Ghana	SSF	L	−1	−1	−1	—	1	2	0.00	−1	−1	1	−1	1	1	0.50	—	—	2	—	1.33	0.61
Guinea	SSF	L	4	−2	1	—	−1	−2	0.00	−2	−1	−1	−1	−3	−1	−1.67	−2	−2	1	1	−0.50	−0.72
Guinea-Bissau	SSF	L	−1	−3	1	—	1	1	−0.60	−2	−2	−1	−1	1	1	−0.67	−2	1	−1	1	−0.25	−0.51
Kenya	SSF	L	−1	1	1	—	1	1	0.60	−1	−1	−1	−1	1	1	0.00	1	—	−1	1	0.33	0.31
Lesotho	SSF	L	−1	1	2	—	−2	—	0.00	−1	−2	−1	−1	−1	1	−0.17	−1	−1	−1	1	−0.50	−0.22
Liberia	SSF	L	—	—	—	—	—	—	—	—	—	—	—	—	—	—	—	—	—	—	—	—

table continues next page

Table 2C.8 Vulnerability Zoning Using Closest-30-Peer Referencing for Low-Income Countries (LICs), 2005 *(continued)*

Vulnerability zoning

Country	Region	IG-C30 L 2005	Macro — GDP growth	Fiscal space — Debt-to-GDP	Fiscal space — ODA/GNI	Structural — Unemployment	SR dependency	Demography	Political economy and governance — ICRG political risk index	Sub-total — Vector mean for external	Commitment to health — GHE/GGE	Health financing level — Log THE PC	Health financing trend — THE growth	Government in health — GHE/THE	Government trend — GHE trend	Coverage — Vaccination	Sub-total — Vector mean for system	Health outcome — IMR	MMR	H4A	W4A	Sub-total — Vector mean for household	Total — Total vulnerability score
Madagascar	SSF	L	−1	1	−1	—	—	−1	1	−0.20	1	−1	−1	2	−1	−1	−0.17	2	—	−2	−2	−0.67	−0.34
Malawi	SSF	L	−1	−1	−1	—	—	−1	1	−1.00	1	−1	1	2	−1	2	0.67	1	—	−1	2	0.67	0.11
Mali	SSF	L	−1	−1	1	—	2	1	1	0.80	−1	1	−1	1	1	1	0.00	−2	1	1	−1	−0.25	0.18
Mauritania	SSF	L	1	−2	1	—	1	1	—	0.25	1	−2	−2	1	1	−1	−1.00	−1	—	—	—	−1.00	−0.58
Mozambique	SSF	L	−1	−1	−1	—	−1	1	—	0.00	−1	−1	3	2	—	1	0.83	−1	—	—	—	−1.00	−0.06
Niger	SSF	L	−1	2	−1	—	2	—	—	1.00	1	−1	−1	1	2	−2	0.67	1	—	—	—	1.00	0.89
Nigeria	SSF	L	−1	1	1	−1	—	−1	−2	−0.17	−1	1	−1	−1	−1	−3	−1.00	−2	—	—	—	−2.00	−1.06
Rwanda	SSF	L	1	1	−1	—	1	1	—	0.50	1	1	1	1	1	2	1.17	−1	−1	−1	1	−0.50	0.39
São Tomé and Príncipe	SSF	L	−2	−4	−3	−2	—	−2	—	−2.60	1	3	−2	1	1	2	1.00	1	2	1	2	1.50	−0.03
Senegal	SSF	L	−1	1	1	—	—	−1	1	0.60	1	−1	−1	1	2	1	0.50	−1	1	2	1	0.75	0.62
Sierra Leone	SSF	L	−1	−1	−2	2	2	—	—	−0.50	−1	2	2	−2	—	−1	0.00	−3	—	−1	−1	−1.67	−0.72
Sudan	SSF	L	1	−1	1	−2	—	−2	−2	−0.33	−1	−1	−1	−1	−1	−1	−0.67	−1	−3	−1	−2	−1.75	−0.92
Tanzania	SSF	L	1	1	1	—	1	−1	1	1.00	1	1	1	1	1	2	0.17	−1	−1	−1	1	−0.50	0.22

table continues next page

Table 2C.8 Vulnerability Zoning Using Closest-30-Peer Referencing for Low-Income Countries (LICs), 2005 (continued)

Vulnerability zoning			Total score for external factors						Sub-total	Total score for system factors						Sub-total	Total score for household factors				Sub-total	Total
			Macro	Fiscal space	Fiscal space	Structural	Demog-raphy	Political economy and governance		Commit-ment to health	Health financing level	Health financing trend	Gov-ern-ment health trend	Gov-ern-ment in HF trend	Cover-age		Health outcome					Total vul-nera-bility score
Country	Region	IG-C30 L 2005	GDP growth	Debt-to-GDP	ODA/GNI	Unem-ploy-ment	SR depen-dency	ICRG politi-cal risk index	Vector mean for exter-nal	GHE/GGE	Log THE PC	THE growth	GHE/THE growth	GHE growth	Vacci-nation	Vector mean for sys-tem	IMR	MMR	H4A	W4A	Vector mean for house-hold	
Togo	SSF	L	−1	2	—	—	−1	−2	−0.20	−1	1	1	−1	−2	1	−0.17	1	—	2	1	1.33	0.32
Uganda	SSF	L	−1	1	—	—	1	−1	0.20	−1	1	2	−2	1	−1	0.00	1	1	1	1	1.00	0.40
Zambia	SSF	L	−1	−1	—	—	1	2	0.00	1	1	1	1	−1	1	0.67	−1	—	—	—	−1.00	−0.11

Note: EAS = East Asia and Pacific (now EAP); ECS = Europe and Central Asia (now ECA); GDP = gross domestic product; GGE = general government expenditures; GHE = government health expenditures; GNI = gross national income; HF = health financing; H4A = height for age; ICRG = International Country Risk Guide; IG-C30 = income group closest 30; IMR = infant mortality rate; L (and LIC) = low-income country; LCN = Latin America and the Caribbean (now LAC); MEA = Middle East and North Africa (now MNA or MENA); MMR = maternal mortality rate; ODA = official development assistance; SAS = South Asia; SR = senior; SSF = Sub-Saharan Africa; THE PC = total health expenditure per capita; W4A = weight for age; — = not available. The color code in the table is based on the description presented in table 2.2.

Table 2C.9 Vulnerability Zoning Using Closest-30-Peer Referencing for High-Income Countries (HICs), 2003

Country	Region	IG-C30 H 2003	Macro GDP growth	Fiscal space Debt-to-GDP	Fiscal space ODA/GNI	Struc-tural Unemploy-ment	Demog-raphy SR depen-dency	Political economy and governance ICRG political risk index	Sub-total Vector mean for external	Com-mitment to health GHE/GGE	Health financing level Log THE PC	Health financing trend THE growth	Gov-ernment in health GHE/THE	Gov-ernment HF trend GHE growth	Cover-age Vacci-nation	Sub-total Vector mean for system	Health outcome IMR	MMR	H4A	W4A	Sub-total Vector mean for house-hold	Total vulner-ability score Total
Australia	EAS	H	-1	2	—	—	1	1	0.80	1	1	1	-1	-1	1	0.00	1	—	—	—	1.00	0.60
Brunei Darussalam	EAS	H	-1	2	—	1	2	-2	0.40	-2	-2	-1	2	-1	1	-0.50	-1	—	—	—	-1.00	-0.37
Hong Kong SAR, China	EAS	H	1	1	—	-1	1	-2	0.00	—	—	—	—	—	—	—	—	—	—	—	—	0.00
Japan	EAS	H	-1	-4	—	1	-2	1	-1.00	—	1	-1	1	-1	-2	0.33	1	—	—	—	1.00	0.11
Korea, Rep.	EAS	H	-1	—	—	2	1	-1	0.40	-2	1	1	-2	1	1	-0.33	1	—	—	—	1.00	0.36
Macao SAR, China	EAS	H	4	—	—	1	2	—	2.33	—	—	—	—	—	—	—	—	—	—	—	2.33	2.33
New Zealand	EAS	H	1	1	—	1	1	2	1.20	2	-1	-1	-1	-1	-1	-0.17	1	—	—	—	1.00	0.68
Singapore	EAS	H	2	-2	—	2	2	1	0.80	-2	2	-2	-3	4	1	0.00	2	—	—	—	2.00	0.93
Austria	ECS	H	-1	-1	—	-1	-1	1	-0.20	-1	-1	-1	1	1	-2	-0.17	1	—	—	—	1.00	0.21
Belgium	ECS	H	-1	-2	—	-1	-1	1	-0.80	1	1	1	1	3	-2	0.83	1	—	—	—	1.00	0.34
Cyprus	ECS	H	-1	-1	—	2	—	-1	0.00	-3	2	-1	-3	2	—	-0.33	1	—	—	—	1.00	0.22
Denmark	ECS	H	-1	-1	—	-1	-1	1	0.20	-1	1	1	1	-1	1	0.33	1	—	—	—	1.00	0.51
Finland	ECS	H	1	1	—	-1	-1	2	0.40	-1	1	1	1	1	1	0.67	1	—	—	—	1.00	0.69

table continues next page

Table 2C.9 Vulnerability Zoning Using Closest-30-Peer Referencing for High-Income Countries (HICs), 2003 *(continued)*

Vulnerability zoning		Total score for external factors							Sub-total	Total score for system factors						Sub-total	Total score for household factors				Sub-total	Total
		Macro	Fiscal space	Fiscal space	Structural	Demog-raphy	Political economy and governance			Commitment to health	Health financing level	Health financing trend	Government in health	Government trend	HF trend / Coverage		Health outcome					Total vulner-ability
Country	Region	IG-C30 H 2003 — GDP growth	Debt-to-GDP	ODA/GNI	Unemploy-ment	SR depen-dency	ICRG political risk index		Vector mean for external	GHE/GGE	Log THE PC	THE growth	GHE/THE	GHE growth	Vaccination	Vector mean for system	IMR	MMR	H4A	W4A	Vector mean for house-hold	score
France	ECS H	−1	−1	—	−1	−1	−1		−1.00	−2	1	1	1	−1	−2	−0.17	1	—	—	—	1.00	−0.06
Germany	ECS H	−1	−1	—	−2	−2	−1		−1.40	1	1	1	1	−1	1	0.67	1	—	—	—	1.00	0.09
Greece	ECS H	2	−1	—	−2	−2	−1		−0.80	1	1	−1	−1	1	1	0.00	1	—	—	—	1.00	0.07
Iceland	ECS H	−1	1	—	2	1	2		1.00	2	1	1	1	−1	2	0.50	2	—	—	—	2.00	1.17
Ireland	ECS H	1	1	—	1	−2	2		1.20	1	1	1	1	1	−1	0.67	1	—	—	—	1.00	0.96
Italy	ECS H	−1	−2	—	−1	−2	−1		−1.40	−1	1	1	1	−1	1	0.00	1	—	—	—	1.00	−0.13
Luxembourg	ECS H	—	—	—	—	—	—		—	—	—	—	—	—	—	—	—	—	—	—	—	—
Netherlands	ECS H	−1	1	—	2	−1	1		0.40	−1	1	1	−1	−1	1	0.33	1	—	—	—	1.00	0.58
Norway	ECS H	−2	1	—	1	1	1		0.20	1	1	1	1	1	1	0.00	1	—	—	—	1.00	0.40
Portugal	ECS H	−2	1	—	1	1	1		0.00	1	1	1	1	−1	1	0.67	1	—	—	—	1.00	0.56
Slovenia	ECS H	−1	1	—	1	1	−1		0.20	1	1	1	1	−1	1	−0.33	1	—	—	—	1.00	0.29
Spain	ECS H	−1	1	—	−2	−1	2		−0.80	2	2	1	−1	2	1	1.00	1	—	—	—	1.00	0.40
Sweden	ECS H	−1	1	—	1	−2	2		0.20	−1	2	1	1	−1	−3	−0.67	1	—	—	—	1.00	0.18
Switzerland	ECS H	−1	−1	—	1	1	1		−0.20	2	1	1	1	1	1	0.00	1	—	—	—	1.00	0.27
United Kingdom	ECS H	1	1	—	1	−1	1		0.60	1	1	1	1	1	1	0.67	1	—	—	—	1.00	0.76

table continues next page

Table 2C.9 Vulnerability Zoning Using Closest-30-Peer Referencing for High-Income Countries (HICs), 2003 *(continued)*

			Total score for external factors							Sub-total		Total score for system factors						Sub-total	Total score for household factors				Sub-total	Total
			Macro	Fiscal space			Structural	Demography	Political economy and governance	Vector mean for external		Commitment to health	Health financing level	Health financing trend	Government in health	Government health trend	Coverage	Vector mean for system	Health outcome				Vector mean for household	Total vulnerability score
Country	IG-C30 H	Region	GDP growth	Fiscal space	Debt-to-GDP	ODA/GNI	Unemployment	SR dependency			ICRG political risk index	GHE/GGE	Log THE PC	THE growth	GHE/THE	GHE growth	Vaccination		IMR	MMR	H4A	W4A		
Bahamas, The	H	LCN	-2	1	—	—	-2	2	—	-0.40	-1	1	-2	-4	-2	-1	-1	-1.50	-4	—	—	—	-4.00	-1.97
Bahrain	H	MEA	2	1	—	—	—	3	-2	1.00	-2	-2	-2	-1	-1	-1	2	-0.83	-2	—	—	—	-2.00	-0.61
Israel	H	MEA	-1	-1	—	—	-2	1	-2	-1.00	-2	-2	-1	-2	-1	-3	1	-1.33	1	—	—	—	1.00	-0.44
Kuwait	H	MEA	4	1	—	—	2	2	-2	1.40	-2	-2	-2	-1	1	-1	2	-0.50	-2	—	—	—	-2.00	-0.37
Qatar	H	MEA	—	—	—	—	—	—	—	—	—	—	—	—	—	—	—	—	—	—	—	—	—	—
United Arab Emirates	H	MEA	—	—	—	—	—	—	—	—	—	—	—	—	—	—	—	—	—	—	—	—	—	—
Canada	H	NAC	-1	—	-1	—	-1	1	1	-0.20	2	2	1	2	1	1	-3	0.67	-1	—	—	—	-1.00	-0.18
United States	H	NAC	-1	—	-1	—	1	1	-1	-0.20	2	2	2	-1	-3	1	1	0.33	-1	—	—	—	-1.00	-0.29

Note: EAS = East Asia and Pacific (now EAP); ECS = Europe and Central Asia (now ECA); GDP = gross domestic product; GGE = general government expenditures; GHE = government health expenditures; GNI = gross national income; H (and HIC) = high-income country; HF = health financing; H4A = height for age; ICRG = International Country Risk Guide; IG-C30 = income group closest 30; IMR = infant mortality rate; LCN = Latin America and the Caribbean (now LAC); MEA = Middle East and North Africa (now MNA or MENA); MMR = maternal mortality rate; NAC = North America; ODA = official development assistance; SAR = special administrative region; SR = senior; THE PC = total health expenditure per capita; W4A = weight for age; — = not available. The color code in the table is based on the description presented in table 2.2.

Table 2C.10 Vulnerability Zoning Using Closest-30-Peer Referencing for Upper-Middle-Income Countries (UMICs), 2003

Vulnerability zoning			Total score for external factors						Sub-total	Total score for system factors						Sub-total	Total score for household factors				Sub-total	Total
			Macro	Fiscal space	Fiscal space	Structural	Demography	Political economy and governance		Commitment to health	Health financing level	Health financing trend	Government in health	Government HF trend	Coverage		Health outcome					
Country	Region	IG-C30 UM 2003	GDP growth	Debt-to-GDP	ODA/GNI	Unemployment	SR dependency	ICRG political risk index	Vector mean for external	GHE/GGE	Log THE PC	THE growth	GHE/THE	GHE growth	Vaccination	Vector mean for system	IMR	MMR	H4A	W4A	Vector mean for household	Total vulnerability score
Malaysia	EAS	UM	−1	1	1	2	2	1	1.00	−1	−1	4	−1	2	1	0.67	1	1	—	—	1.00	0.89
Palau	EAS	UM	−2	—	−4	—	—	—	−3.00	1	−1	−1	2	−1	1	0.50	1	—	—	—	1.00	−0.50
Croatia	ECS	UM	1	1	1	−1	−2	1	0.17	2	1	1	2	—	1	1.40	1	1	—	—	1.00	0.86
Czech Republic	ECS	UM	1	1	—	1	−1	1	0.60	1	1	2	2	1	1	1.33	1	—	—	—	1.00	0.98
Estonia	ECS	UM	2	2	—	−1	−2	1	0.40	1	−1	2	1	—	1	0.83	1	1	—	—	1.00	0.74
Hungary	ECS	UM	1	−1	—	1	−2	2	0.20	1	1	1	1	2	1	1.17	1	1	—	—	1.00	0.79
Latvia	ECS	UM	1	2	—	1	−2	2	0.80	−1	1	1	−1	1	1	0.33	1	1	—	—	1.00	0.71
Lithuania	ECS	UM	2	—	—	−1	−2	1	0.20	2	1	2	2	1	1	1.50	1	1	—	—	1.00	0.90
Poland	ECS	UM	−1	1	—	−2	−1	1	−0.40	−1	−1	1	1	−1	1	0.00	1	1	—	—	1.00	0.20
Slovak Republic	ECS	UM	1	1	—	−2	−1	1	0.00	2	1	1	1	1	1	1.17	1	1	—	—	1.00	0.72

table continues next page

Table 2C.10 Vulnerability Zoning Using Closest-30-Peer Referencing for Upper-Middle-Income Countries (UMICs), 2003 *(continued)*

| | | | Total score for external factors | | | | | | | Total score for system factors | | | | | | | Total score for household factors | | | | | Total |
| | | | Macro | Fiscal space | Fiscal space | Structural | Demography | Political economy and governance | Sub-total | Commitment to health | Health financing level | Health financing trend | Government in health | Government health trend | HF Coverage | Sub-total | Health outcome | | | | Sub-total | Total |
Country	Region	IG-C30 UM 2003	GDP growth	Debt-to-GDP	ODA/GNI	Unemployment	SR dependency	ICRG political risk index	Vector mean for external	GHE/GGE	Log THE PC	THE growth	GHE/THE	GHE growth	Vaccination	Vector mean for system	IMR	MMR	H4A	W4A	Vector mean for household	Total vulnerability score
Antigua and Barbuda	LCN	UM	1	-2	1	—	—	—	0.00	-1	-1	-1	1	1	1	0.00	1	—	—	—	1.00	0.33
Argentina	LCN	UM	1	-3	1	-1	-1	-1	-0.67	1	1	1	-1	1	1	0.67	1	-1	—	—	0.00	0.00
Barbados	LCN	UM	-1	1	—	-1	-1	—	-0.50	1	1	1	-1	-2	1	-0.50	-1	-1	—	—	-1.00	-0.67
Brazil	LCN	UM	-2	-1	1	1	-1	1	0.17	-2	-1	-1	-2	-1	1	-0.67	-1	-1	1	—	-0.33	-0.28
Chile	LCN	UM	-1	2	1	1	1	2	1.00	1	1	2	-2	-2	1	0.17	1	—	—	—	1.00	0.72
Costa Rica	LCN	UM	1	1	1	1	1	2	1.17	4	1	1	2	1	-1	1.33	1	—	—	—	1.00	1.17
Dominica	LCN	UM	1	-2	-1	—	—	—	-0.67	1	-1	-1	-1	—	1	-0.33	1	—	—	—	1.00	0.00
Grenada	LCN	UM	1	-1	-1	1	1	—	0.00	1	1	—	—	—	1	-0.33	1	—	—	—	1.00	0.22
Mexico	LCN	UM	-2	1	1	2	1	-1	0.33	2	-1	—	-2	—	1	0.67	-1	-1	—	-1	-1.00	0.00
Panama	LCN	UM	-1	-1	1	1	1	1	0.33	-1	1	-1	1	-1	1	0.00	1	—	—	-1	0.00	0.11
St. Kitts and Nevis	LCN	UM	-1	-2	1	—	—	—	-0.67	-1	-1	-1	-1	-2	1	-0.83	1	—	—	—	1.00	-0.17
St. Lucia	LCN	UM	-1	1	-1	-2	1	—	-0.40	-1	-1	-1	-1	-1	1	-0.67	1	—	—	—	1.00	-0.02
Trinidad and Tobago	LCN	UM	3	1	—	-1	2	-2	0.60	-2	2	-2	-2	2	-1	-1.00	-2	—	—	—	-2.00	-0.80
Uruguay	LCN	UM	-1	-2	1	-1	-2	1	-0.67	1	2	-2	-1	-2	1	-0.17	1	1	1	-1	0.50	-0.11

table continues next page

Table 2C.10 Vulnerability Zoning Using Closest-30-Peer Referencing for Upper-Middle-Income Countries (UMICs), 2003 (continued)

Country	Region	IG-C30 UM 2003	Macro GDP growth	Fiscal space Debt-to-GDP	Fiscal space ODA/GNI	Structural Unemployment	Demography SR dependency	Political economy and governance ICRG political risk index	Sub-total Vector mean for external	Commitment to health GHE/GGE	Health financing level Log THE PC	Health financing trend THE growth	Government in health GHE/THE	Government health trend GHE growth	Coverage HF trend Vaccination	Sub-total Vector mean for system	Health outcome IMR	MMR	H4A	W4A	Sub-total Vector mean for household	Total Total vulnerability score
Venezuela, RB	LCN	UM	−4	1	1	−1	1	−3	−0.83	−1	1	−1	−2	−1	−1	−0.83	1	−1	—	—	0.00	−0.56
Lebanon	MEA	UM	−1	−3	−1	—	1	−1	−1.00	−1	2	−1	−2	−2	−2	−0.83	1	1	1	—	1.00	−0.28
Libya	MEA	UM	2	1	—	—	2	−2	0.75	−2	−1	—	−1	—	—	−0.50	−1	−1	—	—	−1.00	−0.25
Malta	MEA	UM	−1	−1	—	1	—	1	0.20	2	2	—	—	−1	—	0.83	1	1	—	—	1.00	0.68
Oman	MEA	UM	−1	2	—	—	2	−1	0.50	−2	−2	−1	2	1	1	−0.50	−2	—	—	—	−2.00	−0.67
Saudi Arabia	MEA	UM	1	−1	—	−1	2	−2	−0.20	−2	−2	−1	−1	−1	−1	−0.50	−1	—	—	—	−1.00	−0.57
Botswana	SSF	UM	1	2	1	−2	2	1	0.83	1	1	1	1	1	—	0.33	−2	—	—	—	−2.00	−0.28
Gabon	SSF	UM	−2	−1	—	—	1	−2	−0.60	−2	−2	1	−2	2	−3	−1.00	−3	—	—	—	−3.00	−1.53
Mauritius	SSF	UM	−1	−1	1	1	1	—	0.20	−1	−2	−1	−1	1	1	−0.50	1	1	—	—	1.00	0.23
Seychelles	SSF	UM	−3	−3	1	2	—	—	−0.75	−1	−1	−1	2	1	1	0.17	1	—	—	—	1.00	0.14

Note: EAS = East Asia and Pacific (now EAP); ECS = Europe and Central Asia (now ECA); GDP = gross domestic product; GGE = general government expenditures; GHE = government health expenditures; GNI = gross national income; HF = health financing; H4A = height for age; ICRG = International Country Risk Guide; IG-C30 = income group closest 30; IMR = infant mortality rate; LCN = Latin America and the Caribbean (now LAC); MEA = Middle East and North Africa (now MNA or MENA); MMR = maternal mortality rate; ODA = official development assistance; SR = senior; SSF = Sub-Saharan Africa; THE PC = total health expenditure per capita; UM (and UMIC) = upper-middle-income country; W4A = weight for age; — = not available. The color code in the table is based on the description presented in table 2.2.

Table 2C.11 Vulnerability Zoning Using Closest-30-Peer Referencing for Lower-Middle-Income Countries (LMICs), 2003

Vulnerability zoning			Total score for external factors							Total score for system factors								Total score for household factors					Total
			Macro	Fiscal space	Fiscal space	Structural	Demography	Political economy and governance	Sub-total	Commitment to health	Health financing level	Health financing trend	Government in health	Government trend	Government HF trend	Coverage	Sub-total	Health outcome				Sub-total	Total
Country	Region	IG-C30 LM 2003	GDP growth	Debt-to-GDP	ODA/GNI	Unemployment	SR dependency	ICRG political risk index	Vector mean for external	GHE/GGE	Log THE PC	THE growth	GHE/THE	GHE growth	GHE growth	Vaccination	Vector mean for system	IMR	MMR	H4A	W4A	Vector mean for household	Total vulnerability score
China	EAS	LM	2	2	—	1	—1	1	1.00	—1	—1	1	—1	1	1	—1	—0.33	1	1	—	—	1.00	0.56
Fiji	EAS	LM	—1	1	1	1	1	—	0.60	—1	—1	—1	2	—1	—1	—1	—0.17	1	1	—	—	1.00	0.48
Kiribati	EAS	LM	1	—	—1	—	—	—	0.00	2	2	—	2	—1	—1	—1	0.83	—1	—	—	—	—1.00	—0.06
Micronesia, Fed. Sts.	EAS	LM	—1	—	—4	—	—	—	—1.33	—1	2	—	2	—	—	—	1.33	—1	1	—	—	—1.00	—0.33
Philippines	EAS	LM	1	1	—	—1	—	1	0.67	—1	—2	—	—1	—	—	—	—0.50	1	—	—1	—1	—0.33	—0.06
Samoa	EAS	LM	1	1	—	—	—	—	0.33	1	1	—	2	—	—	—	0.50	1	—	—	—	1.00	0.61
Thailand	EAS	LM	1	—1	2	2	—	1	1.00	1	—2	—	—1	2	—1	—1	0.50	1	—	—	—	1.00	0.83
Tonga	EAS	LM	—1	—	—1	1	—1	—	—0.50	2	—1	—	2	—	—	2	0.83	1	—	—	—	1.00	0.44
Vanuatu	EAS	LM	—1	—	—1	—	—	1	—0.33	1	—2	—	1	—1	—	—2	—0.67	1	—	—	—	1.00	0.00
Albania	ECS	LM	1	—1	—2	—1	—1	1	—0.50	—1	1	—	—2	—	—1	—	0.17	1	1	—	—	1.00	0.22
Belarus	ECS	LM	1	—	—	2	—2	—1	0.00	—1	—	2	2	—	—	—2	0.50	1	1	—	—	1.00	0.50
Bosnia and Herzegovina	ECS	LM	1	1	—2	—3	—2	—	—1.00	1	3	—	1	2	1	—1	1.17	—1	1	1	—	1.00	0.39
Bulgaria	ECS	LM	1	1	—	—1	—3	1	—0.20	2	—	—	—1	—	1	1	1.00	1	1	—	2	1.25	0.68
Kazakhstan	ECS	LM	2	2	1	1	1	1	1.33	—1	—2	—	—1	1	1	1	0.00	—1	1	—	—	0.00	0.44

table continues next page

Table 2C.11 Vulnerability Zoning Using Closest-30-Peer Referencing for Lower-Middle-Income Countries (LMICs), 2003 *(continued)*

Country	Region	IG-C30 LM 2003	Macro space: GDP growth	Fiscal space: Debt-to-GDP	Fiscal space: ODA/GNI	Structural: Unemployment	Demography: SR dependency	Political economy and governance: ICRG political risk index	Sub-total: Vector mean for external	Commitment to health: GHE/GGE	Health financing level: Log THE PC	Health financing trend: THE growth	Government in health: GHE/THE	Government health trend: GHE growth	Coverage: Vaccination	Sub-total: Vector mean for system	Health outcome: IMR	Health outcome: MMR	Health outcome: H4A	Health outcome: W4A	Sub-total: Vector mean for household	Total: Total vulnerability score
Macedonia, FYR	ECS	LM	−1	1	−3	−3	−1	—	−1.40	2	2	1	1	1	1	1.33	1	1	2	2	1.50	0.48
Montenegro	ECS	LM	−1	1	1	—	−2	—	−0.25	2	2	2	2	2	—	2.00	1	—	—	—	1.00	0.92
Romania	ECS	LM	1	1	—	1	−2	1	0.40	1	−1	−1	2	2	1	0.67	1	1	1	1	1.00	0.69
Russian Federation	ECS	LM	−1	1	—	1	−1	−1	0.20	1	1	1	−1	−1	1	0.33	1	1	—	—	1.00	0.51
Serbia	ECS	LM	−1	−1	−3	−1	−2	−1	−1.50	1	1	1	1	−1	1	0.67	1	1	—	—	1.00	0.06
Turkey	ECS	LM	−1	−1	−1	—	−1	−1	0.00	−1	−1	−1	1	2	−2	−0.33	−1	−1	—	—	−1.00	−0.44
Turkmenistan	ECS	LM	3	2	1	—	1	—	1.75	2	2	2	−1	1	1	1.17	−1	1	—	—	0.00	0.97
Belize	LCN	LM	1	−3	1	—	1	—	0.20	−2	−2	−2	2	1	1	−0.33	1	1	—	—	1.00	0.29
Bolivia	LCN	LM	−1	−1	−1	—	−1	−1	−0.20	−1	−2	−1	2	−1	1	−0.33	−2	−2	—	—	−2.00	−0.84
Colombia	LCN	LM	−1	−1	1	1	1	−2	0.17	2	2	2	2	−1	1	1.33	1	−1	—	—	0.00	0.50
Dominican Republic	LCN	LM	−2	1	—	−1	1	−1	−0.17	−1	−1	−2	−2	1	−1	−1.00	2	−3	1	1	0.25	−0.31
Ecuador	LCN	LM	−1	1	—	−1	1	−1	0.33	1	−1	−1	−2	−3	−1	−1.17	−1	−1	−1	−1	−1.00	−0.61
El Salvador	LCN	LM	−1	1	—	−1	1	−1	0.33	2	−1	−1	−1	1	1	0.17	1	−2	−1	−1	−0.75	−0.08
Guatemala	LCN	LM	−1	1	1	2	1	−1	0.50	2	−1	1	−1	1	1	0.50	−1	−1	—	—	−1.00	0.00

table continues next page

Table 2C.11 Vulnerability Zoning Using Closest-30-Peer Referencing for Lower-Middle-Income Countries (LMICs), 2003 *(continued)*

Vulnerability zoning

Column groups: **Total score for external factors** (Macro; Fiscal space; Structural; Demography; Political economy and governance; Sub-total) · **Total score for system factors** (Commitment to health; Health financing level; Health financing trend; Government in health; Government health trend; Coverage; Sub-total) · **Total score for household factors** (Health outcome; Sub-total) · **Total**

Country	Region	IG-C30 LM 2003	Macro — GDP growth	Fiscal space — Debt-to-GDP	Fiscal space — ODA/GNI	Structural — Unemployment	Demography — SR dependency	Political economy and governance — ICRG political risk index	Vector mean for external (Sub-total)	Commitment to health — GHE/GGE	Health financing level — Log THE PC growth	Health financing trend — THE growth	Government in health — GHE/THE	Government health trend — GHE growth	Coverage — Vaccination	Vector mean for system (Sub-total)	Health outcome — IMR	Health outcome — MMR	Health outcome — H4A	Health outcome — W4A	Vector mean for household (Sub-total)	Total vulnerability score
Guyana	LCN	LM	-1	-1	-1	—	1	2	0.00	1	1	-1	2	-1	1	0.50	1	1	—	—	1.00	0.50
Honduras	LCN	LM	1	-1	1	1	1	-1	0.33	3	1	1	1	1	1	1.33	1	—	—	—	1.00	0.89
Jamaica	LCN	LM	1	-2	1	1	-1	1	0.17	-2	-1	-1	-1	-2	-1	-1.33	-1	1	1	1	0.50	-0.22
Paraguay	LCN	LM	-1	1	1	1	1	-2	0.17	2	1	-2	-1	-2	1	-0.17	1	-1	—	—	0.00	0.00
Peru	LCN	LM	-1	1	1	1	1	1	0.67	2	-1	-1	1	-1	-1	-0.17	-1	-1	—	—	-1.00	-0.17
St. Vincent and the Grenadines	LCN	LM	—	—	—	—	—	—	0.00	—	-1	1	1	1	—	0.33	1	—	—	—	1.00	0.44
Suriname	LCN	LM	1	1	1	1	1	1	1.00	-1	1	-1	1	-1	-3	-0.67	-1	—	—	—	-1.00	-0.22
Algeria	MEA	LM	1	1	1	-2	1	-4	-0.33	-1	-2	-1	2	1	1	0.33	-1	-1	—	-3	-1.67	-0.56
Djibouti	MEA	LM	-1	1	-1	—	1	—	0.00	-1	1	-1	1	1	1	0.33	-1	-2	1	—	-0.67	-0.11
Egypt, Arab Rep.	MEA	LM	-1	-2	1	1	1	1	0.17	-1	1	-1	-1	-1	2	-0.17	-1	—	—	—	-1.00	-0.33
Iran, Islamic Rep.	MEA	LM	1	1	1	1	1	-1	0.67	-2	-1	-1	-2	1	2	-0.50	-1	—	1	1	0.33	0.17
Iraq	MEA	LM	-4	—	—	-3	—	-3	-2.25	-2	-2	3	1	4	-1	0.50	1	—	—	—	1.00	-0.25
Jordan	MEA	LM	-1	-1	-1	-1	1	1	-0.33	-1	2	-1	-1	-1	1	-0.17	2	—	—	—	2.00	0.50

table continues next page

Table 2C.11 Vulnerability Zoning Using Closest-30-Peer Referencing for Lower-Middle-Income Countries (LMICs), 2003 *(continued)*

Vulnerability zoning			Total score for external factors							Total score for system factors							Total score for household factors					Total
			Macro	Fiscal space	Fiscal space	Struc-tural	Demog-raphy	Politi-cal economy and gover-nance	Sub-total	Com-mit-ment to health	Health financ-ing level	Health financ-ing trend	Gov-ern-ment financ-ing in health	Gov-ern-ment financ-ing trend	Cover-age	Sub-total	Health outcome				Sub-total	Total vul-nera-bility score
Country	Region	IG-C30 LM 2003	GDP growth	Debt-to-GDP	ODA/GNI	Unem-ploy-ment	SR depen-dency	ICRG politi-cal risk index	Vector mean for exter-nal	GHE/GGE	Log THE PC growth	THE growth	GHE/THE	GHE growth	Vacci-nation	Vector mean for sys-tem	IMR	MMR	H4A	W4A	Vector mean for house-hold	Total score
Morocco	MEA	LM	1	−1	1	−1		2	0.50	−2	−1	1	−2	1	1	−0.33	2	−2	—	—	0.00	0.06
Syrian Arab Republic	MEA	LM	−2	−2	1	1		−1	−0.33	−1	−1	−1	−1	1	−1	−0.67	1	—	—	—	1.00	0.00
Tunisia	MEA	LM	1	−1	1	−1		−1	0.33	−1	−1	1	−1	1	1	0.00	1	—	—	—	1.00	0.44
Maldives	SAS	LM	3	1	1	—		—	1.50	−1	1	2	−1	2	2	0.67	−1	—	—	—	−1.00	0.39
Sri Lanka	SAS	LM	1	—	1	1	−1	−1	0.20	−1	−1	1	−1	−1	1	−0.33	1	1	—	—	1.00	0.29
Cape Verde	SSF	LM	1	−1	−1	−2	−1	—	−0.80	1	1	−1	1	−1	1	0.00	1	—	—	—	1.00	0.07
Equatorial Guinea	SSF	LM	3	2	1	—	2	—	2.00	−1	−4	−4	1	−4	−4	−2.17	−4	−2	−3	—	−3.00	−1.06
Namibia	SSF	LM	−1	1	1	—	1	2	0.80	1	1	1	1	1	−2	0.50	−2	—	—	—	−2.00	−0.23
South Africa	SSF	LM	−1	1	1	−3	2	−1	−0.17	−1	2	−2	−2	1	−2	0.17	−3	−3	—	—	−3.00	−1.00
Swaziland	SSF	LM	1	−1	1			−1	0.50	−1	−1	−2	−1	2		0.00	−4	—	—	—	−4.00	−1.17

Note: EAS = East Asia and Pacific (now EAP); ECS = Europe and Central Asia (now ECA); GDP = gross domestic product; GGE = general government expenditures; GHE = government health expenditures; GNI = gross national income; HF = health financing; H4A = height for age; ICRG = International Country Risk Guide; IG-C30 = income group closest 30; IMR = infant mortality rate; LCN = Latin America and the Caribbean (now LAC); LM (and LMIC) = lower-middle-income country; MEA = Middle East and North Africa (now MNA or MENA); MMR = maternal mortality rate; ODA = official development assistance; SAS = South Asia; SR = senior; SSF = Sub-Saharan Africa; THE PC = total health expenditure per capita; W4A = weight for age; — = not available. The color code in the table is based on the description presented in table 2.2.

Table 2C.12 Vulnerability Zoning Using Closest-30-Peer Referencing for Low-Income Countries (LICs), 2003

Country	Region	IG-C30 2003	Macro space: GDP growth	Fiscal space: Debt-to-GDP	Fiscal space: ODA/GNI	Structural: Unemployment	Demography: SR dependency	Political economy and governance: ICRG political risk index	Sub-total: Vector mean for external	Commitment to health: GHE/GGE	Health financing level: Log THE PC	Health financing trend: THE growth	Government health: GHE/THE	Government health trend: GHE growth	Government HF trend: GHE growth	Coverage: Vaccination	Sub-total: Vector mean for system	IMR	MMR	H4A	W4A	Sub-total: Vector mean for household	Total vulnerability score
Cambodia	EAS	L	2	1	—	—	1	—	0.75	1	1	1	—1	1	1	—1	0.33	—1	—	—	—	—1.00	0.03
Indonesia	EAS	L	1	1	—	—	1	—2	0.50	—2	—2	1	—1	—1	—1	—1	—0.67	—1	—1	1	—1	—0.50	—0.22
Lao PDR	EAS	L	1	—1	—1	—	—1	—	—0.50	1	1	1	—1	—1	—1	—2	—0.83	—1	—	—	—	—1.00	—0.78
Mongolia	EAS	L	1	—	—	1	—	2	0.80	1	—	—	—	—	—	2	0.17	—	1	1	2	0.75	0.57
Papua New Guinea	EAS	L	—1	—	—	—	1	—1	0.00	1	—	—	—1	—1	—1	—	—0.17	—1	—	—	—	1.00	0.28
Solomon Islands	EAS	L	1	1	—	—	1	—	0.50	2	—	—	2	—1	—1	—1	0.00	1	—	—	—	1.00	0.50
Timor-Leste	EAS	L	—2	—	—4	—	1	—	—1.67	4	—	—	2	—1	—1	—1	0.67	—1	—	—	—	—1.00	—0.67
Vietnam	EAS	L	1	1	—	2	—2	—	0.67	—1	—	—	2	—1	—1	2	—0.17	2	—	—	—	2.00	0.83
Armenia	ECS	L	3	—1	—	—3	—3	1	—0.67	—1	1	—	—2	2	1	—2	0.33	—1	—	—	—	1.00	0.22
Azerbaijan	ECS	L	2	1	—	1	—4	1	0.83	—2	—2	4	—2	1	—2	—2	0.00	—	1	1	—1	0.00	0.28
Georgia	ECS	L	1	—	—1	—1	—2	—	—0.75	1	2	2	—2	1	—1	—	0.00	—	—	—	—	1.00	0.08
Kyrgyz Republic	ECS	L	1	—1	—1	—	—2	—	—0.75	—1	—	1	—1	—1	—1	2	0.17	—	—	—	—	1.00	0.14
Moldova	ECS	L	1	—	1	1	—3	2	0.50	—1	2	1	—1	—1	—1	2	0.17	2	—	—	—	1.50	0.72
Tajikistan	ECS	L	2	1	—1	—1	—1	—	0.75	—1	—	—	—1	—1	1	—	—0.50	—	—	1	—	0.00	0.08
Ukraine	ECS	L	2	1	—	1	—4	—1	—0.20	—1	2	2	—1	2	2	—	1.00	—	—	—	—	1.00	0.60

table continues next page

Table 2C.12 Vulnerability Zoning Using Closest-30-Peer Referencing for Low-Income Countries (LICs), 2003 *(continued)*

Country	Region	IG-C30	GDP growth 2003 (Macro)	Debt-to-GDP (Fiscal space)	ODA/GNI (Fiscal space)	Unemployment (Structural)	SR dependency (Demography)	ICRG political risk index (Political economy and governance)	Vector mean for external (Sub-total)	GHE/GGE (Commitment to health)	Log THE PC (Health financing level)	THE growth (Health financing trend)	GHE/THE (Government in health)	GHE growth (Government HF trend)	Vaccination (Coverage)	Vector mean for system (Sub-total)	IMR (Health outcome)	MMR	H4A	W4A	Vector mean for household (Sub-total)	Total vulnerability score (Total)
Uzbekistan	ECS	L	1	1	2	—	−1	—	0.75	−1	—	−1	−1	−1	2	−0.17	1	1	1	—	1.00	0.53
Haiti	LCN	L	−1	1	—	—	−1	−1	−0.50	−1	—	−1	−2	−2	−1	−1.33	−1	−1	—	—	−1.00	−0.94
Nicaragua	LCN	L	−1	—	−2	1	1	1	0.00	2	2	−1	1	−1	1	0.67	1	1	—	—	1.00	0.56
West Bank and Gaza	MEA	L	1	—	−3	—	1	—	−0.33	—	—	—	—	—	—	—	1	—	—	—	1.00	0.33
Yemen, Rep.	MEA	L	−1	1	1	—	—	1	0.60	2	1	1	−1	−1	−1	−0.33	−1	−2	—	—	−1.50	−0.41
Afghanistan	SAS	L	2	—	−2	—	2	—	0.67	2	1	2	−2	3	−2	0.67	−1	—	—	—	−1.00	0.11
Bangladesh	SAS	L	1	—	1	—	−1	−1	0.00	−1	−2	−1	−1	—	−1	−1.17	2	—	—	—	2.00	0.28
Bhutan	SAS	L	1	−1	−1	2	1	—	0.40	1	—	−3	—	−2	1	−0.17	−2	—	—	—	−2.00	−0.59
India	SAS	L	1	—	2	—	−1	1	0.80	−2	−1	−1	−2	−1	−1	−1.33	−1	−1	—	—	−1.00	−0.51
Nepal	SAS	L	−1	—	1	—	−1	—	0.00	−1	−1	−1	−2	−1	−1	−1.17	−1	—	—	—	1.00	−0.06
Pakistan	SAS	L	1	—	2	1	−1	−1	0.50	−2	−2	−1	−2	−1	−1	−1.50	−1	—	—	—	−1.00	−0.67
Angola	SSF	L	−1	−1	1	—	1	−1	−0.20	−2	1	2	2	−1	−3	−0.83	−4	—	—	—	−4.00	−1.68

table continues next page

Table 2C.12 Vulnerability Zoning Using Closest-30-Peer Referencing for Low-Income Countries (LICs), 2003 (continued)

Country	Region	IG-C30 2003	Macro space: GDP growth	Fiscal space: Debt-to-GDP	Fiscal space: ODA/GNI	Structural: Unemployment	Demography: SR dependency	Political economy and governance: ICRG political risk index	Sub-total: Vector mean for external	Commitment to health: GHE/GGE	Health financing level: Log THE PC	Health financing trend: THE growth	Government in health: GHE/THE	Government HF trend: GHE/THE growth	Coverage: Vaccination	Sub-total: Vector mean for system	Health outcome: IMR	MMR	H4A	W4A	Sub-total: Vector mean for household	Total: Total vulnerability score
Benin	SSF	L	−1	—	1	—	1	—	0.50	−1	−1	—	1	1	1	0.67	−1	—	—	—	−1.00	0.06
Burkina Faso	SSF	L	1	1	1	—	2	2	1.40	1	1	1	1	1	1	1.00	−1	—	—	—	−1.00	0.47
Burundi	SSF	L	—	—	—	—	—	—	—	—	—	—	—	—	—	—	—	—	—	—	—	—
Cameroon	SSF	L	1	1	1	—	1	−1	0.60	−1	1	−1	−2	−1	−1	−0.83	2	−3	—	—	−0.50	−0.24
Central African Republic	SSF	L	−3	—	2	—	−2	—	−1.00	1	−2	−1	−1	−1	−1	−0.83	−2	—	—	—	−2.00	−1.28
Chad	SSF	L	2	1	1	—	−1	—	0.75	1	1	−2	−1	−1	−3	−0.17	2	—	—	—	2.00	0.86
Comoros	SSF	L	−1	1	1	—	1	—	0.50	−1	−2	−1	2	−1	−1	−0.67	−1	—	—	—	−1.00	−0.39
Congo, Dem. Rep.	SSF	L	—	—	—	—	—	—	—	—	—	—	—	—	—	—	—	—	—	—	—	—
Congo, Rep.	SSF	L	−1	−4	1	—	1	−2	−1.00	−2	−2	−1	−1	−1	−3	−1.67	−2	—	—	—	−2.00	−1.56
Côte d'Ivoire	SSF	L	−1	1	2	—	1	−2	0.20	−2	−1	−1	−2	−1	−1	−1.33	−2	—	—	—	−2.00	−1.04
Eritrea	SSF	L	−2	−2	−2	—	2	—	−1.00	−2	−2	−1	1	−2	2	−0.67	1	—	—	—	1.00	−0.22
Ethiopia	SSF	L	—	—	—	—	—	—	—	—	—	—	—	—	—	—	—	—	—	—	—	—
Gambia, The	SSF	L	1	−1	−1	—	2	2	0.60	2	−1	−1	1	1	2	0.67	−1	—	—	—	−1.00	0.09
Ghana	SSF	L	−1	−1	−1	—	−1	1	−0.20	−1	−1	−1	−1	−1	1	−0.33	−1	—	—	—	−1.00	−0.51
Guinea	SSF	L	1	−1	1	—	−1	−1	−0.20	−2	−1	−2	−2	—	−1	−0.67	−1	—	—	—	−1.00	−0.62

table continues next page

Table 2C.12 Vulnerability Zoning Using Closest-30-Peer Referencing for Low-Income Countries (LICs), 2003 (continued)

Country	Region	IG-C30 2003	GDP growth (Macro)	Debt-to-GDP (Fiscal space)	ODA/GNI (Fiscal space)	Unemployment (Structural)	SR dependency (Demography)	ICRG political risk index (Political economy and governance)	Vector mean for external (Sub-total)	GHE/GGE (Commitment to health)	Log THE PC (Health financing level)	THE growth (Health financing trend)	GHE/THE (Government health)	GHE growth (Government health trend)	Vaccination (Coverage)	Vector mean for system (Sub-total)	IMR (Health outcome)	MMR	H4A	W4A	Vector mean for household (Sub-total)	Total vulnerability score (Total)
Guinea-Bissau	SSF	L	−2	−3	−2	—	−1	−1	−1.80	−1	−1	−1	−1	−4	1	−1.17	−2	—	—	—	−2.00	−1.66
Kenya	SSF	L	−1	1	1	—	1	1	0.60	−1	−1	−1	−1	−1	1	−0.67	−1	—	1	—	0.00	−0.02
Lesotho	SSF	L	1	1	1	—	−2	—	0.25	−1	1	−1	−1	−1	1	0.00	2	—	—	—	2.00	0.75
Liberia	SSF	L	—	—	—	—	—	—	—	—	—	—	—	—	—	—	—	—	—	—	—	—
Madagascar	SSF	L	1	−1	1	—	1	1	0.20	1	−2	−1	2	−1	−1	−0.33	2	—	—	—	2.00	0.62
Malawi	SSF	L	1	−1	−1	—	−1	1	−0.50	−1	2	1	2	2	1	1.17	3	—	—	—	3.00	1.22
Mali	SSF	L	1	1	1	—	1	1	1.00	1	−1	−1	−1	−1	−1	0.67	−2	—	—	—	−2.00	−0.11
Mauritania	SSF	L	1	−3	−1	—	1	—	−0.50	−2	−1	−2	−1	−1	1	−0.83	−1	—	—	—	−1.00	−0.78
Mozambique	SSF	L	1	−1	−1	—	−1	—	0.00	1	−2	1	2	−1	1	0.17	−2	—	—	—	−2.00	−0.61
Niger	SSF	L	1	1	1	—	2	—	1.25	−1	−2	−1	−1	−1	−2	−1.00	−1	—	—	—	−1.00	−0.25
Nigeria	SSF	L	1	1	2	—	1	−2	0.60	−2	4	4	−2	1	−3	−0.17	−3	—	−1	—	−2.00	−0.52
Rwanda	SSF	L	−1	1	−1	—	1	—	0.00	1	3	3	2	2	2	1.67	−1	—	—	—	−1.00	0.22
São Tomé and Príncipe	SSF	L	1	−4	—	—	−1	—	−1.33	1	3	1	−1	3	1	1.33	−1	—	—	—	−1.00	−0.33

table continues next page

Table 2C.12 Vulnerability Zoning Using Closest-30-Peer Referencing for Low-Income Countries (LICs), 2003 (continued)

Country	Region	IG-C30	GDP growth 2003 (Macro)	Debt-to-GDP (Fiscal space)	ODA/GNI (Fiscal space)	Unemployment (Structural)	SR dependency (Demography)	ICRG political risk index (Political economy and governance)	Vector mean for external (Sub-total)	GHE/GGE (Commitment to health)	Log THE PC (Health financing level)	THE growth (Health financing trend)	GHE/THE (Government in health)	GHE growth (Government trend)	Vaccination (Coverage)	Vector mean for system (Sub-total)	IMR	MMR	H4A	W4A	Vector mean for household (Sub-total)	Total vulnerability score (Total)
Senegal	SSF	L	1	1	1	—	1	1	1.00	1	1	-1	-1	-1	-1	-0.33	-1	—	—	—	-1.00	-0.11
Sierra Leone	SSF	L	1	-1	-2	—	3	—	0.25	-1	1	-3	-1	-1	1	-0.67	-2	—	—	—	-2.00	-0.81
Sudan	SSF	L	1	-1	1	—	1	-2	0.00	-1	-1	1	-1	-1	-1	-0.67	-1	—	—	—	-1.00	-0.56
Tanzania	SSF	L	1	1	1	—	1	1	1.00	1	-1	1	1	1	2	0.83	-1	—	—	—	-1.00	0.28
Togo	SSF	L	1	-1	2	—	-1	-2	-0.20	-1	1	1	-2	2	1	0.33	-1	—	—	—	-1.00	-0.29
Uganda	SSF	L	1	1	1	—	1	-1	0.60	-1	1	1	-1	-1	-1	-0.33	-1	—	—	—	-1.00	-0.24
Zambia	SSF	L	1	-2	-1	—	1	1	0.00	1	1	-1	2	-1	1	0.50	2	—	—	—	2.00	0.83

Note: EAS = East Asia and Pacific (now EAP); ECS = Europe and Central Asia (now ECA); GDP = gross domestic product; GGE = general government expenditures; GHE = government health expenditures; GNI = gross national income; H4A = health financing; H4A = height for age; HF = health financing; ICRG = International Country Risk Guide; IG-C30 = income group closest 30; IMR = infant mortality rate; LCN = Latin America and the Caribbean (now LAC); L (and LIC) = low-income country; MEA = Middle East and North Africa (now MNA or MENA); MMR = maternal mortality rate; ODA = official development assistance; SAS = South Asia; SR = senior; SSF = Sub-Saharan Africa; THE PC = total health expenditure per capita; W4A = weight for age; — = not available. The color code in the table is based on the description presented in table 2.2.

Notes

1. http://hdr.undp.org/en/reports/global/hdr2011/.

2. http://www.doingbusiness.org/.

3. See work on crises and health presented by Chawla (2009), Gottret (2009), and Lewis (2009) at the IHEA (International Health Economics Association) 2009 meeting; by Barros (2012a), Thomas (2012), and Yfantopoulos (2012) at the ECHE (European Conference on Health Economics) 2012 meeting. As a clear sign of increasing interest in lessons and solutions, in 2012 *Health Policy* 106 (1) published a series of studies on the impact of the financial crises on health sector reform in Europe, including some of the most battered countries of the EU in terms of fiscal and macro effects: Italy (de Belvis et al. 2012; Ferrè, Cuccurullo, and Lega 2012), Spain (Gené-Badia et al. 2012), and Portugal (Barros 2012a).

4. http://www.lloyds.com/news-and-insight/risk-insight/reports/microinsurance /global-business-leader-survey.

5. "Managing Risk for Development." 2013. *World Development Report 2014*, World Bank, Washington, DC. http://econ.worldbank.org/WBSITE/EXTERNAL/EXTDEC /EXTRESEARCH/EXTWDRS/0,,contentMDK:20227703~pagePK:478093~piPK:4 77627~theSitePK:477624,00.html. Concept Note, October 30, 2012.

6. See more in a literature review on the impact of the financial crisis on health by Brenzel 2012.

7. See more on nutrition outcomes during crises in a review by Brenzel 2012.

8. Ferreira and Schady (2009) find that the effects of crises may be ambiguous as income and substitution effects are countervailing. In this example, although there is an expected negative income effect during economic shocks, the opportunity cost for exercise is lower, increasing the likelihood that individuals engage in it.

9. Albania, Bosnia and Herzegovina, Bulgaria, Croatia, Estonia, Latvia, Lithuania, the former Yugoslav Republic of Macedonia, Montenegro, and Serbia.

10. Countries are relying much more heavily on data and policy research in making spending decisions when budgets contract, replacing the axe with a scalpel to drive policy and future directions (Lewis and Verhoeven 2010).

11. Food Insecurity and Vulnerability Information and Mapping Systems (FIVIMS), http://www.fivims.org and The State of Food Insecurity in the World 2012, http:// www.fao.org/publications/sofi/en/.

12. The FIVIMS paper (FAO/FIVIMS 2002) distinguishes structural (more permanent) and transitory (temporary) vulnerability.

13. The seven types of crisis are liquidity, solvency, balance of payment, currency, external debt, growth rate, and financial. Laeven and Valencia (2012) explore episodes of financial crises and develop a database for financial crises up to 2012.

14. For example: negative year-on-year GDP growth; debt-to-GDP ratio over 60 percent; a decrease in the value of the local currency greater than or equal to 25 percent, using nominal exchange rate against the U.S. dollar, http://www.hks.harvard.edu/fs /jfrankel/CURRCRSH-WB1.PDF.

15. Following the methods applied in Braun and di Gresia (2003), Velényi and Smitz (2013) implement a descriptive analysis of cyclicality through a five-step process, which is primarily broken down for didactic purposes to be easily understood and applied by noneconomists in the health sector. Applying this method, the authors obtain (a) the Hodrick-Prescott (HP) filtered trends; (b) the cycle trends, which are

defined in terms of the deviation of the observed value of the variable from the stationary trend line; and (c) the cyclical correlations between economic output, fiscal spending, and government health spending. The cyclical correlations calculated for these variables during "bad" and "good" times—defined in terms of output gap, when the cycle is at least 1.5 standard deviations below/above the filtered trend line—enable the exploration of whether the cyclical responses are symmetric or asymmetric during downturns and booms.

16. http://www.prsgroup.com/ICRG_methodology.aspx#PolRiskRating. The political risk rating contributes 50 percent of the composite rating, and the financial and economic risk ratings each contribute 25 percent. The following formula is used to calculate the aggregate political, financial, and economic risk: *CPFER (country X) = 0.5 (PR + FR + ER) where CPFER = Composite political, financial, and economic risk ratings; PR = Total political risk indicators; FR = Total financial risk indicators; and ER = Total economic risk indicators.* The highest overall rating (theoretically 100) indicates the lowest risk, and the lowest rating (theoretically zero) indicates the highest risk. The broad categories of Composite Risk are: (a) very high risk: 0 to 49.9 points; (b) high risk: 50 to 59.9 points; (c) moderate risk: 60 to 69.9 points; (d) low risk: 70 to 79.9 points; and (e) very low risk: 80 to 100 points.

17. See more on ODA and DAH in the literature review section of a paper on business cycles and public health expenditures by Velényi and Smitz (2013) and in a case study on fungibility of development assistance on health by Fairbank (2013).

18. A number of studies aim to disaggregate the drivers of health expenditures (Hartwig 2008; IMF 2010; OECD 2006) so that relevant policy responses at the macro and micro levels could reduce expenditures pressure and keep the health sector as a share of GDP within reasonable bounds. It is critical to have data-driven policy making that aims to maintain a healthy fiscal share of the sector when pressures from a combination of factors (for example, aging, changing disease burden, and more intensive use of advanced technology) lead to upward expenditure spirals. These questions are addressed, among others in the recent literature, by companion papers produced under the umbrella of the Health and Economy Program of the Word Bank (Fleisher, Leive, and Schieber 2013; Liang and Velényi 2013; Tandon et al. 2013; Xu, Saksena, and Holly 2011).

19. $Zs = X - \mu / d$, where X is the value for variable "*j*" for country "*i*"; μ is the group mean (WB income, closest 30, regional, and global benchmark); d is the standard deviation of the group mean.

20. We have calculated the Z scores and mapped them for the full set of variables presented in table 2B.1. For this extended set the aggregate is calculated by averaging through all available variables for the given country in a given year. As data availability varies across countries and years, we list the number of dimensions available to understand what went into the aggregate. Because of the differences in the dimensions, comparisons are not particularly useful. The primary purpose of this analysis was to explore data limitations. Because of missing data for a number of dimensions, we also calculated the Z scores and mapped these for the reduced set, which is discussed in the text and presented in table 2.1.

21. $V_i = (X_i - Min\ X_i) / (Max\ X_i - Min\ X_i)$.

22. Note that there is difference in the dimension between the radar plots prepared for advanced economies and developing countries. In the former we use unemployment rate and in the latter we use official development assistance (ODA) as share of GNI.

This customization makes the plots more relevant as unemployment can be a more precise proxy for fiscal space in more developed countries where the share of the informal sector is relatively smaller, while foreign aid can be material in terms of fiscal space for developing countries.

23. Log transformation is standard procedure with data that have outliers and skewed or exponential distribution, such as income and health expenditures, in order to compact the dispersion of the variable.

24. del Granado, Gupta, and Hajdenberg (2013) find that the cyclicality of government health spending is asymmetric across "good" and "bad" times, defined in terms of output gap relative to potential output. Drawing on this literature, in another paper that focuses on business cycles and government health spending, Velényi and Smitz (2013) construct the variable "output gap," which measures the difference between the observed value for the variable of interest and the value on the filtered trend for the given year in terms of standard deviation from the trends. Good/bad times are defined as positive/negative output gap relative to the trend line. In terms of the measurement approach, output gap is not equivalent to growth crises measures that are provided in terms of negative GDP growth. The difference is that although growth crises are defined in terms of negative year-on-year GDP growth rate, a negative output gap does not necessarily mean that the country has a negative growth rate. For example, a slowdown in economic output for countries with high growth rates and where the trend line would suggest at least maintaining that growth rate, a negative output gap simply means that relative to the expected trend, the country's economic performance is lower, but it does not necessarily mean negative growth rate. In sum, output gap is a relative measure of the country's performance on industrial output.

25. The Fiscal Health Database was compiled by Marc Smitz and Aaka Pande with inputs from Cesar Calderon, John Langenbrunner, Adam Leive, Ece Ozcelik, and Edit V. Velényi.

26. For data on equity and financial protection, the World Bank offers fact sheets: http://web.worldbank.org/WBSITE/EXTERNAL/TOPIC.

Bibliography

Abbas, F., and U. Hiemenz. 2011. "Determinants of Public Health Expenditures in Pakistan." ZEF Discussion Papers on Development Policy 158.

Akitoby, B., B. Clements, S. Gupta, and G. Inchauste. 2004. "The Cyclical and Long-Term Behavior of Government Expenditures in Developing Countries." International Monetary Fund Working Paper, WP/04/202.

Alderman, H., and T. Haque. 2006. "Countercyclical Safety Nets for the Poor and Vulnerable." *Food Policy* 31 (4): 372–83.

Baird, S., J. Friedman, and N. Schady. 2007. *Aggregate Income Shocks and Infant Mortality in the Developing World.* Open Knowledge Repository, World Bank, Washington, DC. https://openknowledge.worldbank.org/handle/10986/7627.

Barros, P. P. 2012a. "Coping with Crisis: The Impact of the Economic Downturn on the Health System of Portugal." Paper presented at Organized Session "Coping with Crisis: The Impact of the Economic Downturn on the Health Systems of Portugal, Ireland and Greece." European Conference on Health Economics (ECHE), Zürich, Switzerland, July 20.

———. 2012b. "Health Policy Reform in Tough Times: The Case of Portugal." *Health Reform Monitor: Health Policy* 106 (1): 17–22.

Bhalotra, S. 2010. "Fatal Fluctuations? Cyclicality in Infant Mortality in India." *Journal of Development Economics* 93 (1): 7–19.

Brahmbhatt, M., and O. Canuto. 2012. *Fiscal Policy for Growth and Development: Economic Premise.* Poverty Reduction and Economic Management (PREM) 19 (October), World Bank, Washington, DC.

Braun, M. 2001. *Why Is Fiscal Policy Procyclical in Developing Countries?* Harvard University.

Braun, M., and L. di Gresia. 2003. "Towards Effective Social Insurance in Latin America: The Importance of Countercyclical Fiscal Policy." Inter-American Development Bank Working Paper 487.

Bredenkamp, C., G. Sølve Sande Lie, and L. Brenzel. 2011. "Rapid Assessment of the Effect of the Economic Crisis on Health Spending in Mongolia." Health, Nutrition, and Population (HNP) Discussion Paper, Human Development Network, World Bank, Washington, DC.

Brenzel, L. 2012. "Literature Review on the Impact of the Global Financial Crisis on Health." Unpublished draft, June 1.

Calderon, C., and K. Schmidt-Hebbel. 2008. "Business Cycles and Fiscal Policies: The Role of Institutions and Financial Markets." Working Paper 481, Central Bank of Chile.

Capaldo, J., P. Karfakis, M. Knowles, and M. Smulders. 2010. "A Model of Vulnerability to Food Insecurity." ESA Working Paper 10-03, Food and Agriculture Organization of the United Nations, Agricultural Development Division, August.

Carter, M. R., and J. A. Maluccio. 2003. "Social Capital and Coping with Economic Loss: An Analysis of Stunting of South African Children." *World Development* 31 (7): 1147–63.

Chawla, M. 2009. "Assessing the Impact of the Recent Global Financial Crisis on Health Financing: Eastern European Perspectives." Paper presented at the Organized Session "Analysis of the Expected Impact of the Current Financial Crisis on Health Revenues and Expenditures," Seventh World Congress of the International Health Economics Association (IHEA), Beijing, China, July 12–15. http://ihea2009.abstractbook.org /session/31.

Chuma, J. 2010. "Rapid Assessment of the Effect of the Economic Crisis on Health Spending in Kenya." Human Development Network, World Bank, Washington, DC.

Conceição, P., K. Namsuk, and Z. Yanchun. 2009. "Economic Shocks and Human Development: A Review of Empirical Findings." UNDP/ODS Working Paper, United Nations Development Programme, New York.

Cuesta, J., and J. Martinez-Vazquez. 2013. "Analyzing the Distributive Effects of Fiscal Policies: How to Prepare (Analytically) for the Next Crisis." In *Is Fiscal Policy the Answer? A Developing Country Perspective,* edited by B. Moreno-Dodson. Washington, DC: World Bank.

Cuesta, J., S. Tiwari, and A. Htenas. 2012. "A Framework to Monitor Food Crises: A Proposal." Unpublished Concept Note, Poverty Reduction and Economic Management (PREM), World Bank, Washington, DC, June.

Cylus, J., P. Mladovsky, and M. McKee. 2012. "Is There a Statistical Relationship between Economic Crises and Changes in Government Health Expenditure Growth? An Analysis of Twenty-Four European Countries." *Health Services Research* 47 (6): 2204–24.

Darby, J., and J. Melitz. 2008. "Social Spending and Automatic Stabilizers in the OECD." *Economic Policy* 23 (October): 715–56.

de Belvis, A. G., F. Ferrè, M. L. Specchia, V. Luca, G. Fattore, and W. Ricciardi. 2012. "The Financial Crisis in Italy: Implications for the Healthcare Sector." *Health Policy* 106 (1): 10–16.

del Granado, J. A., S. Gupta, and A. Hajdenberg. 2013. "Is Social Spending Procyclical? Evidence for Developing Countries." *World Development* 42: 16–27.

Dercon, S. 2001. *Assessing Vulnerability to Poverty*. Report prepared for the Department for International Development (DFID). www.economics.ox.ac.uk/members/stefan .dercon/assessingvulnerability.

Doytch, N., B. Hu, and R. U. Mendoza. 2010. "Social Spending, Fiscal Space, and Governance: An Analysis of Patterns over the Business Cycle." Second Draft, UNICEF Policy and Practice, April.

ECHE. 2012. European Conference on Health Economics, Zürich, Switzerland, July 18–21. http://www.eche2012.ch.

Essama-Nssah, B., and B. Moreno-Dodson. 2013. "Fiscal Policy for Growth and Social Welfare." In *Is Fiscal Policy the Answer? A Developing Country Perspective*, edited by B. Moreno-Dodson. Washington, DC: World Bank.

Fairbank, A. 2013. "Fungibility of Official Development Assistance for Health in Liberia." Draft prepared for the Health and the Economy Program, Health, Nutrition, and Population, World Bank.

FAO (Food and Agriculture Organization). 2003. *Focus on Food Insecurity and Vulnerability: A Review of the UN System Common Country Assessments and World Bank Poverty Reduction Strategy Papers*. Rome: FAO. http://www.fao.org/docrep/006/Y5095E /Y5095E00.htm.

———. 2012. *The State of Food Insecurity in the World 2012: Economic Growth Is Necessary but Not Sufficient to Accelerate Reduction of Hunger and Malnutrition*. Rome: FAO. http://www.fao.org/docrep/016/i3027e/i3027e.pdf.

FAO/FIVIMS (Food and Agriculture Organization/Food Insecurity and Vulnerability Information and Mapping Systems). 2002. *FIVIMS Tools and Tips: Understanding Food Insecurity and Vulnerability*. Rome: Food and Agriculture Organization.

Ferrè, F., C. Cuccurullo, and F. Lega. 2012. "The Challenge and the Future of Health Care Turnaround Plans: Evidence from the Italian Experience." *Health Policy* 106 (1): 3–9.

Ferreira, F. H. G., and N. Schady. 2009. "Aggregate Economic Shocks, Child Schooling, and Child Health." *World Bank Research Observer* 24 (2): 147–81.

Fleisher, L., A. Leive, and G. Schieber. 2013. "Taking Stock of Fiscal Health: Recent Trends in Global, Regional, and Country Level Health Financing." Final draft, Health, Nutrition, and Population (HNP) Anchor, Health and Economy Program, World Bank, Washington, DC.

Food Price Watch. 2012. Poverty Reduction and Equity Group. World Bank. http://sitere sources.worldbank.org/EXTPOVERTY/Resources/336991-1311966520397/Food-Price-Watch-April-2012.htm.

Friedman, J., and N. Schady. 2009. "How Many More Infants Are Likely to Die in Africa as a Result of the Global Financial Crisis?" World Bank Policy Research Working Paper 5023.

Gavin, M., and R. Perotti. 1997. "Fiscal Policy in Latin America." In *National Bureau of Economic Research Macroeconomic Annual*, edited by M. Gavin and R. Perotti, 11–61. Vol. 12. Cambridge, MA: NBER.

Gené-Badia, J. J., P. P. Gallo, C. C. Hernandez-Quevedo, and S. S. Garcia-Armesto. 2012. "Spanish Health Care Cuts: Penny Wise and Pound Foolish?" *Health Policy* 106 (1): 23–28.

Gordon-Strachan, G., and L. Brenzel. 2010. "Rapid Assessment of the Effect of the Economic Crisis on Health Spending in Jamaica." Human Development Department, World Bank, Washington, DC.

Gottret, P. 2009. "Assessing the Impact of the Financial Crisis on Health Systems: Implications Related to Aid-Dependency, Informality, and Out-of-Pocket Spending." Paper presented at the International Health Economics Association meeting "Harmonizing Health and Economics." Beijing, China, July 12–15. http://ihea2009.abstractbook.org/session/31.

Gottret, P., V. Gupta, S. Sparkes, A. Tandon, V. Moran, and P. Berman. 2009. "Protecting Pro-Poor Health Services during Financial Crises: Lessons from Experience." In *Advances in Health Economics and Health Services Research*, edited by D. Chernichovsky and K. Hanson, 23–53. Vol. 21. Emerald Group Publishing. http://www.emeraldinsight.com/books.htm?chapterid=1795482.

Hartwig, J. 2008. "What Drives Health Care Expenditure? Baumol's Model of 'Unbalanced Growth' Revisited." *Journal of Health Economics* 27 (3): 602–23.

IMF (International Monetary Fund). 2010. "Macro-Fiscal Implications of Health Care Reform in Advanced and Emerging Economies." Fiscal Affairs Department, Washington, DC.

Ishihara, Y. 2005. "Quantitative Analysis of Crisis: Crisis Identification and Causality." Policy Research Working Paper WPS3598, World Bank, Washington, DC.

Kaly, U., L. Briguglio, H. McLeod, S. Schmall, C. Pratt, and R. Pal. 1999. *Environmental Vulnerability Index (EVI) to Summarize National Environmental Vulnerability Profiles.* SOPAC Technical Report 275.

Kentikelenis, A., M. Maranikolos, I. Papnicolas, S. Basu, M. McKee, and D. Stuckler. 2012. "Health and the Financial Crisis in Greece: Authors' Reply." *The Lancet* 379 (9820): 1002.

Kirigia, J. M., B. M. Nganda, C. Mvilsia, and B. Cardoso. 2011. "Effects of the Global Financial Crisis on Funding for Health Development in Nineteen Countries of the WHO African Region." *BMC International Health and Human Rights* 11 (4).

Koettl, J., and P. Schneider. 2010. *The Financial Impact of the Economic Crisis on Health Insurance Funds in Eastern Europe.* Washington, DC: World Bank.

Kwon, S., and Y. Jung. 2009. "The Impact of the Global Recession on the Health of the People in Asia." Submitted to the Asian Development Bank and the World Health Organization.

Laeven, L., and F. Valencia. 2012. "Systemic Banking Crises Database: An Update." International Monetary Fund Working Paper 12/163.

The Lancet. 2008. Maternal and Child Undernutrition Series. January 18. http://www.thelancet.com/series/maternal-and-child-undernutrition.

Lewis, M. 2009. "Reflections on the Impact of the Financial Crisis on Health Systems." Paper presented at the International Health Economics Association meeting

"Harmonizing Health and Economics." Beijing, China, July 12–15. http://ihea2009 .abstractbook.org/session/31.

Lewis, M., and M. Verhoeven. 2010. "Financial Crises and Social Spending: The Impact of the 2008–2009 Crisis." Background paper for *Global Monitoring Report 2010*, World Bank, Washington, DC.

Liang, L., and E. V. Velényi. 2013. "Do Sociopolitical Risk and Foreign Aid Explain Cyclicality in Government Health Expenditures? An International Comparison of 123 Countries." Health, Nutrition, and Population Publication Series, World Bank, Washington, DC.

Ligon, E., and L. Schechter. 2004. "Evaluating Different Approaches to Estimating Vulnerability." Social Protection Discussion Paper Series, World Bank, Washington, DC.

Lybbert, T., C. B. Barrett, S. Desta, and D. L. Coppock. 2004. "Stochastic Wealth Dynamics and Risk Management among a Poor Population." *Economic Journal* 114 (498): 750–57.

Mendoza, R. U., and N. Rees. 2009. "Infant Mortality during Economic Downturns and Recovery." Working Paper, SSRN. http://ssrn.com/abstract=1586527 or http://dx.doi .org/10.2139/ssrn.1586527.

Messier, M. C., C. Macdonald, S. Shulman, and J. Bernal. 2012. "How to Protect and Promote the Nutrition of Mothers and Children: A Toolkit for Stable, Crisis, and Emergency Situations." Draft, Health, Nutrition, and Population, World Bank, Latin America and the Caribbean Region, November.

Mladovsky, P., D. Srivastava, J. Cylus, M. Karanikolos, T. Evetovits, S. Thomson, and M. McKee. 2012. "Policy Summary 5. Health Policy Response to the Financial Crisis in Europe." World Health Organization on behalf of the European Observatory on Health Systems and Policies.

OECD (Organisation for Economic Co-operation and Development). 2006. "Projecting OECD Health and Long-Term Expenditures: What Are the Main Drivers?" Economics Department Working Paper No. 477.ECO/WKP(2006)5. http://www.oecd.org/tax /public-finance/36085940.pdf.

Paxson, C., and N. Schady. 2004. "Child Health and the 1988–92 Economic Crisis in Peru." Policy Research Working Paper Series 3260, World Bank, Washington, DC.

Potapchik, E., and L. Brenzel. 2010. "Rapid Assessment of the Effect of the Economic Crisis on Health Spending in Tajikistan." Human Development Department, World Bank, Washington, DC.

Ruhm, C. 2000. "Are Recessions Good for Your Health?" *Quarterly Journal of Economics* 115 (2): 617–50.

———. 2012. "Sick Economies and Healthy Bodies." Presentation prepared for a panel at a workshop organized by the World Bank Institute, "Health System and Economic Downturns: Identifying and Managing the Risks," September 27.

Rukumnuaykit, P. 2003. *Crises and Child Health Outcomes: The Impacts of Economic and Drought/Smoke Crises on Infant Mortality in Indonesia*. East Lansing: Michigan State University.

Schady, N., and M. F. Smitz. 2010. "Aggregate Economic Shocks and Infant Mortality: New Evidence for Middle-Income Countries." *Economics Letters* 108 (2): 145–48.

Sen, A. 1983. *Poverty and Famines: An Essay on Entitlements and Deprivation*. Oxford, U.K.: Clarendon Press.

Simms, C., and M. Rowson. 2003. "Reassessment of Health Effects of the Indonesian Economic Crisis: Donors versus the Data. Viewpoint." *The Lancet* 361: 1382–85.

Skoufias, E., S. Tiwari, and H. Zaman. 2011. "Can We Rely on Cash Transfers to Protect Dietary Diversity during Food Crises? Estimates from Indonesia." World Bank Policy Research Working Paper 5548, World Bank, Washington, DC.

Smith, O., and A. Yazbeck. 2011. "Financial Crisis and Health in Europe and Central Asia." Paper prepared for the International Health Economics Association Conference, Toronto, Canada, July 7–11.

SOPAC (South Pacific Applied Geoscience Commission). 2010. *Environmental Vulnerability Index*. Suva, Fiji Islands. http://www.sopac.org/index.php /environmental-vulnerability-index.

Stuckler, D., S. Basu, M. Suhreke, and M. McKee. 2009. "Commentary: The Health Implications of Financial Crisis: A Review of the Evidence." *Ulster Medical Journal* 78 (3):142–45.

SUN (Scaling Up Nutrition). 2011. "A Framework for Action." Policy brief prepared with Financial Support from the Bill and Melinda Gates Foundation, the Government of Japan, UNICEF, the World Bank, and about 100 other sponsors.

Tandon, A., L. Fleisher, R. Li, and W. A. Yap. 2013. "Re-Prioritizing Government Spending on Health: Pushing an Elephant Up the Stairs?" Paper prepared for the HNP Discussion Paper Series, World Bank.

Thomas, S. 2012. "The Economic Crisis and the Irish Health System: Assessing Resilience." Paper presented at "Coping with Crisis: The Impact of the Economic Downturn on the Health Systems of Portugal, Ireland and Greece." European Conference on Health Economics (ECHE), Zürich, Switzerland, July 20.

Thornton, J. 2008. "Explaining Procyclical Fiscal Policy in African Countries." *Journal of African Economies* 17 (3): 451–64. doi: 10.1093/jae/ejm029.

Velényi, E. V., and M. F. Smitz. 2013. "Cyclical Patterns in Government Health Expenditures between 1995 and 2010: Are Countries Graduating from the Procyclical Trap or Falling Back?" Draft of HNP Working Paper Series, Health, Nutrition, and Population Anchor, World Bank, Washington, DC.

Wagstaff, A., M. Bilger, Z. Sajaia, and M. Lokshin. 2011. *Health Equity and Financial Protection: Streamlined Analysis with AdePT Software*. Washington, DC: World Bank.

WHO (World Health Organization). 2013. "Summary: Health, Health Systems, and Economic Crisis in Europe: Impact and Policy Implications." Draft for review by WHO and European Observatory on Health Systems and Policies.

Wodon, Q., and R. L. Ayres. 2000. "Poverty and Policy in Latin America and the Caribbean." Technical Paper 467, World Bank, Washington, DC.

World Bank. 2012. Fiscal Health Database. Health and Economy Program, Health, Nutrition, and Population Anchor, World Bank, Washington, DC.

Xu, K., P. Saksena, and A. Holly. 2011. "The Determinants of Health Expenditure: A Country-Level Panel Data Analysis." World Health Organization, December 2011.

Yfantopoulos, J. 2012. "Coping with Crisis: The Impact of the Economic Downturn on the Health Systems of Greece." Paper presented at "Coping with Crisis: The Impact of the Economic Downturn on the Health Systems of Portugal, Ireland and Greece."

European Conference on Health Economics (ECHE), Zurich, Switzerland, July 18–21.

Zaridze, D., P. Brennan, J. Boreham, A. Boroda, R. Karpov, A. Lazarev, I. Konobeevskaya, V. Igitov, T. Terechova, P. Boffetta, and R. Peto. 2009. "Alcohol and Cause-Specific Mortality in Russia: A Retrospective Case-Control Study of 48,557 Adult Deaths." *The Lancet* 373 (9682): 2201–14.

CHAPTER 3

Tracking the Impact on Households and Institutions: The Europe and Central Asia Story

The previous chapter illustrated the importance of assessing country vulnerability to crisis and proposed assessment approaches. When a country is facing severe economic hardship, tracking the impact as the crisis unfolds is also important and introduces a unique set of challenges. This chapter explores these issues based on the experiences of the Europe and Central Asia (ECA) region during the 2008–10 global economic crises.

ECA was the region most affected by the global economic downturn of 2008–10. Figure 3.1 captures the dramatic changes in economic growth at the regional level. Only South Asia avoided any decline in economic growth in 2009. East Asia and Africa experienced significant slowdowns but remained in positive territory, while Latin America and high-income countries entered into steep recessions in 2009. But it was ECA that experienced the sharpest decline (more than a 10 percentage point change in growth) and the biggest deceleration in economic activity (a 6 percent contraction on average).

This chapter explores different tools used to track the impact of the economic downturn on the health sector in ECA. It examines how critical actors within the health sector, including households and funding agencies, alter their behaviors and actions during a downturn. The discussion focuses on both "what" and "how" to track the impact of a crisis on health systems, and illustrates with selected findings from a range of data collection efforts that were specifically initiated to track the short-term impact.

What to Track

There are several pathways through which an economic downturn may affect different elements of the health sector. Figure 3.2, originally presented in chapter 1, provides a clear illustration of these channels and emphasizes both demand and supply-side aspects through households and government, respectively.

Figure 3.1 Real GDP Growth, 2008–10

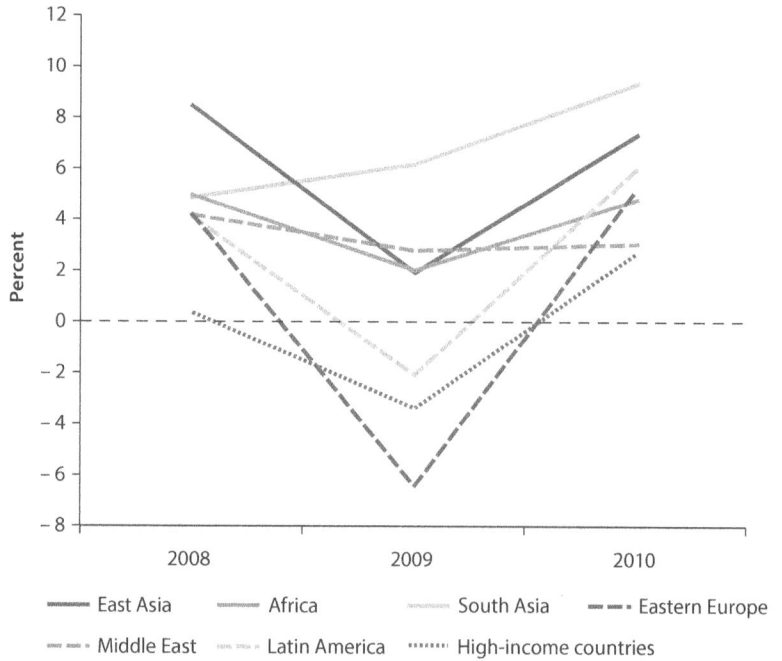

Sources: World Bank, *Global Economic Prospects,* various years.
Note: GDP = gross domestic product.

Figure 3.2 Pathways Framework

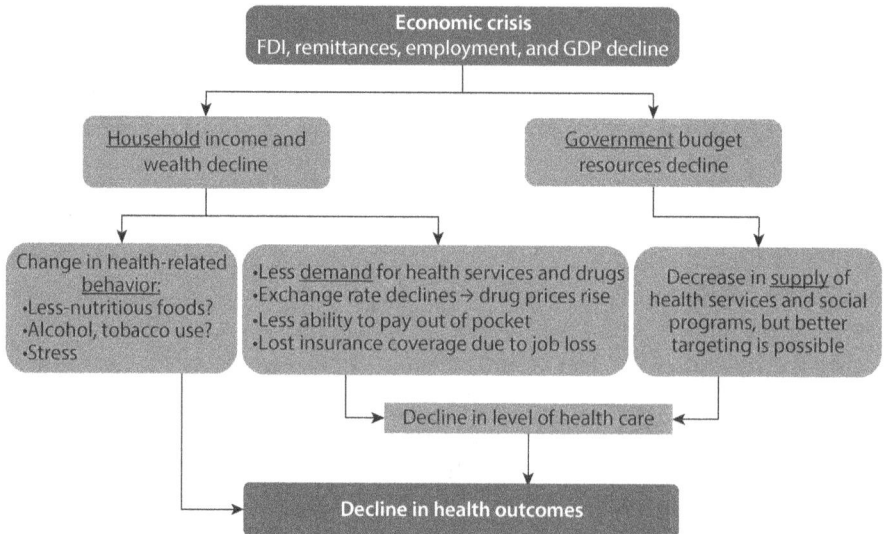

Sources: Adapted from Musgrove 1987; Waters, Saadah, and Pradhan 2003.
Note: FDI = foreign direct investment; GDP = gross domestic product.

The pathways depicted in figure 3.2 offer a list of possible health sector–related candidate measures to track in an economic downturn. These indicators could include:

a. Consumption (for example food): Fewer calories and less-nutritious foods will have an impact on health. But an important challenge here is that standard food consumption modules leave many questions unanswered with regard to the quality and quantity of food consumed both in aggregate and by individual household members. For example, cutbacks to spending on relatively expensive restaurant meals in favor of food cooked at home may in fact have a positive impact on health.

b. Behaviors (for example, tobacco and alcohol consumption): Tobacco use and alcohol consumption can have a long-term impact on health status. Consumption could rise or fall due to the crisis. Passing judgment on the health impact of changes in alcohol consumption is more difficult than for tobacco because moderate consumption of alcohol does not necessarily have bad effects.

c. Health care utilization and expenditure: Fewer visits to health care facilities may result in worse health outcomes, either in the short or long term. Out-of-pocket payments may rise due to cutbacks in government funding as a result of the economic downturn, with implications for financial protection. Out-of-pocket payments could also fall because of fewer health care visits.

d. Health outcomes: Health outcomes are more difficult to track through both routine and specialized data instruments, but if available can provide compelling evidence of the impact of crisis on health. An impact on health outcomes is more likely to manifest itself over the medium to long term, especially in countries where the health burden is primarily due to chronic diseases.

These health indicators are in addition to traditional variables such as income or employment, which may not be directly related to the health sector but can impact the system in several ways. For example, when formal sector jobs are the main vehicle for access to health insurance, a rise in unemployment may result in decreased access. Tracking health indicators in tandem with measures of socioeconomic status, such as consumption, assets, or income, can provide valuable information on the differential impact of the crisis by quintile. This information can help focus attention on the particular vulnerability of poorer households. Indicators of income and employment are usually well tracked outside the health sector, but when crisis-related household surveys are launched, including such indicators in the data collection instrument can provide useful insights.

On the government and health system side, there are a number of measures that should also be tracked during a downturn. The most obvious is national or subnational budget allocations to the health sector. Textbook policy advice would typically argue for countercyclical public expenditure patterns to mitigate income loss for households. The reality is that a pro-cyclical approach has been adopted in most economic downturns, as overall public spending on health has typically declined during economic crises (Gottret et al. 2009). A challenge to countercyclical spending is that as national and local governments face declining revenues, automatic stabilizers (such as unemployment insurance, which constitute part of the safety net) further shrink the fiscal space for health.

Another important health financing indicator to consider during economic downturns is organized pooling of resources through insurance funds. Because most health insurance funds (HIFs) tend to be funded through payroll taxes, a downturn will pose challenges due to employment layoffs and cutbacks. It is likely that insurance funds suffer fiscally during downturns as the returns on any surplus investments are likely to shrink.

An additional potential indicator to track during an economic downturn is the price level of imported health care inputs and their substitutes that may be outside the control of local economies and subject to exchange rate shifts or tariff changes. Particularly important in this regard are pharmaceuticals and imported medical equipment and supplies. A falling exchange rate associated with an economic crisis will tend to increase drug prices, posing an additional financial burden on either government budgets or out-of-pocket spending by households.

How to Track

The standard instrument for tracking household decisions and behaviors is a household survey. Many countries, especially in the ECA region, have a series of integrated household surveys that follow a regular timetable. These surveys tend to have detailed questions that capture socioeconomic status through consumption modules and cover a range of household decisions based on a nationally representative sample. Two key challenges should be addressed if these surveys are to be used to track the impact of an economic downturn on household choices: the timing of the surveys and the specificity of the questions.

Many household survey series have regular schedules with sometimes rotating regional coverage, rotating topics, and rotating target populations. The consistency, timeliness, and wealth of data collected in these surveys are extremely useful for tracking purposes. However, if the timing of the survey is not aligned with an economic downturn, the information may not be as useful as a specifically designed survey. Data processing requirements and political considerations may also result in an extended lag time between data collection and availability for analysis. Moreover, the questionnaire design of repeat surveys does not typically lend itself to editing for the purpose of collecting additional data related to economic downturn. The solution to the timeliness and relevance issue is a standalone survey designed specifically for capturing the impact on household behaviors. The trade-off, however, is the possible loss of information and the long-term ability to track variables offered by regular surveys. A particularly attractive survey format for assessing impact is panel data, in which the same households are monitored over time. This format has been used to gain valuable insights in the Russian context (Nikoloski and Ajwad 2013).

A noteworthy aspect of household survey design for tracking the impact of economic downturns on health is the balance between quantitative and qualitative approaches. The pursuit of "hard numbers" will often be the default position of most researchers. Typically, quantitative modules are invaluable for identifying the magnitude of the impact and capturing the various nuances of how households are affected. However, qualitative approaches offer their own unique benefits, such as the addition of coping modules to household surveys. These modules typically entail a series of "yes-no" questions asking individuals whether they responded to the crisis environment in particular ways (for example, "did you reduce the number of doctor visits due to your household's current economic condition?"). Advantages of this approach include simplicity and convenience, the ability to cast a wide net to cover a range of topics, and the compelling nature of findings for policy advocacy purposes. Of course, other qualitative approaches such as focus group discussions can also be helpful. Whenever possible, using a combination of quantitative and qualitative survey approaches may yield the richest combination of findings.

Tracking the government side of the story is somewhat easier than in the case of household choices. The first step is to track year-to-year budget allocations to the health sector. An economic downturn typically restricts fiscal space available for public expenditures, and therefore most sectors end up with decreased allocations. As noted in chapter 2, the fiscal picture before the economic downturn is an important factor for identifying the level of vulnerability of a health sector to a downturn. If the fiscal house is in order pre-crisis, more resources are usually available for all sectors, including health. The interpretation of health budget trends may vary depending on whether the data are measured in nominal or real terms, as a share of the budget or a share of the gross domestic product (GDP). Careful attention to these details can be important.

It is also important to note that budget allocations alone may be deceptive because there may be significant gaps between what is allocated on paper, what is made available to the relevant spending authority, and what is actually spent. It is important, therefore, not only to track allocations during budget development but also to track budget execution. A standard instrument for tracking public expenditures is the Public Expenditure and Institutional Review (PEIR), which examines the process of budget development, choices in allocation, and execution.

Many countries have mixed public financing systems that include budget allocations from both general tax revenues and various forms of social health insurance funded through payroll taxes. The latter are increasingly important in many ECA countries, especially among new European Union (EU) member states and in the Western Balkans, making it critical to track the impact of the economic downturn on insurance funds. Clearly, a downturn that produces increased unemployment will have an impact on the number of people contributing funds through payroll. It is therefore important to track how insurance funds are impacted with respect to their ability to generate resources and their flexibility to protect spending or replace lost funds by, for example, drawing down reserves. This data tracking can be done through surveys of HIFs.

As a complement to PEIRs and insurance fund surveys, where possible, it is important to also track price changes in critical inputs that may be influenced by exchange rates, such as medicines and imported medical equipment and supplies. Even though the availability of pre-crisis baseline figures may present a challenge, relatively inexpensive drug price surveys can be undertaken to track and compare price trends and customs price data.

Data Collection

As the 2008 crisis hit the ECA region, the regional Human Development Department of the World Bank recognized the need to start monitoring and tracking the social impacts of the crisis on a range of issues. Part of the motivation for doing this work was a recognition that few countries were in a position to track the short-term impact of the crisis on households and institutions. Table 3.1 presents a range of tools and indicators that were mobilized and the number of countries in which these were implemented. This chapter focuses on the last two categories: crisis response surveys and insurance fund surveys. Furthermore, since the scope of this chapter and book is limited to the health sector, only the health-related findings of the household surveys are reported here.

The World Bank team reviewed existing regular survey instruments in nearly every country in the ECA region and concluded that only a minority had instruments that could be helpful in tracking the impact on key social indicators of interest. As a result, household Crisis Response Surveys had to be quickly mobilized in order to begin to tell the empirical story of the household impact. As noted, although stand-alone surveys have the attractive feature of being customizable, they are neither easy nor cheap to implement quickly. Choices had to be made regarding which countries to cover in order to be representative of the different subregions, which were too large to achieve nationwide survey coverage, and in which countries to rely on existing data. The countries in which new

Table 3.1   Data Collection Instruments

Indicator to be monitored	Tool to monitor the indicator	Number of countries for which monitoring results were available as of end-Q1 2010
Household welfare	Microsimulation models for poverty and distributional aspects using aggregate data	8 European and Central Asian countries
Labor market	Labor force survey and administrative data from public employment services offices	25 European and Central Asian countries
Social benefits	Administrative information on social assistance beneficiaries	10 European and Central Asian countries
Human development outcomes and coping strategies	Crisis response surveys and modules	5 European and Central Asian countries
Health insurance funds	Survey of health insurance fund administrators	10 European and Central Asian countries

Table 3.2 Survey Instruments

Country	Survey instrument
Armenia and Romania	Crisis module integrated into regular household surveys
Bulgaria and Montenegro	Stand-alone nationwide surveys
Turkey	Stand-alone survey in selected urban centers
Russian Federation	Ex-post analysis of panel data

tailored survey data pertaining to the health sector were analyzed were Armenia, Bulgaria, Montenegro, Romania, the Russian Federation, and Turkey. Moreover, different survey instruments and techniques were deployed in each setting, as indicated in table 3.2.

A survey on the financial situation of HIFs was conducted in fall 2009. Overall ten countries in the ECA region participated and reported their financial performance for 2008 and the first six months of 2009. The participating countries were Albania, Bosnia and Herzegovina, Bulgaria, Croatia, Estonia, Latvia, Lithuania, the former Yugoslav Republic of Macedonia, Montenegro, and Serbia. The survey questionnaire focused on revenues, expenditures, and the insured population.

Household Impact: Sample Findings

This section provides a sampling of survey findings from the data collection efforts already discussed. They draw upon the ECA experience to illustrate both the opportunities and challenges related to tracking the impact of economic downturns on households and governments.

One dimension of the tracking surveys was to focus on the changes in behavior related to food consumption during the economic downturn. Figure 3.3a shows the percentage of the survey sample in each country that decreased food consumption, by quintile. Figure 3.3b captures quintile responses in terms of substituting cheaper foods. A consistent finding across all countries and both variables is that socioeconomic status is a key predictor of household responses with a clear gradient from the poorest quintile (who are impacted the most) to the richest. It is important to add the caveat that these indicators are imperfect approximations for the actual quantity and quality of food consumed.

Another way to assess household coping behaviors when repeated surveys are available is to track changes in the consumption of specific health-related items and their substitutes over time. Armenia presented that option with a series of repeated surveys that included comprehensive consumption modules. Figure 3.4 captures year-over-year changes for the first nine months of the year at the height of the economic downturn (2008–09) with some revealing variations. While overall per capita household consumption decreased by about 10 percent, alcohol and tobacco consumption were notably better protected than overall food, clothing, or health care expenditures. Alcohol consumption actually rose slightly despite a substantial overall spending decrease. Tobacco and alcohol

Figure 3.3 Coping by Socioeconomic Quintiles: Household Food Consumption

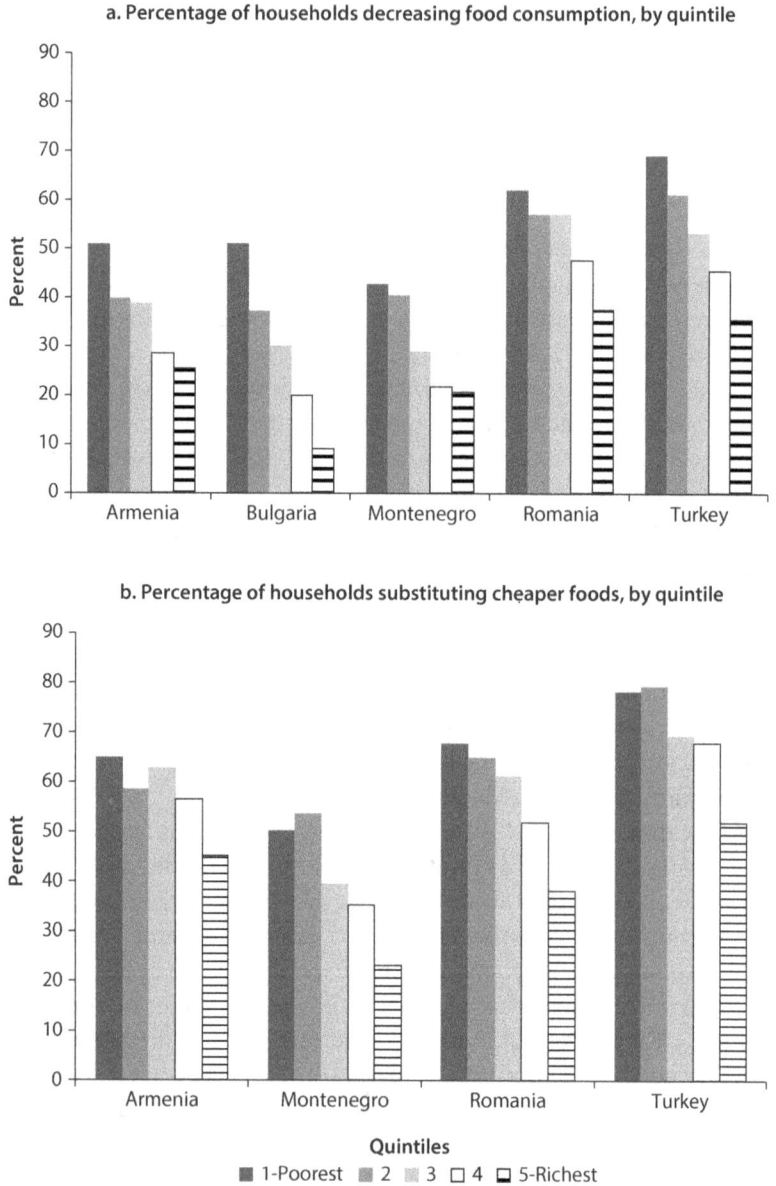

a. Percentage of households decreasing food consumption, by quintile

b. Percentage of households substituting cheaper foods, by quintile

Quintiles
■ 1-Poorest   ■ 2   ▨ 3   ☐ 4   ▤ 5-Richest

Source: Azam 2010.

consumption are significantly higher among men, which raises important issues related to gender and intrahousehold allocation of resources in the context of economic hardship. When households were asked if they thought that the economic situation is having a negative impact on their health and well-being, 51 percent of the respondents said "yes."

Figure 3.4 Changes in Real Per Capita Household Consumption in Armenia, 2008–09

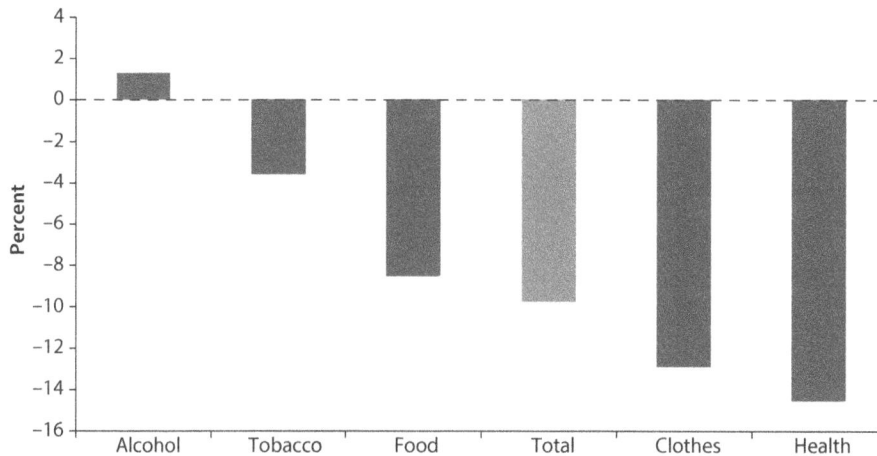

Source: Azam 2010.

The addition of a coping module to the regular collection of consumption data in the Armenian household survey provides an opportunity to consider the reliability of coping modules more closely (Li and Ajwad 2012). More specifically, the binary nature of the questions in a coping module might introduce some concern that they do not adequately capture the impact of a downturn on households and may in fact encourage a "negative" response. However, as shown in figure 3.5, there is some consistency in the messages emerging from both the coping module and consumption data when results are presented together, but the reliability of household responses to simple binary questions on crisis impact remains an issue for further study.

The changes in consumption of health care services in Armenia are also reflected when we look at the other countries covered by the household surveys. Figures 3.6 and 3.7 show the expenditures for overall medical care and for drug purchases, respectively, by socioeconomic quintile. The income gradient is largely consistent, but the magnitude of the cutback in spending is much larger in some countries than in others. The difference is likely a reflection of the availability, generosity, and robustness of consumption smoothing mechanisms such as health insurance. Such findings confirm concerns about country-level vulnerability, as the cross-country variation associated with coverage instruments appears to be at least as important as income-based differences. They also provide evidence supporting the need for countercyclical public expenditure policies for the sector.

An interesting finding with respect to changes in health-related spending is that while the impact is largest in households reporting they have suffered an income shock, the effect is also significant for those who have not been strongly affected by an income shock. Figures 3.8 and 3.9 look at

Figure 3.5 Comparing Coping Modules and Consumption Data in Armenia

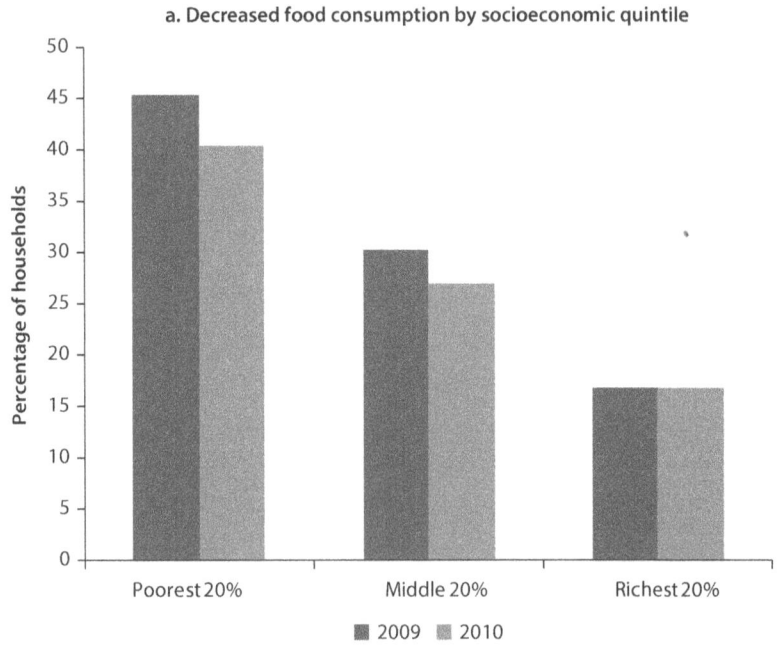

a. Decreased food consumption by socioeconomic quintile

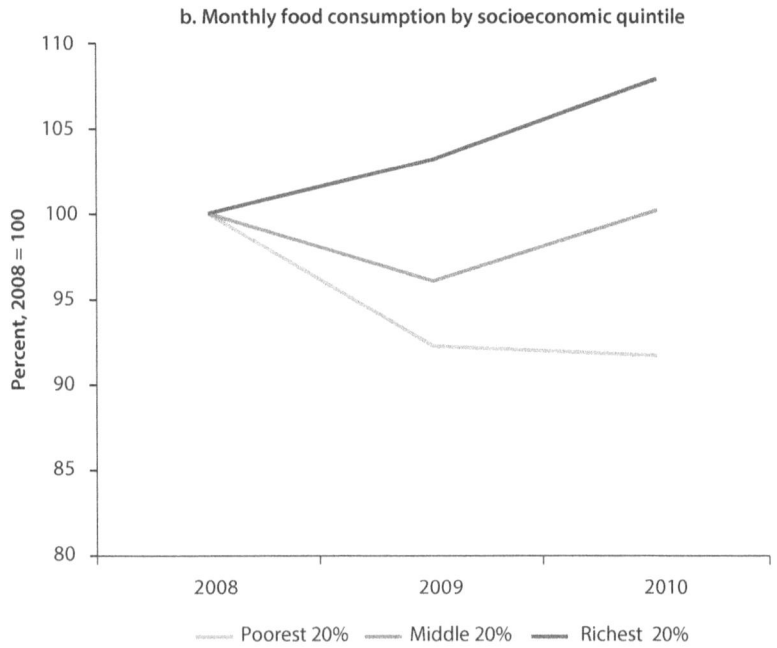

b. Monthly food consumption by socioeconomic quintile

Source: Li and Ajwad 2012.

Figure 3.6 Percentage of Households that Reduced Medical Care, by Socioeconomic Quintile

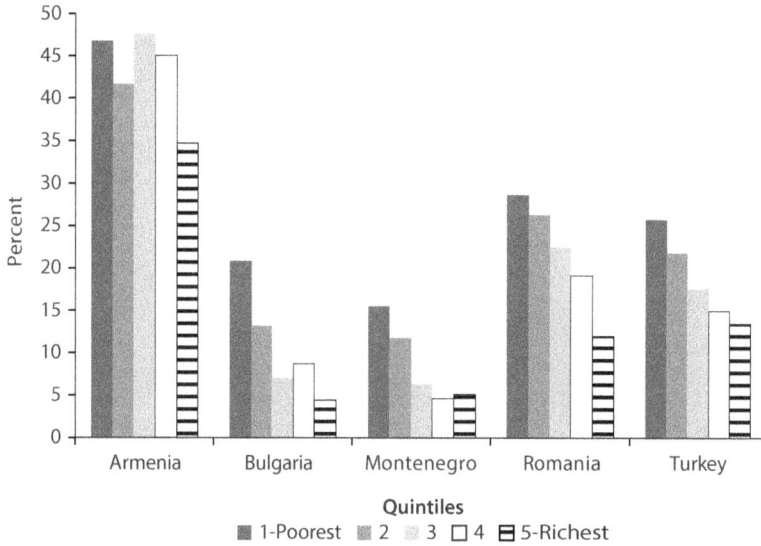

Source: Azam 2010.

Figure 3.7 Percentage of Households that Reduced Drug Purchases, by Socioeconomic Quintile

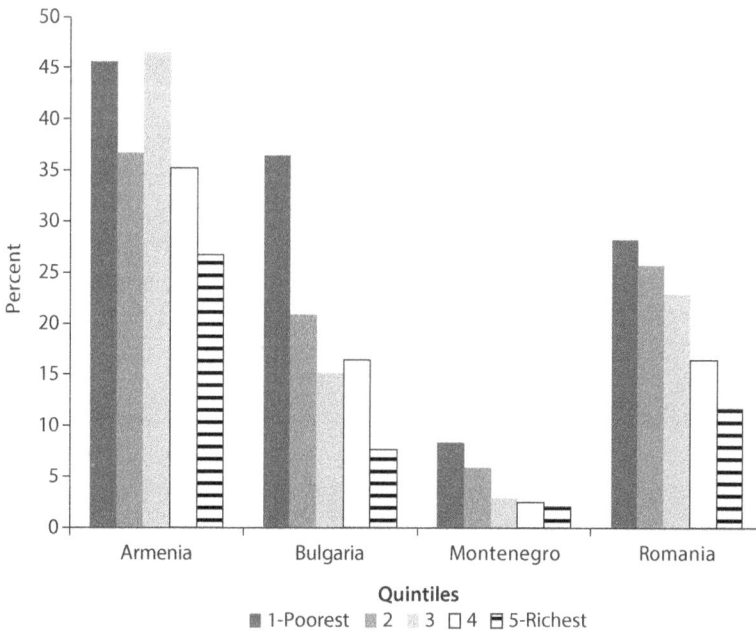

Source: Azam 2010.

Figure 3.8 Percentage of Households that Reduced Medical Care, by whether Affected by Income Shock

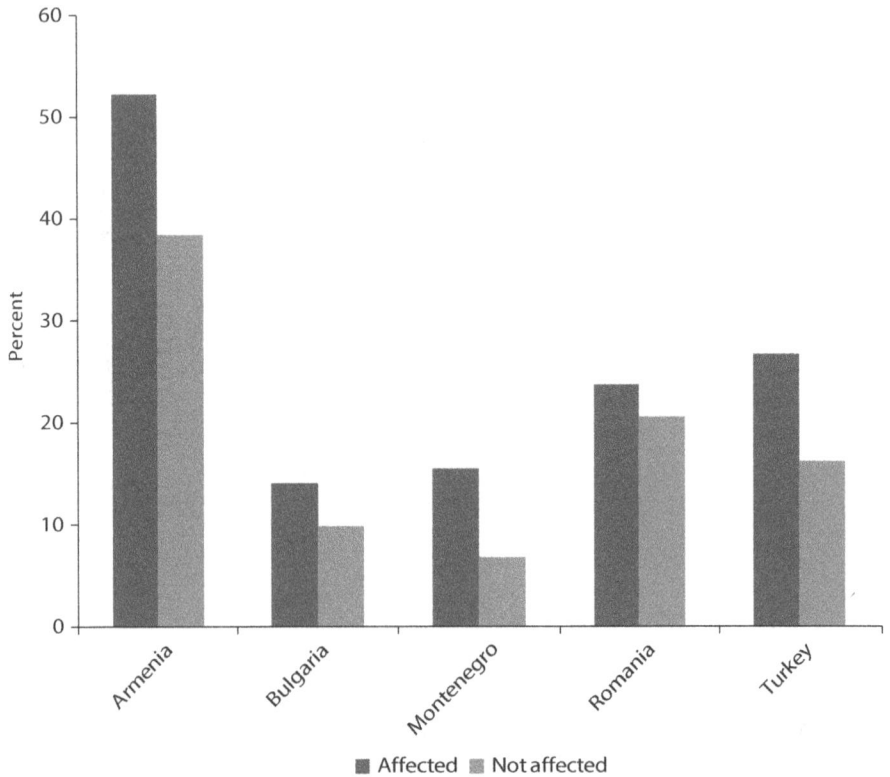

Source: Dasgupta and Ajwad 2011.

the reduction in the consumption of medical care and drugs, respectively, according to whether the household faced an income shock. Once again, the variations across countries appear to be larger than those within countries. The smaller than expected differences between households that have been affected and those that have not been affected may reflect the uncertainty about future household income during a downturn. In other words, health spending appears to be highly responsive to both a decrease in income *and* uncertainty about income.

The distinction between the impact on households that report a large income shock and those that do not takes us one step closer to the issue of attribution. An association between the timing of a crisis and a negative impact on indicators of interest to the health sector does not automatically confirm a causal relationship. Taking this issue one step further, propensity-score matching techniques have been used to help establish the causal link between the economic crisis in ECA and various human development indicators, including health (Dasgupta and Ajwad 2011).

Figure 3.9 Percentage of Households that Reduced Drug Purchases, by whether Affected by Income Shock

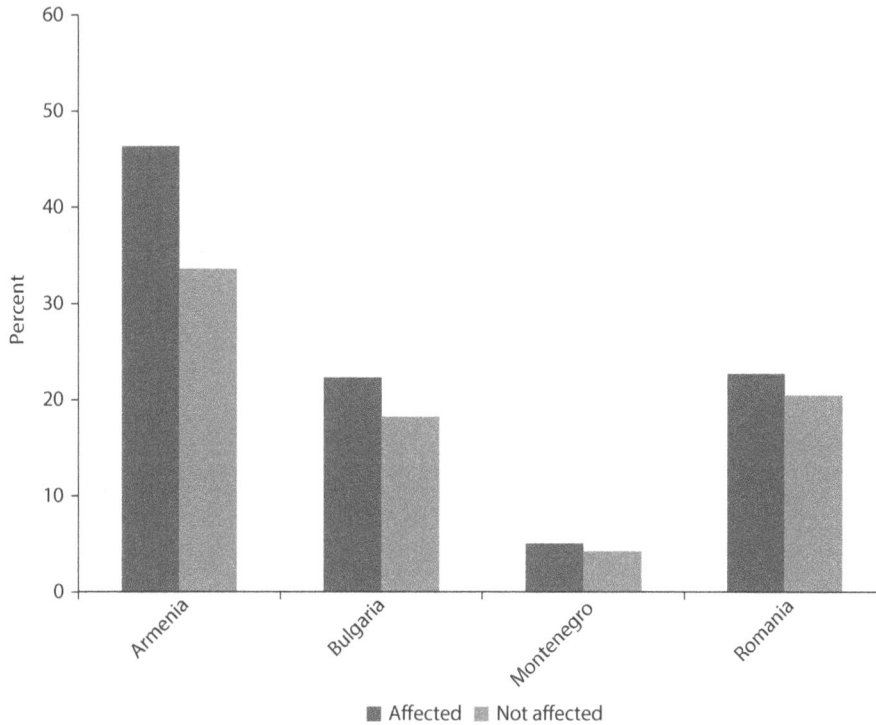

Source: Dasgupta and Ajwad 2011.

Health Insurance Fund Impact: Sample Findings

A second data collection effort focused on governments as opposed to households by surveying national HIFs in several ECA countries. The last 20 years have seen a pronounced shift in the region. The earlier health financing model that followed budget transfers to line ministries is being substituted for a mixed model that uses a combination of direct line ministry financing along with a health insurance approach that is increasingly reliant on payroll taxes tied to formal sector employment. The link between the downturn and resources for health can be exacerbated when the availability of funds is anchored to the level of formal sector employment, which typically decreases in a crisis. The objective of the tracking exercise was to gather empirical evidence examining to what extent revenue for HIFs was impacted by the downturn and how that affected expenditures.

Figure 3.10 shows the total revenue and expenditure picture for a subset of the HIFs in the ECA region. The impact of the crisis on HIFs clearly varied widely across countries, which reflects both differences in the depth of the downturn and the degree of vulnerability of each health financing system to the impact on formal employment. For example, Latvia was one of the countries most affected in the crisis as its GDP declined by more than 15 percent in 2009.

Figure 3.10 Impact of the Downturn on National HIFs: Revenues and Expenditures

Change in revenue growth (percentage points)

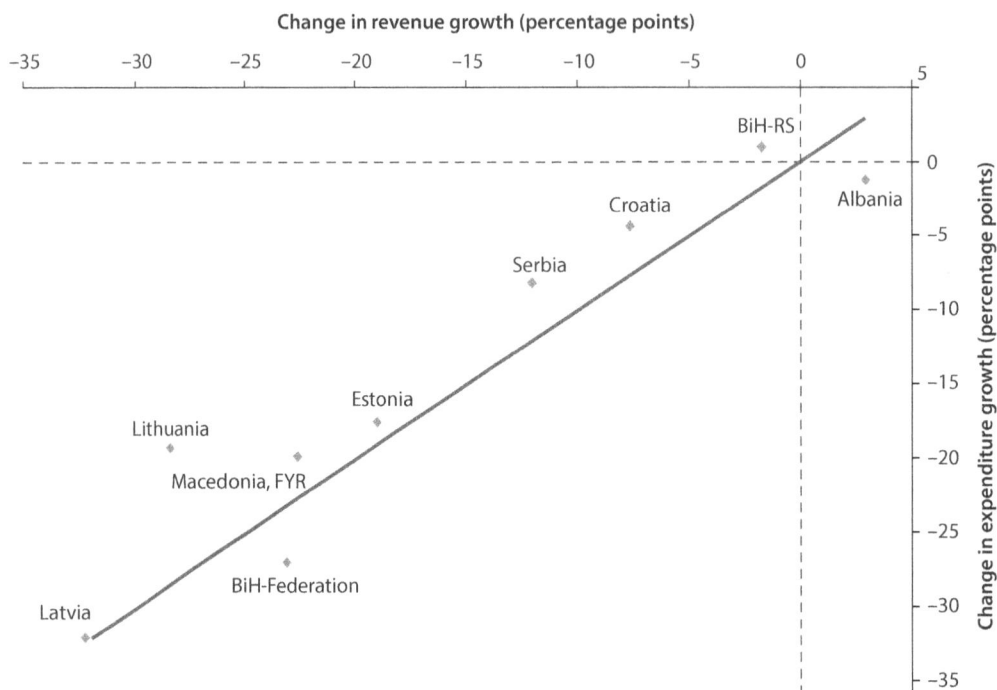

Source: Koettl 2010.
Note: BiH-RS = Federation of Bosnia and Herzegovina-Republika Srpska; HIFs = health insurance funds.

At the same time it was not able to rely on large general budgetary transfers to the health insurance fund due to the extreme nature of the required fiscal consolidation. As a result, the severe drop in revenue is matched almost exactly by a sharp decline in expenditures. Most of the other HIFs show a larger drop in revenue than expenditures because there was scope for general tax revenues to partially cushion the drop in spending. Despite this step, many funds were obliged to make significant expenditure cuts. It is important to note that figure 3.10 shows changes during the first three quarters of 2009 compared to the previous year, and does not capture fourth quarter developments during which additional transfers may have been executed.

Another way to capture certain aspects of the impact on insurance funds is to look at their balance sheets over time. This helps to show which funds had reserves available for use in a downturn and which were much more vulnerable to a major shift in the employment profile. Preliminary evidence based on a three-year horizon for several funds showed large variation in exposure and impact. For example, Albania was not as strongly affected by the crisis and its National Health Insurance Fund maintained a positive position throughout. Estonia and FYR Macedonia entered the downturn with solid reserves, allowing them to manage without necessarily relying heavily on an injection of external resources or resorting to drastic expenditure cuts. Other countries showed a

Figure 3.11　Changes in Subcategories of HIF Expenditures, 2008–09, Cross-Country Average

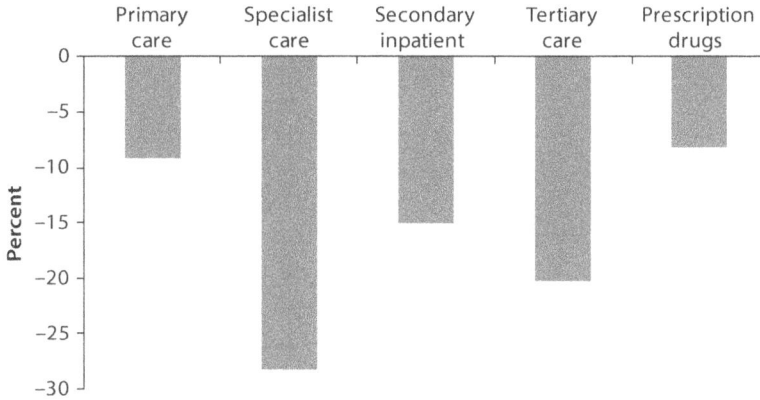

vulnerable balance sheet position that was exposed during the downturn and led to a fiscally unsound position.

The survey of HIFs also revealed how the expenditure slowdown impacted different subcategories of the health sector budget. The largest cuts came in residual expenditure categories typically capturing "others" and cash benefits. As indicated in figure 3.11, among categories related to health care services, the largest cuts were in expenditures on specialist care and tertiary inpatient care while primary care and prescription drug expenditures were better protected.

An exemplary case study of how to cut back during a crisis comes from Estonia. While many countries may reduce spending indiscriminately across the board by cutting all categories equally, Estonia took a more tailored approach in order to lessen the impact. Some of the cost-cutting initiatives were as follows: higher limits on waiting times; a cancellation of dental benefits for adults; reduced sick leave benefits for workers (these are paid by the Estonian HIF) especially for short-duration illnesses; and higher co-payment rates for patients receiving inpatient nursing care. In order to ensure some burden sharing between patients and providers, a 3–5 percent cut in reimbursement prices was also temporarily applied during 2010–11. Drawing down the reserves of Estonia's HIF also helped soften the impact of the crisis. By selectively targeting cuts, the authorities were able to balance sectoral objectives with fiscal imperatives.

Lessons from Tracking during a Crisis

The ECA experience in the recent crisis is instructive on a number of levels. It was clear at the outset that most countries did not have the instruments, or the plans, to rapidly or systematically track how the financial crisis and subsequent economic downturn were impacting the health sector. This deficiency led to an effort to field rapid response surveys in a few countries in order to better understand changes in the demand and supply of health care services and the impact on health-related household behaviors spanning several topics. These surveys produced some consistent findings as well as some important variations:

1. There was a clear impact on intermediate health indicators such as utilization by households and spending by households and government. As would be expected, the impact at the household level is strongest on the poorest segments of society. Perhaps less expected was that the impact extended not only to those who were already impacted through an income decline but also to those who had not suffered an income shock.
2. Differences in key indicators across countries appear to be even larger than variation among households within countries. The differences may be due to the varying depth of recessions across countries or to varying health sector vulnerability and their ability to provide a safety net.
3. The pre-crisis policy environment matters. For example, reliance on out-of-pocket payments or insurance systems that rely on payroll taxes increase the vulnerability of a health sector. Moreover, the absence of poverty-targeted safety net programs in advance of a downturn limits the ability of the health sector to target the most vulnerable during a crisis.

The experience of ECA's health systems and in particular the limited ability to quickly track developments shows the lack of effective management information systems (MIS) in health. Ideally, an effective health management information system should enable regular and frequent reports on health insurance enrollment, health services utilization, and even types of transactions, length of stays, and re-admission rates. It should be able to flag any abnormal changes in any of these aspects during the economic crisis to enable policy makers to react quickly. Understandably, the databases of these information systems usually include only those who have enrolled in the system and do not represent the whole population. In particular, many poor or indigenous people are left out. Therefore, a combination of tracking methods that includes rapid household surveys is essential to obtain sufficient representation and customized information during the crisis. Again, the ECA experience provides a clear message to countries, as well as to development agencies, regarding the importance and necessity of building a system that allows countries to effectively track through MIS and rapid surveys during an economic crisis.

Bibliography

Azam, M. 2010. "Impact of Financial Crisis on Households: How Did Households Deal with the Crisis? Evidence from Europe and Central Asia Countries." World Bank, Washington, DC.

Dasgupta, B., and M. I. Ajwad. 2011. "Income Shocks Reduce Human Capital Investments: Evidence from Five East European Countries." Policy Research Working Paper 5926, World Bank, Washington, DC.

Gottret, P., V. Gupta, S. Sparkes, A. Tandon, V. Moran, and P. Berman. 2009. "Protecting Pro-Poor Health Services during Financial Crises: Lessons from Experience." In *Advances in Health Economics and Health Services Research*, edited by D. Chernichovsky and K. Hanson, 23–53. Vol. 21. Emerald Group Publishing.

Koettl, J. 2010. "The Financial Impact of the Economic Crisis on Health Insurance Funds in Eastern Europe." World Bank, Washington, DC.

Li, Y., and M. I. Ajwad. 2012. "The Impact of the Great Recession on Health Care Utilization in Armenia." Draft Working Paper, World Bank, Washington, DC.

Musgrove, P. 1987. "The Economic Crisis and Its Impact on Health and Health Care in Latin America and the Caribbean." *International Journal of Health Services* 17 (3): 411–41.

Nikoloski, Z., and M. I. Ajwad. 2013. "Do Economic Crises Lead to Health and Nutrition Behavior Responses? Analysis Using Longitudinal Data from Russia." Policy Research Working Paper 6538, World Bank, Washington, DC.

Waters, H., F. Saadah, and M. Pradhan. 2003. "The Impact of the 1997–98 East Asian Economic Crisis on Health and Health Care in Indonesia." *Health Policy and Planning* 18 (2): 172–81.

World Bank. Various years. *Global Economic Prospects* online database.

CHAPTER 4

Mitigating the Effects of Economic Downturns

The ability of any sector to mitigate the impact of an economic downturn is contingent on the existence of instruments, prior to the downturn, that allow for the identification of the most vulnerable groups, as well as the ability to target interventions toward them. Successful mitigation programs in the health sector have been synchronized with social safety net programs and have used the existing targeting instrument to scale up coverage and ensure the take-up of services, particularly preventive care. At the health care system level, this implies the need to take a long-term approach in order to make the system more resilient. This can also be seen as an opportunity to make the financing and organization of health care more efficient.

The objective of this chapter is to identify successful global experiences in health and related sectors, such as social protection, in order to help countries develop programs that can withstand future economic downturns. Specifically, the chapter analyzes four country case studies that illustrate different mitigation strategies that were successful in minimizing the adverse effects of the recent downturn on health care utilization, especially among poor and marginalized groups.

The Country Case Studies: An Overview

A large number of primary and secondary sources were consulted to identify developing countries whose innovative health care policies were adapted to successfully meet the challenges of economic downturns. This exercise showed that although every mitigation strategy is unique and has a different combination of effects, all successful strategies have two salient attributes. The first attribute of a successful strategy is the specific response or the ability to adapt to an economic downturn. The second attribute is the ability to improve quality of service and/or expand access to the target population.

Mitigation strategies typically focus on one of these attributes. Some attempt to respond to a downturn primarily with efficiency improvements such as changing management practices, staff incentives, and co-payment regimes. Other strategies focus more on increasing the quality and accessibility of health care.

The four countries selected for the study all employed context-specific mitigation strategies that reflected both of these attributes in various combinations.

a. Indonesia's post-downturn mitigation strategy used existing data on the poor to ensure greater access to the health care system in real time, as the crisis was unfolding. It was successful because of strong political will and the availability of data.

b. Thailand had reformed its health care system to increase access and treatment for the poor during East Asia's rapid growth period. These reforms helped mitigate the effects of the East Asian financial crisis on health care utilization. Because of these reforms, Thailand was the only country in which health care utilization did not initially decline when the crisis hit.

c. The Kyrgyz Republic was able to increase health care access and treatment during a succession of economic downturns because of a sustained reform effort to adapt to long-term budget constraints that began in the 1990s. The reforms implemented during and after the economic contraction made it possible to mitigate the effect of budget cuts on the poor. The reforms also ensured that sufficient international donor funds were received to increase health expenditure during the period of contraction.

d. Colombia made sweeping health sector reforms in 1993 that increased the proportion of poorer groups who were insured and subsequently had regular access to the health care system. Most of the studies evaluating the success of these reforms do not explicitly take into account the possible effects of the economic contraction and political instability that plagued the country in the late 1990s and early 2000s. However, the evaluations clearly show an increase in the number of poor Colombians accessing the public health system and demonstrate that economic downturns and political crises are not always barriers to effective structural reforms.

Adapting to an Economic Downturn: Implementing Pro-Poor Health Care in Indonesia

The Asian financial crisis gripped Indonesia in July 1997 and escalated into a full economic and political crisis by May 1998, as the country's gross domestic product (GDP) declined by 14 percent over the duration of the downturn (1997–99) (Rana 1999). The downturn caused a set of demand and supply-side shocks that, if left unaddressed, would have caused steep declines in health care utilization and expenditure, especially among marginalized groups.

Specifically, the financial downturn had the following direct economic effects:

a. Massive devaluation of the rupiah. The currency was worth 20 percent of its trade-weighted value by the end of 1998, which resulted in inflation (80 percent in 1998) and made the importation of health care products significantly more expensive (Levinsohn, Berry, and Friedman 2003).
b. Rapid contraction in employment conditions. The unemployment rate surged past 15 percent in 1998, with more than 8 million people losing their jobs.
c. Increase in the poverty rate from 11 percent before the crisis to 18–20 percent postcrisis (Saadah, Pradhan, and Sparrow 2001).

The effects of the economic downturn resulted in a significant decrease in health care expenditure by households and the public sector. This decrease is evidenced by the following statistics:

a. Household utilization of health care services decreased by 25 percent between 1997 and 1998 (Waters, Saadah, and Pradhan 2003).
b. There was a 9 percent reduction in public health spending due to decreased revenue from 1997 to 1998 (Knowles and Marzolf 2003).
c. Household expenditure allocated to health care declined by 16 percent, from 1.9 percent to 1.6 percent of total household expenditure, during the same period (Frankenberg, Thomas, and Beegle 1999).

Given the rapidly declining level of health care utilization associated with the downturn and the political instability caused by the economic collapse, the Indonesian government launched the Indonesian Social Safety Net Program (Jaring Pengaman Sosial Bidang Kesehatan, or JPS-BK) in August 1998. One of the critical components of the program was the scaling up of a previously minor program, the Health Card program (Saadah, Lieberman, and Juwono 1999).

Design and Implementation of the JPS-BK: The Health Card

The Health Card program was effectively a targeted price subsidy, as all household members who received the card were entitled to subsidized care by public health care providers (Yazbeck 2009). It entitled users to "free services at public health care providers consisting of: (a) outpatient and inpatient care; (b) contraceptives for women; (c) prenatal care; and (d) assistance at birth" (Sparrow 2008).

The Health Card program existed prior to the Asian financial crisis. However, its uptake was negligible and lacked robust assessments as to whether the program was in fact successfully targeting low-income groups (Sparrow 2008). The decision to massively scale up the program was aimed at increasing access of financially distressed and marginalized households to public health care.

The distribution of the Health Cards was strategically focused on the poor. Public providers in the local communities identified as likely to receive a surge in demand for services were given additional funds. Specifically, primary health centers (*puskesmas*) and village midwives (*bidan di desa*) were given an additional US$29 million for FY98 (Sparrow 2008). Although this amount was not sufficient to cover all of the new demand created by the expansion in coverage, it helped to ensure that the quality of treatment would not be significantly affected by increased health care utilization.

Pro-Poor Targeting in Times of Downturn
Given how quickly the targeted scheme was scaled up and rolled out, the JPS-BK program followed a two-pronged strategy to ensure that it reached the poorest groups:

First, funds were targeted according to the results of a prosperity index of 307 districts (urban *Kota* and rural *Kabupaten*). The index classified a household as poor if it failed to meet one or more of the following criteria (Yazbeck 2009):

a. Have freedom to worship
b. Eat two basic meals a day
c. Have different clothing for different occasions school/work and home/leisure
d. Have a home floor that is not earthen (Sparrow 2008)

Second, the distribution of Health Cards was guided by local health officials and community leaders who could apply their knowledge to target pro-poor groups within their specific communities.

The program followed a partly decentralized targeting process, involving both geographic and community-based targeting instruments. It was, however, not perfect in its execution. In hindsight, policy makers may have wished to have made the following modifications to the Health Card distribution process—assuming their objective was to ensure pro-poor targeting:

a. The use of household expenditure data to determine who was poor. The prosperity index is correlated to indicators of poverty, but it is still a proxy indicator and therefore a more noisy measure of who can be classified as poor. Ideally, a more efficient measure of the poverty headcount could have allowed for even more efficient targeting. However, given the speed with which the program needed to be rolled out, the prosperity index was the most appropriate up-to-date indicator available at the time.
b. The use of local elites to make distribution decisions. Allowing local officials to make decisions about distribution of Health Cards resulted in some leakage to higher-income groups. However, the majority of cards were distributed to lower-income groups (Galasso and Ravallion 2005).

Impact: Sustaining the Social Safety Net
By February 1999, 22 million Indonesians, or approximately 10.6 percent of the population, had received the Health Card. By 1999 the incidence of Health Card ownership was clearly skewed toward the poorest groups: 93 percent of those in the poorest quintile (the 20 percent of the population classified as poorest) had

Figure 4.1 Incidence of Health Card Coverage by Income Group in Indonesia, 1999

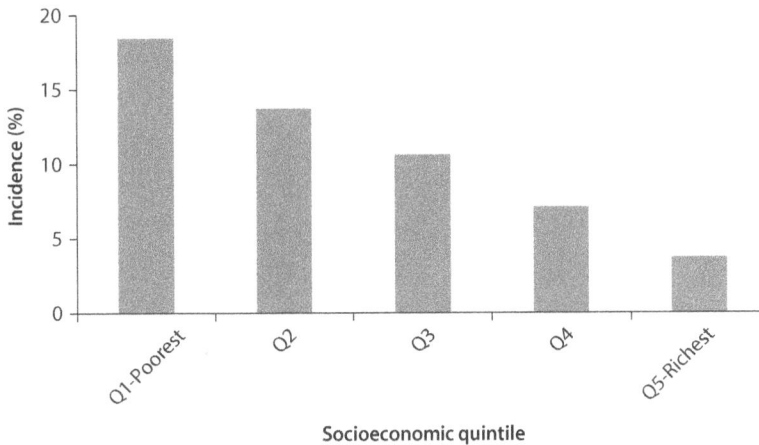

Source: Sparrow 2008.
Note: The figure shows the percentage of the population in each income group that received the Health Card.

received the Health Card (figure 4.1). This suggests that despite reliance on the prosperity index, the rapid scale-up of coverage, and the discretion of local elites in distributing the cards, the program was moderately successful in increasing the coverage of marginalized groups, even though a majority of them still remained outside the formal health care system. However, almost 4 percent of the wealthiest Indonesians also received a Health Card.

The success of the targeting becomes more mixed when examining the percentage of total cardholders in each income quintile, rather than the incidence of card ownership by income group. Figure 4.2 shows that although 34 percent of the cards did reach the poorest quintile and 60 percent reached the two lowest quintiles, a very large 40 percent went to the top three income quintiles.

Nevertheless, considering that the scheme was scaled up during and immediately after an economic and political crisis in one of the largest developing countries in the world, its relative success should not be dismissed. At the very least, the results suggest that it is possible to implement, albeit imperfectly, a pro-poor health mitigation program in a very short period of time despite significant economic, political, and geographical obstacles.

Despite the limitations noted, the rapid scale-up of the Health Card program helped to ensure that the fall in health care utilization caused by the economic crisis was partly reversed.

Outpatient visits to all types of medical facilities (public, private, and modern[1]) declined among all poor households between 1997 and 1998, but among the subset of households that received Health Cards, this trend was reversed by 1999 (figure 4.3). Conversely, outpatient visits continued to decline among households that had not obtained the cards. Among cardholding households,

Figure 4.2 Distribution of Health Card by Income Group in Indonesia, 1999
Percent

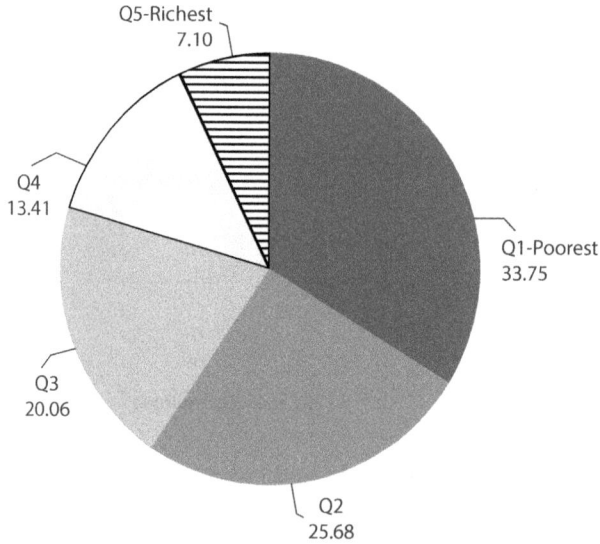

Source: Sparrow 2008.

Figure 4.3 Outpatient Visits by the Poor in Indonesia, 1997–99

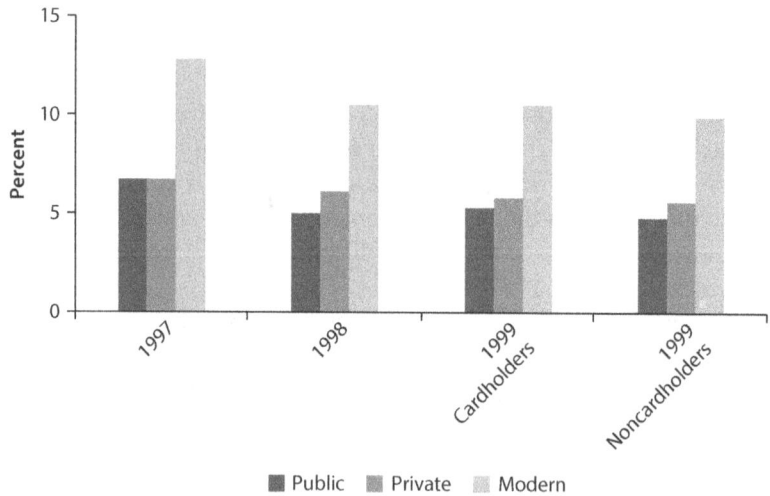

Source: Saadah, Pradhan, and Sparrow 2001.

although outpatient visits in 1999 had not recovered to their pre-crisis levels, there was a notable recovery in the use of public sector outpatient services (5.3 percent in 1999 versus 5 percent, on average, in 1998). There was also stabilization in the use of modern facilities (Sparrow 2008) (at 10.5 percent). As the Health Card did not cover private sector facilities, it is not surprising that

Figure 4.4 Health Card Use by Income Group in Indonesia, 1999

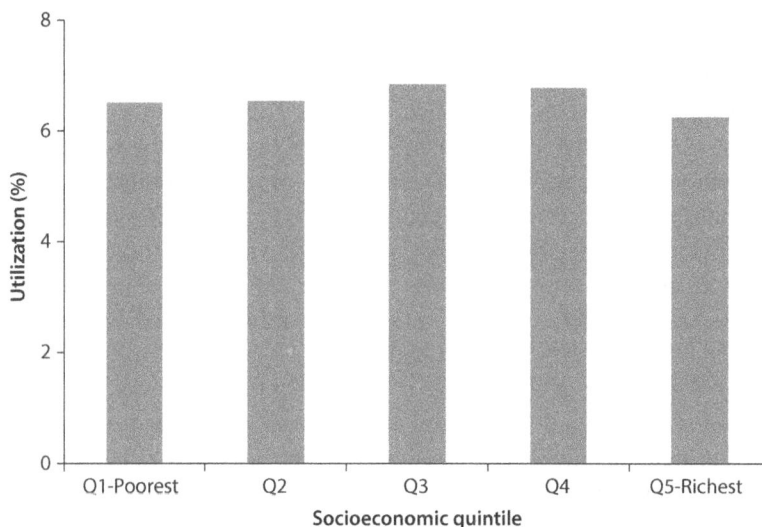

Source: Sparrow 2008.

the rate of utilization continued to fall, from 6.1 percent in 1998 to 5.8 percent in 1999, in households with Health Cards. However, in poor households without the Health Card, the decline in utilization continued unabated over the one-year period, with public sector outpatient visits declining from 5.0 percent to 4.8 percent in 1999, and the use of modern outpatient services declining from 10.5 percent to 9.9 percent.

Further, as shown in figure 4.4, cardholders in the 3rd and 4th quintiles were more likely to make use of the card when visiting a facility than were cardholders in the two poorest quintiles.[2] There is evidence that middle-income groups are more likely to utilize the Health Card because they have better access, in terms of physical proximity, to public health facilities. Therefore, in order to make the scheme more pro-poor, it would have been necessary to ensure better access to public health care facilities by reducing the transportation costs that limit the poor's access to health care (Sparrow 2008).

Limitations

The Health Card program faced the following limitations (adapted from Sparrow 2008):

a. Evidence shows that patients who received treatment using a Health Card received a poorer quality of service compared with other patients.
b. Approximately one-third of Indonesian Health Card users did NOT present their cards when attending an eligible health care institution.
c. Due to the imperfect distribution of the Health Card to the poor as well as barriers to accessing the health centers, the effect of the program on health care utilization by marginalized groups was more limited than the successful dissemination of the cards would have otherwise ensured (Johar 2009).

Lessons and Recommendations

According to the International Labour Organization, in 2005, the Health Card program was modified in order to increase its reach and effectiveness (ILO 2008). Specifically, the Health Card began to be issued by Askes,[3] with the government paying premiums on behalf of cardholders. This program was also designed to be expanded quickly. Two targets were specifically established to aid the rapid expansion of the program. The first phase of the expansion, January–May 2005, established a target of reaching 36.1 million people, which was equivalent to 17 percent of the total population and equivalent to the estimated number of people in absolute poverty in the country. As in the initial program, districts were allocated cards based on the estimated number of poor. Local authorities provided lists of qualifying individuals to Askes branches. During the second phase, June–December 2005, a higher target of 60 million was set and a simplified transfer of funds, directly from the Ministry of Finance to health care clinics rather than through Askes, was developed to maximize efficiency. Despite lingering problems in identifying and reaching the poor, by 2007 the program covered more than 76.4 million people (ILO 2008).

Prior to the Asian financial crisis, the Indonesian Health Card scheme was a minor program designed to help marginalized groups gain access to health care. The onset of the Asian financial crisis in 1997 and its associated political aftershocks, including the fall of the Suharto regime in May 1998, created an adverse environment in which health care utilization fell by more than 9 percent during 1997–98.

The massive scaling-up of the Health Card program during this period was no small accomplishment. Access to the Health Card did not fully compensate for the effects of the crisis, but it did stop and begin to reverse the fall in health care utilization among the poorest groups. Despite the pro-poor distribution objectives, more than 40 percent of Health Cards were distributed to middle- and upper-income groups, who were more likely to use the Health Card than the poorer groups.

Coverage Expansion during the Economic Boom Time: The Case of Thailand

Access to health care institutions in Thailand has been closely linked historically to economic growth. In 1963 politically powerful civil servants were the first to receive medical benefits through insurance schemes designed to target the formal sector. Insurance schemes designed to target the rural poor officially commenced in the 1970s (Wibulpolprasert 2010). The end of the Vietnam War and political instability in neighboring countries, coupled with fast economic growth in the 1980s, resulted in an expansion of insurance schemes. For example, in 1981 the voluntary health card was introduced, and concerted efforts to train and retain medical professionals commenced. The effectiveness of government reforms and expansion was limited because of persistent corruption, especially with respect to construction contracts and pharmaceutical procurement (Wibulpolprasert 2010). Furthermore, while economic growth reduced the level of absolute poverty from 23 percent in 1988 to 11 percent in 1996, growth was accompanied by exacerbated inequality, which created new challenges in the implementation of successful social protection programs (Wibulpolprasert 2010).

Both health sector and social protection programs expanded quickly with the support of the government. Yet, at the time of the Asian financial downturn in 1997, Thailand did not have a comprehensive and universal social protection scheme (World Bank 1999).

The crisis had a significantly adverse effect on the Thai economy and resulted in severe public expenditure restrictions. Specifically, the downturn had the following effects:

a. GDP growth slowed significantly, from an average rate of about 7–9 percent in the late 1980s and early 1990s to 0.6 percent in 1997 and a contraction in 1998 (Supakankunti 2000).
b. The Thai baht fell by more than 70 percent, which resulted in inflation of more than 10 percent.
c. The unemployment rate more than doubled, from 2 percent in 1996 to 5 percent in 1998 (Supakankunti 2000).
d. Real wages fell by almost 6 percent with a disproportionate loss of income among poor members of society (World Bank 1999).

This economic downturn resulted in the following adverse effects on health care utilization:

a. Medical drugs and devices became more expensive. The cost of domestically produced drugs increased by 12–15 percent, and imported drug prices rose even faster at 18–20 percent during 1997–98 (World Bank 1999).
b. Budgetary restrictions grew due to falling revenue and rising demands for social services. Specifically, the health care budget was slashed by 15 percent in 1998 and by just under 1 percent in 1999.

To minimize the impact of the downturn on actual health utilization, most cuts focused on capital expenditure, although substantial cuts were also made to many programs, including HIV/AIDS treatment and antitransmission programs.

Despite these constraints, the expansion of coverage during the boom period meant that Thailand was one of the few countries affected by the Asian financial crisis in which health care utilization did not decline during 1997–98. In fact, outpatient visits to public health facilities increased by 22 percent between 1996 and 1998 (Waters, Saadah, and Pradhan 2003). Several studies have found that the increase was due in part to the expansion of the Health Card program. The program made access to public health facilities more affordable to households, especially poor households, during the crisis (Waters, Saadah, and Pradhan 2003).

Further, the program received financial support from the development agencies during the crisis, which enabled it to increase provision to poor groups during the downturn.[4]

The Health Card: Better Health?

The Ministry of Health introduced the voluntary Health Card in 1983. The program goal was to enable poor households to access health services. The purchase of a card enables up to five members of the same household to obtain care at public health institutions at no additional expense. The Health Card provides coverage for outpatient and inpatient care, as well as maternal and child care services (Supakankunti 2000).

In 2000 the average cost of an annual voluntary Health Card was 1,000 baht, half of which was covered by the government. This subsidy made the program affordable and attractive for lower- and middle-income households. The card did not provide coverage for privately run medical institutions. This restriction seems to have virtually eliminated leakage to wealthier groups, although data on the demographics of cardholders are not always reliable. More recent studies, such as one conducted in the rural Khon Kaen province, have found that proxies for household poverty are generally good indicators of whether a household purchased a Health Card (Supakankunti 2000). As in Khon Kaen province, Supakankunti (2000) found that on average, the household income of a card-owning household was approximately 50,000 baht, or 12,000 baht less than non–card-owning households (average income 62,000 baht), and this difference was highly statistically significant (at the 1 percent level). However, statistical analyses have generally found that the best predictor of whether a card is purchased is not income, but rather the presence of illness and/or the existence of nearby health facilities. This suggests that the structure of the program incentivizes adverse selection (Supakankunti 2000). Furthermore, when it comes to utilization of health services, Health Card holders who access public hospitals have a lower income than non-cardholders who access public hospitals, but this difference is not statistically significant once other factors are controlled for. This suggests that while the initial distribution of Health Cards is relatively pro-poor, the actual use of Health Cards is by no means restricted to the poorest groups in society. Middle-income groups who own cards are just as likely to use them as their poorer peers (Supakankunti 2000).

Impact: What Has the Health System Contributed to Health Improvement?

The purchase of Health Cards increased 60 percent during the Asian financial crisis, from approximately 5 million in 1996 to 8.6 million in 1998. Outpatient visits doubled from just under 11 million to just under 21 million during the same period (figure 4.5).

Empirical analyses have generally concluded that the expansion of this affordable program was one of the key factors in preventing the crisis from having a negative impact on health care utilization (Waters, Saadah, and Pradhan 2003).

Figure 4.5 Health Card and Health Care Utilization in Thailand, 1996–98

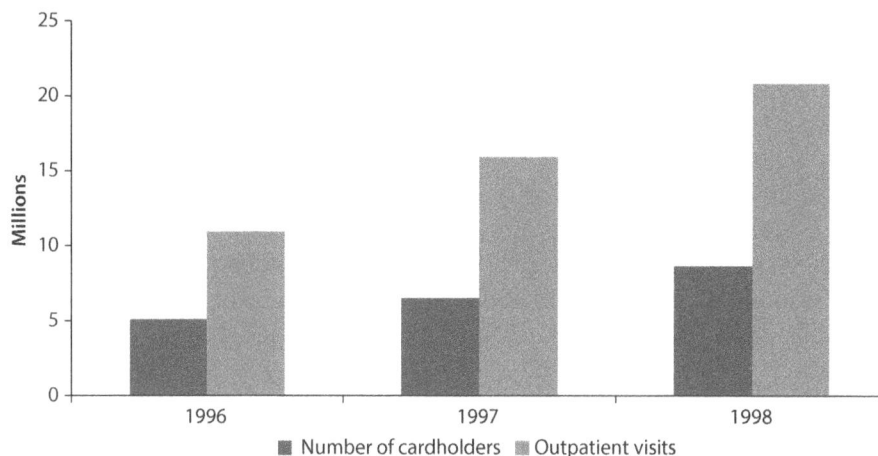

Source: World Bank databank, as adapted from the Thai Ministry of Health, 1999.

This finding was in stark contrast to the experience of Indonesia and other affected countries, where patient utilization declined as the crisis took hold.

Limitations: Agenda Setting for the Future

Despite its success, the Health Card scheme was criticized because it did nothing to ensure the quality of services. Moreover, the best predictor of Health Card purchase was the anticipation of illness rather than any measurable socioeconomic indicators.

Lessons and Recommendations

Despite the relative success of the program, it did not provide universal coverage. Marginalized groups remained uninsured and dependent on out-of-pocket payments to access health care. Following the election of Prime Minister Thaksin Shinawatra in 2001, the card was replaced by a universal health scheme in 2002. The scheme automatically enrolled all uninsured Thais, approximately 18.5 million of a total population of 62 million, and provided treatment for a flat 30 baht fee per visit (Towse, Mills, and Tangcharoensathien 2004). The experience of utilizing the Health Card, especially in rural areas, made it easier to roll out this larger plan (Towse, Mills, and Tangcharoensathien 2004).

By continuously expanding access to health care through various insurance schemes, Thailand did not experience a decline in health care utilization during 1997–98 (Waters, Saadah, and Pradhan 2003). The evidence suggests that this was due in no small part to the existence and expansion of the Health Card program in the preceding years. While the targeting toward the poor was not perfect, the program was broadly successful in protecting access to the health care system for lower-income groups.

Adapting to a Protracted Downturn: The Case of the Kyrgyz Republic

Following the collapse of the USSR and the subsidies it provided, the Kyrgyz Republic suffered a protracted five-year recession from 1991 to 1996. Per capita GDP declined by an astounding 40 percent. In such a context, policy makers had to increase the efficiency of public service provision in order to try to maintain standards in a constantly contracting budgetary situation. By pursuing a successful round of reforms that enhanced both efficiency and equity, the Kyrgyz health care system was in a good position to receive international aid to soften the impact of the financial crisis that started in 2008 (World Bank 2008). The example of the Kyrgyz Republic provides evidence of the policy options available to decision makers in times of extreme and persistent economic distress.

The Recession and Health Reforms

The 1991–96 recession resulted in a massive decline in health expenditures—from 3.6 percent of GDP in 1991 to 1.9 percent of GDP by 2000—a 47 percent decrease in expenditure (World Bank 2008). Compounding this dire downturn was that the majority of health care expenditure, 75 percent, went to administrative costs, leaving few resources for actual patient care (Purvis et al. 2005). Since the collapse of the Soviet Union, the Kyrgyz economy has been adversely affected by the Asian financial crisis (1997–98), a winter crisis and drought in 2008–09 (UNDP 2012), and the current economic downturn (2008–12).[5]

Political instability, which seemed to plague the country, further compounded these economic downturns. The instability culminated in April 2010 with uprisings by protesters against the incumbent president Kurmanbek Bakiyev and his ultimate ouster. The transition was ultimately successful, but the violence (more than 1,000 injuries), displacement (more than 400,000 people), deaths (at least 100), and political uncertainty it engendered did not, initially, facilitate the stabilization of the country, even though it did provide a possible basis for further reforms (UNDP 2012).

Due to the shortage of funds, in 2008 the average out-of-pocket expense faced by a typical patient was the equivalent of US$46. This amount was five times the average monthly level of individual consumption. In effect, more than 50 percent of health care expenditure in the country was raised by out-of-pocket payments, with patients contributing to the cost of medicines, equipment, and the salaries of health care professionals (Kutzin 2001). As a result, health care was unaffordable for a large percentage of the population (Yazbeck 2009).

In 2001 the Kyrgyz Republic began implementing a five-year health system reform program. The "Manas Health Sector Reforms" were part of a 10-year reform program aimed at increasing the efficiency of the health system and reducing out-of-pocket expenses, especially for the poor (Yazbeck 2009).

The main logic behind these reforms was to split the purchase and provision of services in order to realize efficiency gains. The Mandatory Health Insurance

Fund (MHIF) would become the main purchaser of individual health insurance, which was financed by general taxation and payroll taxes. The main elements of the reform were:

a. Rationalization of Health Financing. Before the reforms, there had been separate health care financing schemes at the national, regional, and oblast (district) levels, resulting in duplication and waste. The reform organized financing at the regional level and abolished municipal and city-level resource pools. It was hoped that such a reform would allow for the more efficient allocation of resources across oblasts.

b. Consumer-Focused Purchasing Methods. Prior to the reforms, providers had been paid based on input criteria and line-item budgeting. Managers had little leeway to shift spending across line items. By shifting to capitation and case-based payments to hospitals, based on actual demand, the reforms aimed to create incentives for resources to be focused on the needs of patients (Yazbeck 2009).

c. A More Transparent Benefits Regime. By clearly defining services covered under the benefit package and introducing a flat co-payment regime, reform aimed to displace informal payments, which had become highly regressive. Furthermore, because hospitals would receive higher payments for treating the uninsured (mostly the poor), this reform was expected to enhance equity of access.

d. Downsizing the Hospital Sector. By reducing the number of hospitals from 1,464 to 784, the reforms potentially could have increased barriers to health care. However, by focusing on eliminating inefficiencies (excess administrative costs and duplication of services), the reforms aimed to free up more resources to finance patient care. As a result of this reform, the percentage of the health budget devoted to administration fell below 75 percent for the first time since independence.

Impact: Effective Reform Can Attract Funding for Continued Reform

As the reforms were rolled out sequentially in different oblasts, it was possible to identify the impact of the reforms across the country and over time. By carrying out a baseline survey in all parts of the country before any reforms were implemented, and then conducting a survey when the reforms had been implemented in half the oblasts, it became possible to identify the treatment effect of the reforms.[6] The following effects were identified:

a. The introduction of a transparent co-payment scheme resulted in a slower growth rate of out-of-pocket expenses, which grew by only about US$5 in reformed oblasts, compared to US$15 in unreformed oblasts, between the years 2000 and 2003 (World Bank 2008).

b. In particular, out-of-pocket expenses declined for low-income groups in reformed oblasts, compared to a slight increase with out-of-pocket payment in unreformed oblasts.

c. At the district level, there was an 84 percent reduction in nonmedical expenditures among reformed oblasts between the years 2000 and 2003, which resulted in the release of extra funds for medical care.

d. The initial success and effectiveness of the health reforms, coupled with continued political support, made it easier to attract external funding from international development agencies prior to and after the subsequent economic downturn (box 4.1).[7] Although the economic downturn resulted in a dramatic decrease in public health expenditure in 2008—from 3.2 percent of GDP in 2007 to 2.7 percent in 2008—this decline was more than compensated for by 2009 (figure 4.6). Expenditure rose to 3.5 percent of GDP as a result of donor support coupled with deficit spending by the government (Mogilevsky et al. 2011).

Box 4.1 Effective Reform in the Kyrgyz Republic Attracts International Donors

The decline in resources devoted to health, coupled with the first stage of the Manas reforms, attracted resources from international donors. In 2004, 10 donors, led by the International Development Association, adopted a sectorwide approach (SWAp) focusing on health expenditure (the first of its kind in the Europe and Central Asia region). In return for continued government commitment to expand the Manas reforms, the donors agreed to provide financial support to improve access and ease the effects of the sharp economic downturn on health care utilization. As recent evaluations have shown, both the SWAp and the Manas reform schemes have been successful in reducing the financial barriers to health care access. In short, reacting to the effects of an economic downturn by increasing efficiency, the Kyrgyz health care system was able to attract financial support from abroad to ease the budget burden.

Source: World Bank 2008.

Figure 4.6 Public Health Expenditure in the Kyrgyz Republic, 2006–09

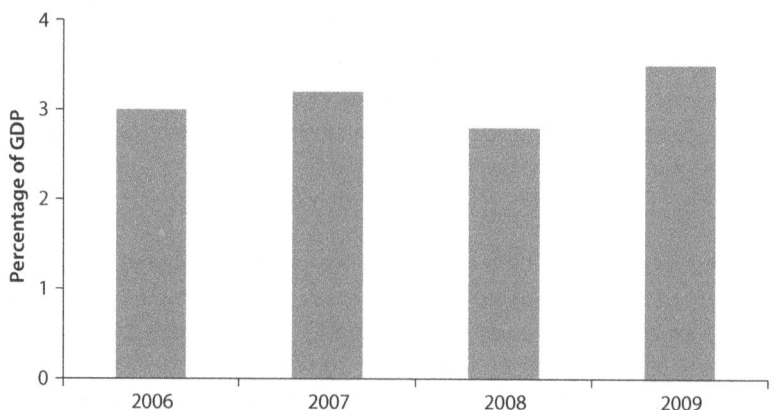

Source: Mogilevsky et al. 2011.
Note: GDP = gross domestic product.

Limitations: Dependence on Donor Support

The reform programs did not address the lack of qualified medical professionals, whose numbers have been declining since before the collapse of the USSR. This deficit could result in severe cost and access problems in the future (International Crisis Group 2011). Moreover, given the significant budgetary constraints and dependence on donor support, the gains from the reforms remain vulnerable to changes in donor priorities (Mogilevsky et al. 2011).

Lessons and Recommendations

The relative success of the health reforms provided incentives for development partners to support the Kyrgyz health care system during the current economic downturn. The example of the Kyrgyz Republic demonstrates that even when faced with a severe and protracted budgetary crisis, the pursuit of reforms can directly mitigate the adverse effects on health care utilization and show a commitment to reform that attracts partnership and assistance from development agencies.

Targeting System for Social Programs: The Case of Colombia

Colombia illustrates how the allocation of resources in a more efficient and equitable manner in a pre-crisis context can mitigate the adverse effects of an economic downturn. Colombia's 1993 reforms to the health care system helped to reduce the system's vulnerability to crisis by expanding access and efficiency of the system, and reducing the need for out-of-pocket payments. The reforms further established a versatile and sophisticated mechanism—the Selection System of Beneficiaries for Social Programs (SISBEN)—for identifying and potentially targeting the poor.

According to the Colombian Constitution (1991), public health care provision is a constitutional right:

> Public health ... [is a] public service for which the state is responsible. All individuals are guaranteed access to services that promote, protect, and rehabilitate public health. It is the responsibility of the state to organize, direct, and regulate the delivery of health services ... to the population in accordance with the principles of efficiency, universality, and cooperation.

Despite this formal mandate, before the 1993 reforms, the health care system in Colombia was characterized by low efficiency, lack of access by the poor, and large out-of-pocket payments (Escobar et al. 2010).

In fact, barriers to health care access among the poorest groups were so significant that, in 1992, only one in six people sought medical care when they became ill. Of all those treated in public hospitals, only 20 percent came from the poorest quintile, with middle-income groups being responsible for more than 60 percent of public health care utilization (Yazbeck 2009). As figure 4.7 indicates, the lack of private health insurance resulted in further inequity because 91 percent of the poorest quintile made out-of-pocket payments as compared to 69 percent of richest quintile users (Escobar 2005).

Figure 4.7 Incidence of Out-of-Pocket Payments for Inpatient Care by Income Group in Colombia, 1992

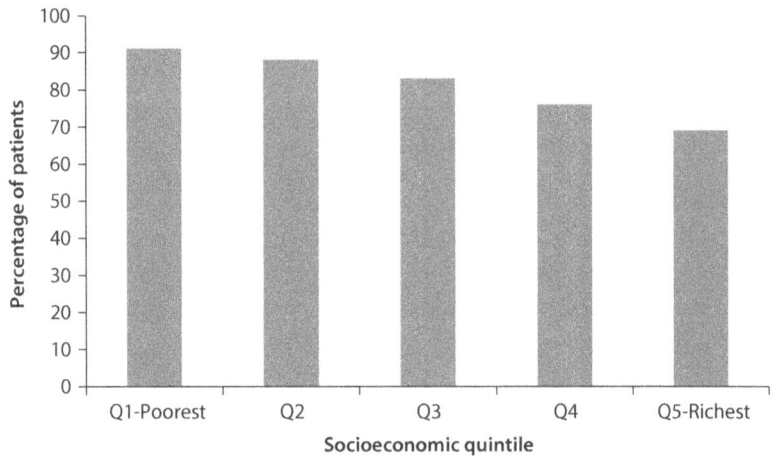

Source: Escobar 2005.

The Reforms: Using Proxy Means Testing to Expand Health Insurance

By focusing on mitigating inefficiencies in the management of health care resources, the 1993 Colombian health care system reforms represent one of the most ambitious attempts by a developing country to expand health care access, especially for marginalized groups.

The efforts were predominantly focused on governance reform or changing how the health care system worked, not just on expanding access. This mix of reforms represents a contrast to many reform programs around the world that focused exclusively on expanding access to health care without significantly altering the governance of the health care system (Miller, Pinto, and Vera-Hernández 2009).

The 1993 health care sector reforms improved the access to and quality of health care received by the poor by establishing an income threshold. Those citizens whose income fell below the threshold were eligible for a fully subsidized health insurance scheme (Miller, Pinto, and Vera-Hernández 2009). Quality of care was improved as insurance agents were allowed to allocate funding or purchase health care from different providers, thereby enabling them to avoid hospitals that were likely to provide poor-quality services.

To realize these changes, Colombia took steps to develop an efficient poverty index, and to shift subsidies from hospitals to patients. The poverty index, SISBEN, was absolutely pivotal in ensuring that households eligible for the subsidy scheme were identified. The SISBEN index included the following measures (Yazbeck 2009):

a. Access to and quality of a household's living accommodations
b. Access to and quality of essential public services
c. The number of durable goods the household possesses

d. Education attainment
e. Income level[8]

Shifting the subsidy from hospitals to patients was supposed to empower patients to shop for the best-quality treatment by hospitals that made the most efficient use of resources. However, this element of the reform was not fully implemented and its expected positive effects were therefore not fully realized (Escobar et al. 2010).

Impact

Between 1992 and 2007, the share of insured Colombians rose from 20 percent to 80 percent of the population (CENDEX 2008). Furthermore, as figure 4.8 indicates, these gains were concentrated among the poorest income groups. Access to health care among the poorest quintile increased especially quickly—from 9 percent of the poorest in 1992 to 49 percent in 2003. This increase resulted in a significantly smaller percentage of potential patients claiming that they could not access health care because of a lack of money (Yazbeck 2009).

The reforms halved the out-of-pocket expenses of the poor. While the uninsured poor spent 8 percent of their income on out-of-pocket expenses in 2003, the insured poor spent only 4 percent.

By 2003 the percentage of respondents in every income group who indicated a lack of money as the reason not to seek health care was significantly lower among the insured compared to the uninsured (figure 4.9). This was particularly true among the lowest income groups.

Furthermore, the creation of the SISBEN index encouraged local municipalities to share information with the central government, thereby facilitating better coordination and distribution of benefits across the country (Yazbeck 2009).

Figure 4.8 Insured Population by Income Group in Colombia, 1992 and 2003

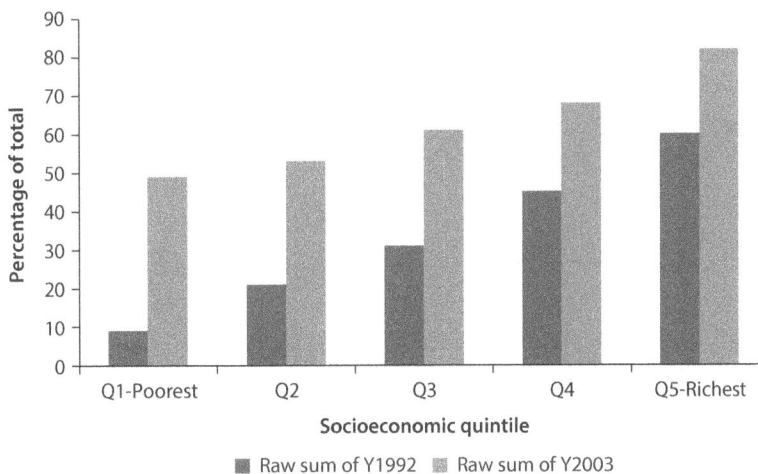

Source: Escobar 2005.

Figure 4.9 "Lack of Money" Prevents Health Care Utilization by Income Group in Colombia, 2003

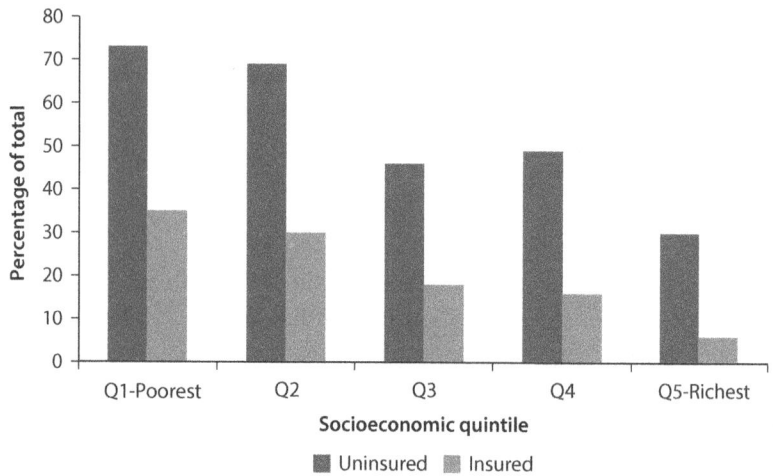

Source: Escobar 2005.

The reforms increased not only the percentage of the poor who were insured and had access to public health care facilities but also their use of these facilities. Using a matching technique, a recent evaluation study found that the reforms significantly increased the utilization of public health facilities by the poor and previously uninsured (Trujillo, Portillo, and Vernon 2005).

Finally, there is evidence that the scheme significantly reduced extreme expenditures on health care by one-third, thereby reducing the susceptibility of the poor to the effects of income shocks (Miller, Pinto, and Vera-Hernández 2009). The evidence for this is that despite a deteriorating economy (GDP declined by 4.3 percent between 1997 and 1998) and rising unemployment (from 8.5 percent in 1995 to 20.2 percent in 2000), implementation of the program continued to bring health care to Colombians in increasing numbers, even during the period of escalating political violence in the early 2000s (Escobar et al. 2010).

Limitations

Despite its success, the impacts of the reforms are of a more limited scope than would have been possible for the following reasons:

a. The complexity of reforms, duplication, and to some extent a loss of political will to implement the reforms over time affected results. This has meant that initial efficiency gains were not as great as hoped. The reforms have not mitigated the issue of strong union membership—generating resistance to change and/or the lack of managerial expertise in the public health care system limited the efficient component of the reforms (Escobar et al. 2010). Until resistance from unions to limit reforms is abated and managerial expertise is improved, the ability to realize the full potential of the reforms will remain constrained.

b. In many cases, an individual insurer enjoyed a geographical monopoly, which reduced the efficiency effects that might be associated with competition for patients (Miller, Pinto, and Vera-Hernández 2009).

c. There is evidence that households and local officials may have manipulated the SISBEN index to obtain coverage. The scheme generated revenue for the municipalities based on the number of participants. This provided incentive for local government officials to inflate the number of eligible households (Camacho and Conovor 2009).

d. Expansion of the program is conditional on overcoming financial constraints (Yazbeck 2009).

e. Although more insulated from economic shocks than before, the insurance system ultimately relies on payroll taxes and general government revenues, both of which decline during times of crisis.

Lessons and Recommendations

The governance and targeted nature of the health reforms undertaken in Colombia significantly expanded the coverage of and access to public health care by poor and marginalized groups. The scheme was not perfect, but the reforms did reduce the necessity of out-of-pocket expenses for the poor seeking health care and thereby increased health care utilization. Further, the scheme was successful despite the onset of an economic downturn in 1997, and the political instability and conflicts from 1995 to 2003 (Escobar et al. 2010). This suggests that over a long period of time, similar reforms can result in improvements in the utilization of health care by the poor despite economic contractions and significant political instability.

Lessons across Sectors: Health and Social Protection

The country case studies illustrate that there are numerous methods of mitigating the effects of economic downturns on population health and the health delivery system. Reforms to improve efficiency and increase system resilience are but one way to stabilize and strengthen health sectors. There are ample opportunities for the health sector to collaborate with other sectors to further improve equity and accessibility to health services for the poor and vulnerable, particularly during economic downturns. The country case studies show that countries with social protection systems, particularly the social safety net programs, were able to develop responses more effectively before and during the global economic crisis. Countries that did not have an effective social safety net program found it more difficult to identify and protect the most vulnerable when the economic downturn hit. In light of these findings, the discussion turns to collaboration between the two sectors and the possible benefits.

The social protection sector has become increasingly important over the past two decades among developing countries. The financial crisis in 2008 has made it even more relevant as it has become one of the key driving sectors in poverty reduction and development. Social protection is seen as "public interventions that assist individuals, households, and communities to manage risk better and that provide support to the critically poor" (World Bank 2001). In response to the financial crisis in 2008, and to better link with essential services, the UN System Chief Executives Board (CEB 2009) established the Social Protection Floor (SPF) Initiative as a joint effort to promote access to essential services and social transfers. An SPF is the first level of a comprehensive national social protection system guaranteeing universal access to essential services, including health services, and providing social transfers to guarantee income and food security. The most recent World Bank social protection and labor strategy paper (World Bank 2012a) stressed that social protection and labor programs *"improve resilience, equity and opportunity by helping people insure from different types of shocks, reducing poverty and destitution and promoting opportunity through more investment."* The following discussion focuses more on the social safety net, one of the most important pillars within the social protection system (Robalino, Rawlings, and Walker 2012)[9] because of its close linkage with the health sector and the relevance in mitigating the impact of economic downturns.

The linkages between social safety net programs and health are wide and deep. Social safety net programs directly affect health status. Beneficiaries in social safety net programs, including those in the cash transfer programs or public work programs, receive additional income with which they can purchase more food. The evaluation of some cash transfer programs finds that beneficiaries eat more and eat better (Hoddinott and Skoufias 2004). Social safety net programs can lead to an increase in the use of health services, particularly for women and children when the regular seeking of preventive care is a condition or co-responsibility for receiving cash benefits. This results in greater uptake of preventive health services, which ultimately contributes to a lower infant and maternal mortality rate. Social safety net programs can have a direct impact on the removal of social and economic barriers to basic health services in the form of insurance, cash transfers, or granting direct access to public facilities for the poor and thereby helping to achieve more equitable outcomes in the health sector. Not only does the social safety net directly affect the ultimate goal of health status and risk protection, but also it directly or indirectly interacts with health financing, payment, and delivery systems.

Such close collaboration has manifested in designing and implementing the targeted or government-subsidized health insurance in a few countries. However, based on a 24-country survey in the World Bank Universal Coverage for Health (UNICO), only a minority are using the same targeting approach for the health insurance program as in the social protection targeted programs (World Bank 2012b). This sends a clear message that there is still ample space for further collaboration between the two sectors. Two key areas for intersector collaboration are targeting and integrated systems.

A Targeted Approach to Improving Health

Mitigating the impact of economic crisis on access to health for the poor and the vulnerable can be achieved by providing direct access to health services. Another form of mitigation is to provide the poor and vulnerable with access to some forms of health insurance, so that they can purchase health services. In either case, there is a need for an effective way to identify the poor and vulnerable during or before the economic crisis. The most successful mitigation programs in the health sector are those that are able to link with social safety net programs and use the existing targeting instrument to scale up coverage. Grosh et al. (2008) have laid out different methods for targeting. Table 4A.1 in annex 4A presents the main targeting methods along with the associated advantages and disadvantages.

Integrated System to Improve Efficiency and Effectiveness

There are significant similarities among different types of social programs in the delivery of services or transfers to the poor (Palacios 2013). Today's technology can enable an effective management information system (MIS) to facilitate inter-sector collaboration and improve the overall governance and transparency of the system. Such integrated systems can assist all the relevant programs including assessing eligibility, identifying and registering beneficiaries, providing information on availability and quality of services, supporting and monitoring delivery of benefits, and facilitating coordination of different programs at different levels (UNICEF 2012).

Integrated systems or database collaboration between the health and social protection sectors would complement targeting by improving identification efforts and ensuring that benefits go to unique individuals. Further, integrated systems help reduce duplicate or ghost beneficiaries and overlap of similar benefit packages. The biometric identification initiative described in Gelb and Clark (2013) is an example that can facilitate such identification.

On the other hand, information and communication technology (ICT) systems also offer new opportunities and challenges for the design and delivery of social programs. The system permits a one-stop shop for all social programs, including social protection programs and health programs, due to its multicapacity to make transactions, transfer cash to beneficiaries, and utilize health services or other forms of social assistance in a more transparent manner. India, for example, uses biometric information integrated smart cards to identify beneficiaries and accomplish cashless transactions when RSBY[10] beneficiaries seek health services in the empanelled hospitals. Overall, encouraging social safety net programs and health programs to share the same database and same identification technology can greatly improve information accuracy, enable effective monitoring and tracking, increase the efficiency and effectiveness in service delivery, and thus ultimately create the desperately needed fiscal spaces and improve the program governance and accountability.

The health sector interacts both directly and indirectly with many sectors and cannot operate within a vacuum. In fact, reticence to collaborate with other sectors would most likely result in inefficiency and ineffectiveness. The continued and increased collaboration between the social protection and health sectors will allow a more inclusive, equitable, and efficient social system for the poor.

Annex 4A Advantages and Disadvantages of Different Targeting Methods

Table 4A.1 Advantages and Disadvantages of Different Targeting Methods

Type	Advantages	Disadvantages
Means tested: Eligibility is based on income. Information on household income and/or wealth are collected and verified.	Rigorous indication of eligibility; administratively demanding.	It usually requires a high level of literacy and documentation of economic transactions; costly to verify the accuracy of the information; it measures the current income, not the more permanent welfare status.
Proxy means tested: Eligibility is based on a score, which is statistically derived from household survey data based on observable characteristics such as location and quality of housing, ownership of goods, demographic structure of household, education of members.	Depending on construction of the score, this method can provide a more multidimensional measurement of poverty; since based on easily observable characteristics, it can be easier to collect than income data; asset indicators (economic, social and human) may better reflect poverty over time, compared to income.	Requires recent and national representative sample for statistical derivation and testing; administratively intensive to collect information required to compute the score; insensitive to the quick change of household welfare; exclusion errors if particular causes of vulnerabilities are not considered in the score formulation.
Community-based targeting (CBT): Community members are part of the eligibility assessment and/or verification based on assumption that they are familiar with the welfare of the households in the community.	May increase ownership and validation of program and in some contexts strengthen existing community mechanisms; relies on local information on individual circumstances; less costly to collect necessary information.	A subjective targeting method: Local actors may have other incentives besides good targeting of the program; difficult to apply in urban settings; may increase tensions between selected and unselected groups.
Categorical: Eligibility defined based on broad social categories and/or groups such as age, physical ability, gender, ethnicity, social status.	Administratively simple; some specific health services can be better targeted (like immunization).	Verification of status may be a challenge in some cases; may not address structural vulnerabilities and/or impacts of particular risks on families and communities that are not strongly associated with the categories; stigma associated with targeting particular groups.
Geographical: Selection of beneficiaries based on location, often through mapping to identify poorest regions or districts.	Low administrative costs as household level assessment is not required; efficient where poverty or vulnerability is geographically concentrated; have no direct labor disincentives.	Requires sufficiently reliable data to poverty map estimation; can be politically more complicated as geography or vulnerability are correlated with other political or social dimensions; performs poorly if poverty is not spatially concentrated.

table continues next page

Table 4A.1 Advantages and Disadvantages of Different Targeting Methods *(continued)*

Type	Advantages	Disadvantages
Self-selection: Program design components (size or type of transfer, timing of benefits, location of payments, etc.) make the program attractive only to specific groups who self-select to participate.	Limited technical capacity required.	The noncoverage and leakage rate could be high; certain self-selection criteria can be stigmatizing or impose heavy costs on participants.

Sources: Based on Grosh et al. 2008; UNICEF 2012.

Notes

1. This term has been defined as "more recently constructed public and private facilities" (Saadah, Pradhan, and Sparrow 2001).

2. While the difference in utilization is not statistically significant, the similarity in the rate of use suggests that, in practice, the Health Card was not as pro-poor as the initial distribution might have suggested.

3. Askes (PERSERO) are organizations that traditionally provide the health insurance schemes of public sector employees.

4. A substantial portion of this development loan was allocated to mitigating the social impacts of the crisis, including providing support for the Health Card (World Bank 1999).

5. Although, unlike many other countries in the region, the current economic downturn did not cause an actual downturn but only an economic slowdown in GDP growth.

6. Original results are from Jakab (2007) and World Bank (2008). Because the rollout of the reforms was not random the baseline survey was absolutely crucial in ensuring that the causal effect of the reforms could be identified.

7. The importance of ensuring countercyclical development aid in order to ensure health care utilization is noted in Schneider (2011).

8. Income was initially included as a variable but was dropped.

9. That is, we do not discuss unemployment, disability, and pension, which all fall under the social protection arena.

10. RSBY (Rashtriya Swasthya Bima Yojna) is a health insurance program for poor households (households below the poverty line) in India.

Bibliography

Camacho, A., and E. Conovor. 2009. "Manipulation of Social Program Eligibility: Detection, Explanations, and Consequences for Empirical Research." CEDE Working Paper 19, Universidad de Los Andes, Bogotá, Colombia.

CEB (UN System Chief Executive Board for Coordination). 2009. *The Global Financial Crisis and Its Impact on the Work of the UN System.* New York: United Nations.

CENDEX (Projects Center for Development). 2008. *Resultados de la Encuesta Nacional de Salud 2007.* PowerPoint Presentation.

Escobar, M.-L. 2005. "Health Sector Reform in Colombia." *Development Outreach* 7 (2).

Escobar, M.-L., U. Giedeón, A. Giuffrida, and A. Glassman. 2010. "Colombia: After a Decade of Health System Reform." In *From Few to Many: Ten Years of Health Insurance Expansion in Colombia*, edited by A. Glassman, M.-L. Escobar, A. Giuffrida, and U. Giedeón. Washington, DC: Inter-American Development Bank and Brookings Institution.

Frankenberg, E., D. Thomas, and K. Beegle. 1999. "The Real Costs of Indonesia's Economic Crisis: Preliminary Findings from the Indonesia Family Life Surveys." Papers 99-04, RAND-Labor and Population Program.

Galasso, E., and M. Ravallion. 2005. "Decentralized Targeting of an Antipoverty Program." *Journal of Public Economics* 89 (4): 705–27.

Gelb, A., and J. Clark. 2013. "Identification for Development: The Biometrics Revolution." http://www.cgdev.org/publication/identification-development -biometrics-revolution-working-paper-315.

Grosh, M., C. del Ninno, E. Tesliuc, and A. Ouerghi. 2008. *For Protection and Promotion: The Design and Implementation of Effective Safety Nets*. Washington, DC: World Bank.

Hoddinott, J., and E. Skoufias. 2004. "The Impact of PROGRESA on Food Consumption." *Economic Development and Cultural Change* 53 (1): 37–61.

ILO (International Labour Organization). 2008. *Providing Health Insurance for the Poor.* United Nations, Bangkok.

International Crisis Group. 2011. *Central Asia: Decay and Decline.* Asia Report 201, Brussels, Belgium.

Jakab, M. 2007. "An Empirical Evaluation of the Kyrgyz Health Reform: Does It Work for the Poor?" PhD thesis, Harvard University, Cambridge, MA.

Johar, M. 2009. "The Impact of the Indonesian Health Card Program: A Matching Estimator Approach." *Journal of Health Economics* 28 (1): 35–53.

Knowles, J., and J. Marzolf. 2003. Unpublished. "Health Financing for the Poor in Indonesia." World Bank, Washington, DC.

Kutzin, J. 2001. "A Descriptive Framework for Country-Level Analysis of Health Care Financing Arrangements." *Health Policy* 56 (3): 171–204.

Levinsohn, J. A., S. T. Berry, and J. Friedman. 2003. "Impacts of the Indonesian Economic Crisis: Price Changes and the Poor in Managing Currency Crises in Emerging Markets." In *National Bureau of Economic Research Conference Report*, edited by M. P. Dooley and J. A. Frankel. Chicago: University of Chicago Press.

Miller, G., D. Pinto, and M. Vera-Hernández. 2009. "High-Powered Incentives in Developing Country Health Insurance: Evidence from Colombia's Regimen Subsidiaro." Working Paper 15456, National Bureau of Economic Research, Cambridge, MA.

Mogilevsky, R., A. Chubrik, M. Dabrowski, and I. Sinitsina. 2011. "The Impact of the Global Financial Downturn on Public Health Expenditure in the Economies of the Former Soviet Union." CASE Network E-Briefs 09/2011, Warsaw, Poland.

Palacios, R. 2013. "Framework for Implementing Social Programs (FISP)." Working Paper, World Bank, Washington, DC.

Purvis, G. P., S. Chinara, M. Jakab, K. Kojokeev, G. Murzalieva, K. Djemuratov, J. Kutzin, D. Cochrane, S. Mukeeva, T. Schuth, R. Uchkemirova, S. O'Dougherty, S. Chakraborty, L. Murzakarimova, and N. Kadyrova. 2005. "Evaluating Manas Health Sector Reforms (1996–2005): Focus on Restructuring." Manas Health Policy Analysis Project, WHO/ DFID, Policy Research Paper 30, London.

Rana, P. B. 1999. "East Asian Financial Crisis—An Agenda for Economic Recovery." EDRC Briefing Notes 7, Asian Development Bank, Manila.

Robalino, D. A., L. Rawlings, and I. Walker. 2012. "Building Social Protection and Labor Systems: Concepts and Operational Implications." Social Protection and Labor Discussion Paper 1202, World Bank, Washington, DC.

Saadah, F., S. Lieberman, and M. Juwono. 1999. "Indonesian Health Expenditure during the Crisis: Have They Been Protected?" Indonesia Watching Brief Issue 5, World Bank, Washington, DC.

Saadah, F., M. Pradhan, and R. Sparrow. 2001. "The Effectiveness of the Health Card as an Instrument to Ensure Access to Medical Care for the Poor during the Crisis." *World Bank Economic Review*, World Bank, Washington, DC.

Schneider, P. 2011. *ECA Knowledge Brief: Mitigating the Impact of the Economic Downturn on Public Sector Health Spending*. Washington, DC: World Bank.

Sparrow, R. 2008. "Targeting the Poor in Times of Crisis: The Indonesian Health Card." *Health Policy and Planning* 23 (3): 188–99.

Supakankunti, S. 2000. "Future Prospects of Voluntary Health Insurance in Thailand." *Health Policy and Planning* 15 (1): 85–94.

Towse, A., A. Mills, and V. Tangcharoensathien. 2004. "Learning from Thailand's Health Reforms." *British Medical Journal* 328: 103–05.

Trujillo, A. J., J. E. Portillo, and J. A. Vernon. 2005. "The Impact of Subsidized Health Insurance for the Poor: Evaluating the Colombian Experience Using Propensity Score Matching." *International Journal of Health Care Finance and Economics* 5 (3): 211–39.

UNDP (United Nations Development Programme). 2012. *Kyrgyzstan: From 'Compound' to Socio-Economic Crisis?* New York: UNDP.

UNICEF (United Nations Children's Fund). 2012. *Integrated Social Protection System: Enhancing Equity for Children*. New York: UNICEF.

Waters, H., F. Saadah, and M. Pradhan. 2003. "The Impact of the 1997–1998 East Asian Economic Crisis on Health Care in Indonesia." *Health Policy and Planning* 18 (2): 172–81.

Wibulpolprasert, S. 2010. "Thai Healthcare System: Past, Present, and Future." Presentation prepared for "One Century of Development: Four Main Eras of Continuous Investment: Learning and Reform," Bangkok, Thailand, August 26.

World Bank. 1999. *Thailand Social Monitor: Challenge for Social Reform*. World Bank, Washington, DC.

———. 2001. *Social Protection Sector Strategy: From Safety Net to Springboard*. Washington, DC: World Bank.

———. 2008. "Reducing Financial Burden of Healthcare for the Poor: The Case of Kyrgyz Health Financing Reform." Reaching the Poor Policy Brief 43722, World Bank, Washington, DC.

———. 2012a. *The World Bank 2012–2022 Social Protection and Labor Strategy*. Washington, DC: World Bank.

———. 2012b. "Universal Health Coverage Studies Series (UNICO)." World Bank, Washington, DC.

Yazbeck, A. 2009. *Attacking Inequality in the Health Sector: A Synthesis of Tools and Evidence*. Washington, DC: World Bank.

CHAPTER 5

Lessons from the European Union

The recent global economic crisis (GEC), which started as early as 2007, has shown that no country is immune to external challenges. When policy controls are missing or not used efficiently, crises can reverse progress and positive performance even in advanced economies with AAA credit ratings. This crisis has been unique. It emanated from advanced economies and led to prolonged stagnation and, in some cases, contraction. The depth and length of the crisis have led to fiscal turbulence that affected health sectors across a number of developed countries, requiring strategic consolidation and efficiency gains to fit the declining health sector budget.

Prior to the GEC, the Europe and Central Asia region (ECA) displayed robust economic performance. When the crisis hit, it was expected that this relatively stable, economically robust region would have the means and tools to tackle the downturn. However, many countries in ECA did not cope well. This unexpected outcome increases concerns about the ability of health sectors in low- and middle-income countries to prepare for future economic downturns.

As the crisis deepened[1] over time, a number of countries in Europe stood on the fiscal brink, engaging in pro-cyclical fiscal policy. These policies have affected the health sector and resulted in reduced fiscal space for health. This dynamic is atypical as, in general, advanced economies have been known for their counter-cyclical behavior. However, the emerging literature shows that stereotypical cyclical behavioral patterns associated with income levels are slowly changing. There has been an observed graduation from pro-cyclicality in lower-income countries confirming that countercyclical responses are possible at lower income levels (Brahmbhatt and Canuto 2012; Braun and di Gresia 2003; Frankel, Végh, and Vuletin 2011; IMF 2009; Lewis and Verhoeven 2010). On the other hand, there is evidence of "fallback" into pro-cyclicality at the higher end of the income distribution (Frankel, Végh, and Vuletin 2011; Velényi and Smitz 2013). In other words, advanced economies may respond in a pro-cyclical manner, especially if the crisis is deep and protracted.[2] Thus, lessons illustrating crisis navigation are important, regardless of where a country is on the development trajectory.

By 2009 the effects of the shock on the health sector were undisputable, but policy reactions at the global and national levels lagged. In 2009 the World Health Organization (WHO) held high-level consultations known as "The Financial Crisis and Global Health" and "Health in Times of Global Economic Crisis: Implications for the WHO Europe Region" in an attempt to catalyze policy and technical responses. Objectives were proposed to mitigate the effect of crises on global health, such as building awareness of how an economic downturn may affect health spending, health services, health-seeking behavior, and health outcomes (Chan 2008). In addition, various actions were identified as helpful to mitigating the negative impact of economic downturns and increasing future health sector resilience. Such actions included the monitoring of early warning signs.

The country case studies presented in this chapter are aligned with these objectives. First, the studies illustrate how the health systems in Ireland and Portugal responded to the crisis with policy changes that affected their systems and health outcomes during a prolonged negative economic cycle. Second, the studies explored the data, monitoring, and warning signs that were used to inform health policy discussions and how system resilience has been affected. The cases also illustrate the differences in the political economic dynamics of country responses, their priority-setting processes, and reform management.

Case Study 1: The Economic Crisis and the Irish Health System: Assessing Resilience

Sara Burke, Sarah Barry, and Stephen Thomas

Economic Context

The Irish economic crisis that began in 2008 is unparalleled in terms of the speed of its arrival and the severity of the contraction. In 2010 Ireland recorded the single worst annual government deficit of any country in Europe since World War II (Barret 2011). Ireland's crisis is multidimensional, spanning banking, public finance, the economy, social welfare, and Ireland's reputation abroad (Cinnéide 2009). It was caused by a combination of national and international factors. As a small open economy, Ireland was severely affected by the global financial crisis. Its participation in the euro project meant the availability of cheap credit, which contributed to an unsustainable property bubble. Combined with poor regulation of the banking sector the bubble created a banking crisis. Poor national economic management resulted in Ireland being one of the lowest taxing and spending economies in the European Union (EU) 27 up to 2008 (Burke and Pentony 2011). While Ireland had growth levels of over 5 percent consistently in the early 2000s, between 2008 and 2011 the country experienced negative real growth rates of –3, –7, and –0.4 percent (Thomas, Keegan, Barry, and Layte 2012). An additional million people entered the workforce during the economic boom, and in October 2008 unemployment was at 4 percent. In contrast, since September 2010, unemployment has been above 14 percent (Thomas, Keegan, Barry, and Layte 2012).

In September 2008 the Irish government announced a banking guarantee scheme, which meant banking debt became national debt and put further pressure on the country's contracting economy. The overreliance on consumption taxes meant that the tax base was eroded. In December 2010 Ireland entered into a European Union/European Central Bank/International Monetary Fund (EU/ECB/IMF) financial agreement, worth €85 billion. The government's response to the crisis, under the close scrutiny and direction of the Troika (EU, ECB, and IMF), has been largely focused on austerity measures with €23.9 billion in budgetary adjustments over six budgets between October 2008 and December 2011 (ESRI 2012). Budget 2013, which was announced in December 2012, planned to make another €3.5 billion in budgetary adjustments. Fiscal adjustments made since 2008 have been two-thirds cuts and one-third revenue raising (Burke and Considine 2012).

There was a change in government in February 2011, but the new coalition government largely continued the previous economic policy of austerity. Their ambitious Program for Government states that "by the end of our term in Government [2016], Ireland will be recognised as a modern, fair, socially inclusive and equal society supported by a productive, prosperous economy" (Government of Ireland 2011). However, the Irish government is hugely constrained in what it can accomplish due to the memorandum of understanding it has with the Troika, which is revised on a quarterly basis.

Brief Overview of the Irish Health System

Ireland has a tax-funded system of health care, but unlike other tax-funded systems, there is no entitlement to free care and no universal access (Thomas and Burke 2011). It has a complicated mix of public, private, and voluntary care, which often charges at the point of access, depending on what services one is accessing. The public health system has been run by the Health Service Executive (HSE) since 2005. While everyone is eligible for public hospital care at a maximum cost of €700–750 per year, if one has a medical card, one is entitled to public hospital and general practitioner (GP) care without charge (Burke 2009). Before the economic crisis, more than half of the population had private health insurance. Having private health insurance can enable people to gain faster access to the public hospital system, and their care in the public hospital system is subsidized by public money (Burke 2009). Primary care is very underdeveloped in Ireland with a mismatch between the location of GPs and population health need (McDaid et al. 2009; Thomas and Layte 2009). Anyone who does not have a medical card has to pay €40 to €60 each time they see a GP. They also pay a large proportion out-of-pocket for prescription medicines. Some services are provided universally, such as public health nurse visits to newborns, vaccinations, and palliative care. However, these services have come under increasing pressure in recent years, despite an aging population with an increasing burden of disease (Burke and Considine 2012).

The Program for Government adopted in March 2011 committed to providing free GP care for all and universal health insurance by 2016. If achieved, this will be the first time in the history of the state that universal access will be based on need and not ability to pay (Government of Ireland 2011).

Government and System Response

In 2008 a range of new revenue-raising measures were introduced into the health system. These measures included increased charges for inpatient bed days, emergency department visits, and long stays. Nevertheless, the health budget for 2009 rose from €16.1 billion to €16.3 billion indicating some initial protection of health spending or perhaps lags in spending allocations. Health budgets since then have fallen; by €1.1 billion in 2010, €747 million in 2011, and €750 million in 2012 (Burke and Considine 2012) (figure 5.1). Further, in each of these years, the capital budget was cut by 25 percent. Although initial cuts were absorbed through efficiencies and wage reductions, recent data show overspending of €399 million for the first eight months of 2012 (HSE 2012a). This deficit was made up of €207 million of hospital overspending, €180 million of community schemes overspending, and €22 million of community services' overspending (HSE 2012a). In November 2012 the government announced a supplementary health budget in order to curtail spending by year-end. While the budget for 2013 has been maintained in nominal terms (DPER 2013), it masks the need for more cost-cutting of around €700 million just to cope with the increased spending associated with an aging population and increasing chronic disease prevalence.

Figure 5.1 GDP and Health Funding in Ireland

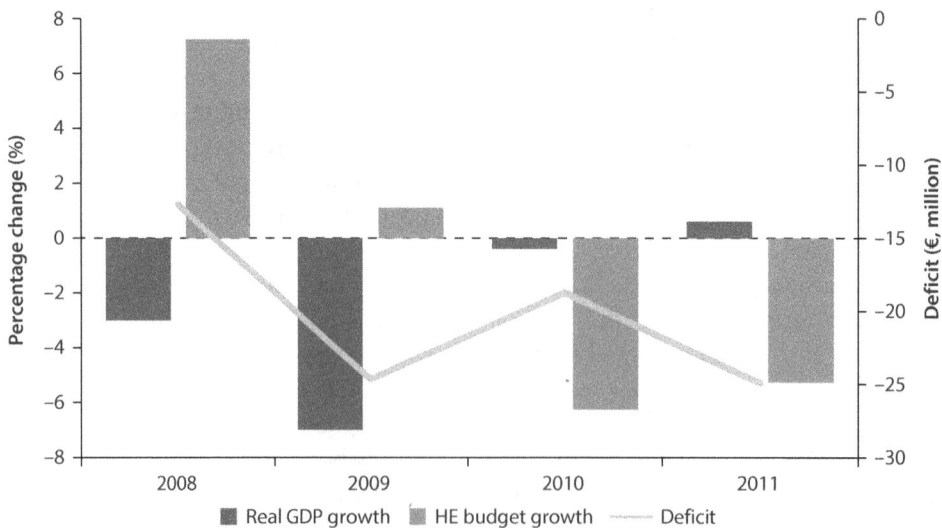

Note: GDP = gross domestic product; HE = health expenditure.

Impact

Efficiency Gains

It appears that the austerity drive produced, at least initially, some efficiency gains. In 2010, €660 million was saved by cuts to the wages of all public sector staff, which were high by European standards. Pay cuts were progressive and ranged from 5 percent to 15 percent. Since the emergency budget in October 2008, there has also been a strong emphasis on cost-cutting through reducing fees paid to professionals such as GPs and pharmacists, through efforts (largely unsuccessful) to cut the drugs budget, and through efficiencies in areas such as procurement and "doing more with less" (Burke and Considine 2012; Thomas, Keegan, Barry, and Layte 2012). Indeed, the HSE has managed to provide more care to more people over the past four years with increased activity levels in public hospitals (Thomas, Keegan, Barry, and Layte 2012). In interviews senior health system managers endorsed this: "the very fact that [the crisis] made us focus on efficiency I think is a benefit."

To date, service levels have been maintained in the face of serious efficiency cuts. It seems that "there was too much padding in the system ... there wasn't enough emphasis on measuring outputs, what we were getting for the resources that went in."

There has also been protection of the "most vulnerable" through continuing to provide medical cards on the basis of need (HSE 2012b) (figure 5.2). On October 1, 2012, more than 1.8 million people were covered by medical cards,

Figure 5.2 Financial Resilience: Trends in Coverage and Entitlements in Ireland, 2000–12

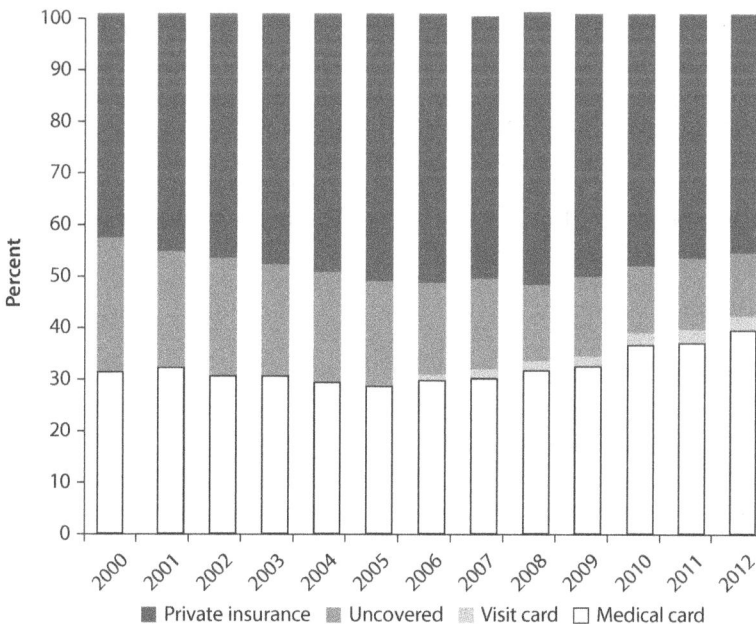

a huge increase of 558,000 or 44 percent of the number eligible for medical cards compared to January 2008 (HSE 2008, 2012a). By October 2012, 40 percent of the population were covered by this scheme (HSE 2012a).

System Risks

Nevertheless, the austerity poses several risks to the health system. A central plank of budget reduction has been to reduce the numbers of staff in the public health system and the public sector wage bill. Even before the economic crisis was recognized by government, in September 2007 HSE management announced cost-cutting measures, including an embargo on staff recruitment (Burke 2009). In January 2008 there were almost 111,000 HSE staff (HSE 2008). In September 2012 HSE staffing was below 102,000, a reduction of over 9,000 staff in under five years caused largely by the public sectorwide staff embargo and a voluntary redundancy scheme introduced in 2010 (HSE 2012a). The expectation is that HSE staff numbers will continue to decline despite increased activity and a growing and aging population.

Furthermore, there has been a continued debate over universalization of health care. The October 2008 budget removed a universal entitlement to medical cards for everyone over age 70 and established a means test. The result of the means test is that about 40,000 people over 70 now no longer get medical cards. Successive budgets have increased co-payments to essential health care. In 2007 the charge upon arrival in an emergency department was €70, whereas now it is €120. In 2008 people without medical cards had to pay €80 per month for their prescription drugs, after which the costs were covered by the state. In 2012 the threshold stood at €132 per month (Burke and Considine 2012). Furthermore, the 2010 budget introduced a 50 cent per item charge for drugs for those on medical cards and cut back their dental services (Burke and Considine 2012).

Yet universalization of health care is now a central pillar of government policy. Looking forward, there are big questions over the ability of the system to manage and implement stated change within this context of continued austerity (Thomas, Keegan, Barry, and Layte 2012).

Case Study 2: Changes in the Health Sector under Economic Crisis and Financial Rescue: Portugal

Pedro Pita Barros

How Did We Get Here?

The global crisis that began late in the first decade of the 21st century hit Portugal the same way it did other European countries. In Portugal, however, the crisis added to an already existing domestic crisis, as gross domestic product (GDP) growth had been stagnant from early in the decade. When the global crisis began, the Portuguese economy was characterized by decreasing real growth rate of GDP, an increasing external deficit in the current account, and a decreasing savings rate. This was coupled with a loss of competitiveness of exports, increasing debt with external creditors, and too much investment in nontradable goods and services. The small productivity gains achieved were reached by lower use of labor and not by adding value through technological progress and innovation. The growth rate of GDP was close to zero in 2008, became negative in 2009 but was less than in other European countries impacted by the crisis. In 2011 and 2012 the economy saw a more severe recession (−1.6 and −3.2 percent were the growth rates of GDP, respectively).[3] The current account has systematically been below −5 percent of GDP; and often close to 10 percent of GDP during the last 15 years.

The high and persistent deficit in the current account implied that consumption was funded from loans from abroad and not by higher domestic production. It is important to note that trend GDP, as estimated by the European Commission, has been decreasing since 2006, prior to the global crisis.

GDP per employed worker is low in Portugal because of low output per hour (as average annual hours worked per person employed are similar to other countries and above that of Germany, for example).

The consumption surge was largely determined by a strong positive wealth effect in consumers' expectations from the euro birth. During the decade of preparation for the euro, inflation rates in Portugal dropped from 13 percent in 1990 to less than 4 percent after 2002, and moved since then, in line with the Euro Area's inflation. A similar drop occurred in interest rates. From a value of 16 percent in 1986, interest rates fell to 4 percent and lower after Portugal participated in the foundation of the euro and continued until the start of the sovereign debt crisis. The decrease in inflation and interest rates, anticipated as permanent, created a wealth effect and had a strong impact on consumption decisions.

After entering the Euro Area, the low growth in output, coupled with the same high consumption expectations, were bound to create a problem. Economic growth was too low to finance the higher consumption pattern.

The growth in permanent income fueled a persistent increase in consumption, with a production shift to nontradables and with imports as a response to increased demand.

To sum up, before the international crisis Portugal already had problems, and the international crisis did not help. It implied no further available credit to fund imports and the consumption patterns. The initial government response in 2009 and 2010 was to increase public expenditure to keep economic activity going, an option that turned out to be problematic for the deficit in the government budget.

The Financial Rescue Plan

The memorandum of understanding (MoU) between Portugal and the Troika (the European Union, the European Central Bank, and the International Monetary Fund) defined a wide range of policy measures aimed at the health care sector (within the public sector). Many measures were adopted, some with immediate impact, but structural reforms lagged considerably behind. Table 5.1 reports major areas of policy intervention defined in the MoU.

Learning from Economic Downturns • http://dx.doi.org/10.1596/978-1-4648-0060-3

Table 5.1 Key Demands Defined in Portugal's Memorandum of Understanding

Area of intervention	Key demands
Pharmaceuticals	Cap public pharmaceutical expenditures at 1.25 percent of GDP in 2012 and 1 percent of GDP in 2013.
	Change structure and value of retail distribution margins.
	Revise international reference pricing system.
	Increase price discount of first generic relative to originator drug.
User charges	Increase levels and differentiate between primary care and emergency department user charges.
	Revise exemptions to user charges.
Management of the National Health Service (NHS)	Reorganize hospital network.
	Publish medical guidelines and monitor prescription patterns.
	Develop centralized procurement procedures.
	Reduce transportation costs with patients.
Primary care	Increase use of primary care by expansion of Family Health Units.
Tax system adjustments	Reduce fiscal benefits by two-thirds.
Health subsystems	Change public funding rules to make them self-sustainable.
Human resources	Have full description of human resources distribution by geographic location, institution, and health profession.
Public-private interface	Obtain lower prices from private service providers to the NHS.

The Pharmaceutical Market

In the pharmaceutical market, policy measures included removal of barriers, entry of generics, change of regulated margins, pharmaceutical distribution (moving to regressive margins from the standard constant percent markup), and targets of public expenditure with pharmaceutical products. The impact of these measures was a decrease in public health expenditure.

The target level of public pharmaceutical expenditures for 2012 was achieved as an agreement between the government and the association of the pharmaceutical industry (APIFARMA) to meet the target, with a payback clause. The overall target for 2012 was divided into ambulatory and hospital markets. The ambulatory market target was achieved without the use of the payback mechanism, and in the hospital market the payback mechanism was activated.

These two markets have evolved in different ways. The public expenditure of pharmaceutical products in ambulatory care has decreased considerably in recent years. It actually started to decrease before the financial rescue plan was instituted in Portugal. On the other hand, pharmaceutical expenditures in public hospitals continue to increase, moving away from the target value. The difficulties in meeting the 2012 target suggest further problems in meeting the 2013 target, as it requires a 20 percent decrease in total pharmaceutical public expenditure relative to 2012.

The change in the regulated margins in pharmaceutical product distribution attempted to save €50 million. Although no final value has been yet provided, the sixth evaluation of the MoU does not mention the issue, an implicit recognition that the target has been achieved. The implications of pharmaceutical price reductions in ambulatory care and pharmaceutical distribution margins have caused economic distress in retail pharmacy. Current estimates suggest that revenues per prescription are below its marginal cost. Thus, further price decreases of pharmaceutical products in the context of distribution margins linked to prices will put the pharmacy network at risk. As prices of pharmaceuticals will continue to experience a downward pressure, a change in the way pharmacies are remunerated for dispensing pharmaceuticals must occur to avoid disruption in the existing network.

User Charges

User charges are traditionally a hot topic because they may constitute a barrier to health care access. The levels of user charges doubled in January 2012. At the same time, exemption categories were revised and enlarged to include a greater number of citizens covered by some type of exemption (table 5.2). In 2006 an estimated 4.2 million people were covered by exemptions. Under the new exemption system, as of March 2013, 5.6 million of the total population of Portugal is covered. An important change in the exemption system is that income-related exemptions must be requested rather than automatically granted.

Organization of the National Health Service

A significant part of the measures from the memorandum of understanding involves the restructuring of the National Health Service (NHS). One major issue to be resolved is the recovery of arrears, which amounted to €3,100 million at the end of 2011. As a point of reference, the total NHS budget of Portugal for 2012 was €7,500 million. To deal with this issue, measures have been instituted requiring the preauthorization of expenditures based on near-future available funds and past debt. The recovery of arrears involves bargaining with the pharmaceutical industry, the main creditor, for ex-post discounts on prices.

Other actions required by the MoU are more general, such as the requirement to set a benchmarking process to assess hospital performance, the need to

Table 5.2 User Charges Exemptions in Portugal

	2006	2011	2012 (forecast)	2012 (November)	2013 (March)
Income related	1,900,055	1,807,854	5,189,209	2,926,279	3,001,889
Pregnant women and children under age 13	1,501,210	1,390,857	925,961	1,411,086	1,401,969
Significant incapacity to work	3,861	230	81,711	100,112	116,999
Firemen	34,225	32,947	59,387	25,844	26,014
Blood donors	160,606	196,408	74,692	121,120	116,231
Other	24,761	227,220	50,000	3,135	6,781
Specific medical conditions	572,019	890,120	890,120	890,120	890,120
Total	4,196,737	4,545,636	7,271,080	5,477,696	5,560,003

Sources: Administração Central do Sistema de Saúde (except 2006); Comissão para a Sustentabilidade Financeira do SNS (2006).
Note: Portuguese population in 2011 (census by Statistics Portugal): 10,562,178.

Learning from Economic Downturns • http://dx.doi.org/10.1596/978-1-4648-0060-3

reorganize and rationalize the hospital network, and further development of primary care activities.

Public-Private Interface

Another area in which the MoU will impact the Portuguese health system is the public-private interface, both on the funding side and on the delivery side. On the funding side, the pre-2012 fiscal credits to health expenditures must be revised. In economic terms these fiscal credits are additional public health insurance granted to private health expenditures. Taxpayers were able to deduct 30 percent of their documented private health expenditures from taxes. The MoU called for a reduction in this fiscal credit. The 2012 government budget reduced the fiscal credit to 10 percent of documented private health expenditures and eliminated the fiscal credit for the two upper-income brackets in personal income tax.

Also on the funding side, the civil servants' health insurance plan, Assistência na Doença aos Servidores do Estado (ADSE), has traditionally been largely paid by government budget transfers. Only a small share of it is financed by contributions from beneficiaries. This protection scheme has no direct health care provision and contracts both public and private providers. Discussions continue on whether to move it out of the government budget and sustain it by payments of beneficiaries only.

This movement, if accompanied by a redefinition of benefits, may have a serious impact on private health care providers because the civil servants' health protection system represents a significant share of their activities. The exact conditions and terms of this change have yet to be defined. Until recently, all civil servants were required to contribute to the health protection system. Since 2009 civil servants have the ability to opt out. Contributions to the ADSE system are income-related. Currently, contributions are made by the employee and the public sector employer. Moving to a fully optional system may create attrition by the healthiest and/or the wealthiest, changing the risk pool and the funding requirements. Currently, the contribution from government departments constitutes a significant subsidy (2.5 percent of wages, against a worker's contribution of 1.5 percent of wages). As the government contribution decreases over time, attrition is likely to increase.

On the provision side, the NHS contracts and buys several health care goods and services from the private sector. Pharmaceuticals are one of the main examples. Three other relevant areas include imaging services, laboratory tests (blood, urine, and so forth), and renal dialysis. The NHS imposed significant price reductions in these areas (10 percent in 2011 and again in 2012) and is putting a more competitive procurement system into place.

Effect on the Population

The global crisis has had significant economic and health-related impacts on the Portuguese. Some of the most significant measures of the impacts can be seen in the areas of usage of care, waiting list times, and suicide rates.

Use of Care

According to the sixth evaluation provided by the European Commission on the MoU compliance, the data point to a reduction in the use of emergency room services and an increase in the use of primary care services.

Additionally, the price reductions in retail pharmaceutical products resulted in smaller payments by the population and by the government. The price effect was strong enough to allow an increase in consumption of pharmaceuticals with lower overall direct spending by the population.

Waiting Lists

Data showed a slight increase in waiting list times. Median waiting time was 3.10 months in the first semester (January through June) of 2010, 3.13 in the first semester of 2011, and 3.30 in the first semester of 2012. Rising waiting times for surgical interventions are an early warning sign that the performance of the health system may be deteriorating. The more recent information, up to the first semester of 2012, points to an increase in median waiting times from the beginning of 2011. The reason was an increase in the number of patients that received an indication for surgery rather than a cut in activity to save costs. The total number of patients that required surgery experienced a slight increase.

Suicides

As typical of economic crisis periods, there are signs pointing to a slight increase in suicides and reduced number of accidental deaths (traffic accidents and work accidents). An increase in mental health problems, as measured by higher consumption of antidepressants, is also reported.

Final Remarks

The policy responses associated with the economic downturn have been largely determined by the MoU. They have acted primarily in the price dimension, with measures aimed at the quantity dimension being slow to define and to implement let alone produce results. Table 5.3 provides a preliminary and brief summary.

The impact of price-related measures on the population is, so far, likely to be beneficial in financial terms. The user charges for public services have increased, but so have exemptions from these user charges. The financial impact of user charges is relatively small (about 2 percent of total NHS budget). Pharmaceutical prices have, on average, declined considerably, benefiting both the NHS and the patients.

One current risk is the threat to retail pharmacies' economic fundamentals. Some pharmacies have started to go bankrupt, and the risk to the network of pharmaceutical retail distribution needs to be assessed.

In hospital activities, budget cuts, including wage cuts, have been met with resilience of health care professionals. The threat is the end of such resilience and personal disinvestment and reduced commitment of health professionals in case of further wage cuts.

Table 5.3 Summary of Policy Response Impacts in Portugal

Area	Positive impacts	Negative impacts	Risks
Pharmaceuticals	Lower spending for both government and patients		Retail pharmacy network faces economic viability issues
User charges	More adequate use of emergency room services		Access limitations due to economic barriers may result
Management of the National Health Service (NHS)	Efficiency gains; more adequate prescription pattern	Increase in waiting times	Decrease in quality of care due to lack of investment; disengagement of health professionals
Tax system adjustments	Lower government spending	Higher out-of-pocket payments	Impact on household budgets
Human resources	Better planning of training and deployment of human resources		
Public-private interface	Lower NHS spending in private services		

For the moment, there is not much information on the impact upon the population. Immediate impacts such as lack of access seem to have been avoided, but long-term effects on population health have not been addressed.

Conclusions

Overall, there have been clear efficiency gains across the country case studies. However, as with all complex reforms, it is difficult to find cases of absolute success. Conflicting objectives have led countries to backtrack on the breadth and depth of coverage.

Two main conclusions can be drawn from the country cases presented here. First, the political economic dynamics of reform processes between the health sector and the Ministry of Finance, as well as within the sector, are critical. Political economy is especially important if there is not enough time for evidence-based priority setting. Second, further developing and applying country-level monitoring tools and early warning systems could help evidence-based responses. These tools must consider changes in inputs (for example, health financing), outputs (for example, utilization), and outcomes (for example, mental health, suicide rates, chronic conditions, and so forth) to understand the effects throughout the result chain. Some impacts of crises, such as population health outcome indicators, require longer periods of time to be fully realized. Thus, crisis effect monitoring is not a short-term engagement. It requires a systematic and long-term impact assessment approach.

Because of the vicious cycle of pro-cyclical fiscal behavior, pro-cyclical social spending, and consequently reduced potential for long-term equitable growth, a growing body of evidence is emerging on the importance of effective fiscal and social policies. To highlight two recent additions in this domain by the World Bank, both the Bank's Social Protection and Labor Strategy (World Bank 2012) and the *World Development Report (WDR) 2014* (World Bank 2013) focus on risk, resilience, opportunity, and equitable growth.

It is important to continually explore the sector-specific aspects of and tools for risk management to more effectively cope with economic downturns. The ability of any sector to mitigate the impact of an economic downturn is contingent on the existence of established instruments that allow for the identification of the most vulnerable groups and the ability to target interventions toward them. In the pursuit of exercising more risk mitigation at the sector level, the A.T.M. (assessing, tracking, mitigating) framework was designed to help countries identify and track system-level failures early and thereby mitigate adverse and long-term effects on the population.

The expected effects of economic downturns on the health sector are mixed. On the one hand, increasing fiscal pressures could provide incentive to increase efficiency in the health system.[4] On the other hand, governments must take a thoughtful, long-term approach to reform in order to ensure sustained health system resilience. The Spanish crisis has raised concerns related to this very issue. Recent reforms have achieved the immediate goal of balancing annual budgets but may prove to have negative long-term effects, which may adversely impact the system (Gené-Badia et al. 2012). This is a perfect example of the old adage "penny-wise and pound-foolish." Given the long-term implications of crisis-catalyzed system reforms, navigating through economic turbulence and building health system resilience have become important global issues.

Because of the heterogeneity and changing nature of crises, as well as the changing landscape of (cyclical) responses to economic downturns and their impact on populations, it is important to consider and apply the A.T.M. framework irrespective of which income group a country is in. Advanced economies have relied more on automatic stabilizers and have more-developed social safety nets. The global crisis has shown that there is no place for complacency.

Crises vary in terms of their trigger, geographic origin and scope, length, and depth. These crisis parameters, the extent of structural preparedness, and policy reactions by governments jointly determine the severity of outcomes and the length of the impact horizon. A global lesson from these crises is that the health sector must build systems that can effectively assess vulnerability, track system changes, and synthesize the information to improve mitigation efforts. These structural changes can, and must, happen and cannot come soon enough.

Notes

1. To operationalize crisis depth, we can apply the concept of "output gap," which can be measured in terms of standard deviation from the Hodrick-Prescott filtered trend line for GDP per capita. "Good" time is defined as economic output 1.5 standard deviations above the trend line (economic output potential), and "bad" time is when the economic performance is at least 1.5 standard deviations below the filtered trend line (see, for example, del Granado, Gupta, and Hajdenberg 2013; Velényi and Smitz 2013).

2. With respect to health system and population vulnerability to shocks, intuitively, shorter crises may be easier to absorb but they leave little time for adjustment. Longer crises provide ample time for policy makers and system reform (that is, structural or "transformative" change), but they may come at a high (political) cost. The more buffer that governments and systems have, the more populations can withstand shocks and the less they suffer from the negative implications of crises on health and illness-related financial protection.

3. Statistics Portugal, http://tinyurl.com/cu87rnk.

4. There are various references in the empirical literature regarding how crises could be used as an opportunity to improve sector performance, including terms such as "liposuction" (Thomas, Keegan, Barry, Layte, Jowett, Portela, and Normand 2012), "cutting the fat but not the muscle" (Smith and Nguyen 2013), and "cutting wisely" (Mladovsky et al. 2012). Mladovsky et al. provide examples from across 45 countries in Europe.

Bibliography

Administração Central do Sistema de Saúde. http://tinyurl.com/bxrvohd.

Barret, S. 2011. "The EU/IMF Rescue Programme for Ireland: 2010–2013." *Economic Affairs* 31 (2): 53–57.

Brahmbhatt, M., and O. Canuto. 2012. "Fiscal Policy for Growth and Development: Economic Premise." Poverty Reduction and Economic Management (PREM) 19 (October), World Bank, Washington, DC.

Braun, M., and L. di Gresia. 2003. "Towards Effective Social Insurance in Latin America: The Importance of Countercyclical Fiscal Policy." Inter-American Development Bank Working Paper 487.

Burke, S. 2009. *Irish Apartheid: Health Care Inequality in Ireland.* Dublin: New Island.

Burke, S., and M. Considine. 2012. *Annual National Report 2012. Pensions, Health and Long-term Care: Ireland.* http://www.socialprotection.eu/files_db/1242/asisp _ANR12_IRELAND.pdf.

Burke, S., and S. Pentony. 2011. *Eliminating Health Inequalities: A Matter of Life and Death.* Dublin: TASC. http://www.tascnet.ie/upload/file/HealthWeb.pdf.

Chan, M. 2008. "Impact of the Global Financial and Economic Crisis on Health." Statement by WHO Director-General Dr. Margaret Chan. November 12. http:// www.who.int/mediacentre/news/statements/2008/s12/en/index.html#.

Cinnéide, S. Ó. 2009. *Pensions, Health and Long-term Care: Ireland.* Annual National Report 2009. http://www.socialprotection.eu/files_db/292/asisp_ANR09_Ireland.pdf.

Comissão para a Sustentabilidade Financeira do SNS (Commission on the Financial Sustainability of the National Health Service). 2007. Portugal, Ministry of Health. http://tinyurl.com/dyn7nfd.

del Granado, J. A., S. Gupta, and A. Hajdenberg. 2013. "Is Social Spending Procyclical? Evidence for Developing Countries." *World Development* 42: 16–27.

Department of Health and Children. 2011. *Health in Ireland: Key Trends 2011.* Dublin: Department of Health and Children.

———. 2012. *About the Special Delivery Unit.* Dublin: Department of Health and Children. http://www.dohc.ie/about_us/divisions/special_delivery_unit.html.

DPER (Department of Public Expenditure and Reform). 2013. http://per.gov.ie /databank/.

ESRI (Economic and Social Research Institute). 2012. *Quarterly Economic Commentary* (Autumn). Dublin: ESRI. http://www.esri.ie/UserFiles/publications/QEC2012AUT .pdf.

Frankel, J., C. Végh, and G. Vuletin. 2011. "On Graduation from Procyclicality." NBER Working Paper 17619, National Bureau of Economic Research, Cambridge, MA. http://www.nber.org/papers/w17619.

Gené-Badia, J. J., P. P. Gallo, C. C. Hernandez-Quevedo, and S. S. Garcia-Armesto. 2012. "Spanish Health Care Cuts: Penny Wise and Pound Foolish?" *Health Policy* 106 (1): 23–28.

Government of Ireland. 2011. *Government for National Recovery 2011–2016.* Dublin: Fine Gael/Labour Party.

HSE (Health Service Executive). 2008. *HSE Performance Report.* Dublin: HSE.

———. 2011. National Clinical Programmes. http://www.hse.ie/eng/about/Who/clinical /natclinprog/listofprogrammes.html.

———. 2012a. *HSE Performance Report.* Dublin: HSE. http://www.hse.ie/eng/services /Publications/corporate/performancereports/PRSept.pdf.

———. 2012b. *National Service Plan 2012.* Dublin: HSE. http://www.hse.ie/eng/services /Publications/corporate/nsp2012.pdf.

IMF (International Monetary Fund). 2009. *Regional Economic Outlook. Sub-Saharan Africa: Withstanding the Storm.* Washington, DC: IMF.

IMPACT [trade union]. 2012. *The Future of Healthcare in Ireland: Position Paper on the Health Crisis and the Government's Plans for Healthcare.* Dublin: IMPACT.

Layer, R., A. Nolan, and B. Nolan. 2007. *Poor Prescriptions: Poverty and Access to Community Health Services.* Dublin: Combat Poverty Agency.

Lewis, M., and M. Verhoeven. 2010. "Financial Crises and Social Spending: The Impact of the 2008–2009 Crisis." Background paper for *Global Monitoring Report 2010*, World Bank, Washington, DC.

McDaid, D., M. Wiley, A. Maresso, and E. Mossialos. 2009. "Ireland: Health System Review." *Health Systems in Transition* 11 (4): 1–268.

Mladovsky, P., D. Srivastava, J. Cylus, M. Karanikolos, T. Evetovits, S. Thomson, and M. McKee. 2012. "Policy Summary 5: Health Policy Response to the Financial Crisis in Europe." World Health Organization on behalf of the European Observatory on Health Systems and Policies, Geneva.

OECD (Organisation for Economic Co-operation and Development). 2012. *Health at a Glance.* OECD Publishing. http://www.oecd.org/document/30/0,3746 ,en_2649_34631_12968734_1_1_1_1,00.html.

Smith, O., and S. N. Nguyen. 2013. *Getting Better.* Washington, DC: World Bank.

Stuckler, D., S. Basu, M. Shurcke, A. Coutts, and M. McKee. 2009. "The Public Health Effect of Economic Crises and Alternative Policy Responses in Europe: An Empirical Analysis." *The Lancet* 374 (9686): 315–23.

Thomas, S., and S. Burke. 2011. *Ireland Case Study for the "Resilience Project."* Dublin: Centre for Health Policy and Management, Trinity College.

Thomas, S., C. Keegan, S. Barry, and R. Layte. 2012. "The Irish Health System and the Economic Crisis." *The Lancet* 380 (9847): 1056–57.

Thomas, S., C. Keegan, S. Barry, R. Layte, M. Jowett, C. Portela, and C. Normand. 2012. *Resilience in the Irish Health System: Surviving and Utilising the Economic Contraction, Year 1 Report of the Resilience Project*. Dublin: Centre for Health Policy and Management, Trinity College.

Thomas, S., and R. Layte. 2009. "General Practitioner Care." In *Projecting the Impact of Demographic Change on the Demand for and Delivery of Health Care in Ireland*, edited by R. Layte. Dublin: Economic and Social Research Institute (ESRI).

UNICEF (United Nations Children's Fund). 2012. *Integrated Social Protection System: Enhancing Equity for Children*. New York: UNICEF.

United Nations. 2009. *United Nations Chief Executive Board. The Global Financial Crisis and Its Impact on the Work of the UN System*. New York: United Nations. http://www.ilo.org/gimi/gess/RessShowRessource.do?ressourceId=12603.

Velényi, E. V., and M. F. Smitz. 2013. "Cyclical Patterns in Government Health Expenditures between 1995 and 2010: Are Countries Graduating from the Procyclical Trap or Falling Back?" Draft for HNP Working Paper Series, Health, Nutrition, and Population Anchor, World Bank, Washington, DC.

World Bank. 2001. *Social Protection Sector Strategy: From Safety Net to Springboard*. Washington, DC: World Bank.

———. 2012. *The World Bank 2012–2022 Social Protection and Labor Strategy*. Washington, DC: World Bank.

———. 2013. *World Development Report 2014*. Washington, DC: World Bank.

Environmental Benefits Statement

The World Bank is committed to reducing its environmental footprint. In support of this commitment, the Publishing and Knowledge Division leverages electronic publishing options and print-on-demand technology, which is located in regional hubs worldwide. Together, these initiatives enable print runs to be lowered and shipping distances decreased, resulting in reduced paper consumption, chemical use, greenhouse gas emissions, and waste.

The Publishing and Knowledge Division follows the recommended standards for paper use set by the Green Press Initiative. Whenever possible, books are printed on 50 percent to 100 percent postconsumer recycled paper, and at least 50 percent of the fiber in our book paper is either unbleached or bleached using Totally Chlorine Free (TCF), Processed Chlorine Free (PCF), or Enhanced Elemental Chlorine Free (EECF) processes.

More information about the Bank's environmental philosophy can be found at http://crinfo.worldbank.org/wbcrinfo/node/4.

green press
INITIATIVE

www.ingramcontent.com/pod-product-compliance
Lightning Source LLC
Chambersburg PA
CBHW080612270326
41928CB00016B/3024